MW01124514

THE FEELING OF LETTING DIE

THE FEELING OF LETTING DIE

NECROECONOMICS AND VICTORIAN FICTION

Jennifer MacLure

THE OHIO STATE UNIVERSITY PRESS

COLUMBUS

Library of Congress Cataloging-in-Publication Data
Names: MacLure, Jennifer, author.
Title: The feeling of letting die : necroeconomics and Victorian fiction / Jennifer MacLure.
Description: Columbus : The Ohio State University Press, [2023] | Includes bibliographical references and index. | Summary: "Explores how Victorian novels by Elizabeth Gaskell, Harriet Martineau, Charles Dickens, William Morris, and George Eliot depict feelings that both fuel and are produced by a capitalist economic system that capitalizes upon death"—Provided by publisher.
Identifiers: LCCN 2023029921 | ISBN 9780814214855 (hardback) | ISBN 0814214851 (hardback) | ISBN 9780814283301 (ebook) | ISBN 0814283306 (ebook)
Subjects: LCSH: English fiction—19th century—History and criticism. | Capitalism in literature. | Capitalism and literature—Great Britain—History—19th century. | Economics—Great Britain—History—19th century. | Gaskell, Elizabeth Cleghorn, 1810–1865—Criticism and interpretation. | Martineau, Harriet, 1802–1876—Criticism and interpretation. | Dickens, Charles, 1812–1870—Criticism and interpretation. | Morris, William, 1834–1896—Criticism and interpretation.| Eliot, George, 1819–1880—Criticism and interpretation.
Classification: LCC PR878.C25 M33 2023 | DDC 823/.809—dc23/eng/20230817
LC record available at https://lccn.loc.gov/2023029921

Cover design by Larry Nozik
Text composition by Stuart Rodriguez
Type set in Minion Pro

CONTENTS

ACKNOWLEDGMENTS

I begin by offering a wholly inadequate thank you to the people without whom this book would not exist.

I am enormously grateful to the faculty, staff, and students at University of Wisconsin–Madison, especially Susan Bernstein, Mario Ortiz-Robles, Ellen Samuels, and Jenell Johnson for their insightful feedback and generous mentorship, as well as Jessie Reeder, Mattie Burkert, and Sharon Yam for their support and expertise. I offer my particular thanks to Anne McClintock, without whose well-timed encouragement I may well be in a different profession right now. Any expression of gratitude to Caroline Levine must fall short of the mark; I can only thank her for her insight and wisdom and hope to emulate her unparalleled generosity.

This project and my life have been enriched by the INCS and NAVSA communities. I am especially grateful to Pamela Gilbert for her generous feedback in the early stages of this project and to Deborah Morse for inspiration years ago and continued mentorship today. Like so many, I am indebted to Dino Felluga and Emily Allen for doing the hard and often thankless work required to create inclusive academic communities. And for formative conversations and sustaining friendships, I thank Greg Brennan, Emma Davenport, Michael Harwick, Phil Stillman, and especially Stefan Waldschmidt, whose feedback on this project has been invaluable.

I am aware how rare it is to join a department and feel immediately valued and supported; I am immensely grateful to have found that at Kent State. Special thanks are owed to Tammy Clewell and Jen Cunningham for their mentorship and support. I also wish to express my gratitude to department staff Sheri McMahon and Jenni Nikolin-Meyer for their indispensable help. This project has been enriched by conversations with graduate students, particularly Muhammad Farooq and Alex Coleman, and by the contributions of my 2018–19 undergraduate research assistants, Alyssa Fernandez and Nathan Seres.

I extend my warmest thanks to everyone who made this book's publication possible: to the anonymous readers who reviewed the manuscript with such care, whose insightful questions made this a better book; to Becca Bostock, whose editorial guidance and continued belief in this project have been vital; and to the entire team at The Ohio State University Press who have helped shepherd this book to publication.

For the friends and family who have carried me through a task that has at times seemed interminable, words do not suffice. My deepest thanks to the women of Serious Writing Group for advice and support; to Jacquelyn Fox-Good for teaching me to think like a scholar; to Joey Thomas for being someone who is on my side; and to Clay Cogswell for countless conversations that have made this book (and my life) better. This project would never have made it across the finish line without the impossibly generous support of my parents. And where would I be without Maggie and Tess, who have sprawled all over the archive? This book is for them to knock off the table.

Chapter 2 is derived in part from an article published in *Nineteenth-Century Contexts* (2016), copyright Taylor & Francis, available online: https://www.tandfonline.com/doi/full/10.1080/08905495.2016.1219199.

INTRODUCTION

Death by Invisible Hand

Victorian fiction is haunted by the problem of letting die. Over the course of the nineteenth century, as laissez-faire ideology hardened into economic policy, novelists repeatedly returned to the murky distinction between killing and letting die. Where should the line be drawn, they asked, between outright murder and passive complicity? When Bulstrode, in *Middlemarch,* discovers that a well-meaning nurse is providing the blackmailer Raffles with the wrong medical treatment, he chooses not to intervene, standing by as she unknowingly hastens Raffles's death. Dickens's greedy and irresponsible Skimpole indifferently sells out an ailing Jo for five pounds and contributes to the young boy's death. Though he never engages in direct violence, Godfrey Cass refuses to acknowledge his secret wife, Molly, which leads to her unmourned death by exposure in the snow in *Silas Marner.* He is followed by a whole spate of Hardy characters—Sergeant Troy, Alec D'Urberville, Michael Henchard, Clym Yeobright—whose actions indirectly lead to the deaths of women they sometimes loved, sometimes despised. The line between "letting die" and killing reads as anxiously unstable in these scenes: the Middlemarch rumor mill interprets Bulstrode as a murderer; Clym proclaims himself the killer of his wife and his mother; in *Daniel Deronda,* Gwendolen Harleth will turn a similar judgment on herself, reading her own hesitation to rescue her abusive husband as murder.

Even outright villains are curiously indirect. Quilp clearly brings about the much-mourned deaths of Nell and her grandfather, but he does so through predatory lending rather than direct violence. *The Woman in White's* Sir Percival Glyde goes to absurd lengths to avoid directly murdering his wife, Laura, for her money; instead, he kidnaps her doppelgänger, Anne Catherick; waits for Anne to die; buries her corpse as Laura; gaslights Laura into believing she is actually Anne; and then checks her into an asylum under Anne's name. Instead of killing the friendless Oliver Twist and claiming the full inheritance, Monks enlists Fagin to turn the child into a criminal so that he will forfeit his claim on his own. On the other side of the coin, guiltless bystanders go to extraordinary lengths to avoid letting others die, even against their own interests and at the risk of their own safety. Walter Hartright makes a desperate attempt to break into a burning church to save a man who is trying to kill him; John Barton pawns his last remaining belongings to help a family he does not even know; Esther Summerson risks her own health to care for Jo. Even the universally despised Rogue Riderhood becomes an object of "extraordinary interest" and keen "anxiety" when on the verge of death; the entire crowd leaps into action around his nearly drowned body, and "everybody present lends a hand, and a heart and soul" (Dickens, *Our Mutual Friend* 443–45).

This trend, I argue, speaks to a particular anxiety about pathological inaction that becomes pressing in the context of Victorian capitalism's codification of laissez-faire ideology. Even examples that do not seem directly connected to the capitalist marketplace, I suggest, express an anxiety that is at its root economic. The "let alone" capitalism that informed such Victorian economic policy as the New Poor Law of 1834 contains a necroeconomic mandate to let people die in service of market freedom—what I call "death by invisible hand." This book explores the complicated feelings produced by and circulating around this mandate—the reluctance, fear, sadism, pleasure, sympathy, sadness, guilt, and identification that accompany, motivate, or complicate the act of letting die. Looking closely at these necroeconomic feelings provides insight into how capitalism works with and through feeling—and how the Victorian novel works for and against capitalism.

"NECROECONOMICS"

In *The Condition of the Working-Class in England,* Engels argues that capitalism commits murder:

When society places hundreds of proletarians in such a position that they inevitably meet a too early and an unnatural death, one which is quite as much a death by violence as that by the sword or bullet; when it deprives thousands of the necessaries of life, places them under conditions in which they *cannot* live—forces them, through the strong arm of the law, to remain in such conditions until that death ensues which is the inevitable conse-quence—knows that these thousands of victims must perish, and yet permits these conditions to remain, its deed is murder just as surely as the deed of the single individual; disguised, malicious murder, murder against which none can defend himself, which does not seem what it is, because no man sees the murderer, because the death of the victim seems a natural one, since the offence is more one of omission than of commission. But murder it remains. (95–96)

Capitalism kills—but it does so in a roundabout, elusive way. Industrial capi-talism creates and requires a proletariat class that is deprived of the fruits of its own labor; thus, when proletarians die younger than their bourgeois counterparts due to deprivation, Engels calls foul play. "Malicious murder" is disguised as natural death because responsibility is dispersed across a sys-tem; murder is carried out not by sword or bullet but by the invisible hand of poverty, unnaturally created by capitalism and kept in place by a legal system designed to protect property. Marx detaches culpability even further from an individual actor when he assigns a kind of murderous capacity to capital itself. Capital, he claims, "is dead labour which, vampire-like, lives only by sucking living labour, and lives the more, the more labour it sucks" (342). Capital itself, in its vampiric extraction of surplus value from laboring bodies, is a necroeco-nomic mechanism.[1]

Of course, the Victorian system of free-market industrial capitalism[2] that Marx and Engels indict here is by no means the first or only economic sys-tem to produce or capitalize upon death. Sven Beckert emphasizes the vio-lence of the preceding economic era in Europe by renaming what is generally termed "mercantilism" as "war capitalism" (xv–xvi). This system, which accu-mulated wealth largely by means of slave trade and labor and the exploitation,

---

1. For an elaboration of the vampiric metaphor in Marx's *Capital*, see Neocleous.
2. While I emphasize the concept of "market freedom" because of its ideological signifi-cance, it is important to note that the Victorian economy never approached the entirely unregu-lated capitalist marketplace that the phrase "laissez-faire" implies. Paul Johnson's *Making the Market* is particularly effective in revealing just how far the complex historical reality of Victo-rian capitalism diverged from the rational ideal of the free market that Smith and Ricardo posit.

expropriation, and genocide of Indigenous peoples, was quite literally engaged in systematic murder in the service of economic growth. Nor is this death function limited to capitalism; the totalitarian socialism of twenty-first-century North Korea could certainly be said, in Engels's words, to deprive "thousands of the necessaries of life" and place them "under conditions in which they *cannot* live."

And yet, while death-by-economics is not unique to the nineteenth century, I will make the case here that necroeconomics emerges in a unique form in the period that this book investigates. I focus here on literature written between the 1820s and 1890s, a period famously marked by dramatic economic development and change in England. The steam power that set off the Industrial Revolution in the eighteenth century now powered mechanical production in factories and the railroad system that transported products to consumers; a growing population moved from farms to industrial centers; England transformed from a primarily agricultural economy to an industrial one, increasingly dependent on international trade to feed its population. These historical shifts were both the result of and the impetus for new developments in economic thought. While the broader story of Victorian economics is well known, I highlight how two of its key preoccupations—nonintervention and the population problem—combined in complex, sometimes contradictory ways to produce the uniquely Victorian necroeconomic anxieties that this book investigates.

Nonintervention

While the phrase "laissez-faire" originates with the French physiocrats, the principle of economic nonintervention comes to British economics largely through the work of Adam Smith. Due in part to William Pitt and Edmund Burke's readings of Smith in the decades following his death in 1790, the name has come to function as a metonym for economic freedom. But invocations of Smith as an uncompromising advocate for absolute market freedom belie the complexity and nuance of his writings. Smith could not have foreseen how his work would be taken up by future free-market evangelists, from direct followers like David Ricardo to twentieth-century Thatcherite conservatives to twenty-first-century anarcho-capitalists. He published his seminal text, *The Wealth of Nations*, in 1776, before the effects of the industrial revolution could be fully known. Over the course of his work's dynamic afterlife, Smith has been interpreted as everything from a radical Jacobin sympathizer to a providential theologian to a conservative demagogue.[3] This wide variety of interpretations points to internal contradictions in his oeuvre. Much has been made, for example, of the apparent conflict between the philosophy of ethical social cohesion Smith elaborates in *The Theory of Moral Sentiments* (1759) and his defense of individual self-interest in *The Wealth of Nations*.[4] In this book, I focus specifically on Smith's role in the emergence of the Victorian moral conundrum of necroeconomics.

While the actual Adam Smith was considerably less militant on nonintervention than many of his followers, his work played a crucial role in the public's understanding of the market as a mechanism that functioned best when unfettered by government intervention. In *The Wealth of Nations*, Smith posits his famous paradox: the surest way to promote the public good is to encourage individuals to pursue their private self-interest. "Without any intervention of law," he claims, "the private interests and passions of men naturally lead them to divide and distribute the stock of every society among all the different employments carried on in it; as nearly as possible in the proportion which is most agreeable to the interest of the whole society" (book 4, chapter 7). In this model, the public good cannot be pursued directly; it is an emergent product of self-interested individual action on a large scale. The mechanism by which individual self-interest is converted into public good is the metaphorical "invisible hand." While Smith uses the phrase only three times across his works—and while scholars such as Rothschild have suggested that he used it at least somewhat tongue-in-cheek[5]—the metaphor has taken on a life of its own. His most influential invocation of the invisible hand appears in his discussion of foreign trade in *The Wealth of Nations*. In explaining why self-interest will lead investors to employ their capital domestically without the need for government regulation, Smith claims that the capitalist

---

3. See Rothschild. Particularly interesting is Rothschild's explanation of how Edmund Burke co-opts and integrates Smith's economic liberalism into his own social conservatism in a way that lays the groundwork for the reinterpretation of Smith as a conservative thinker. On the other side of the coin, Marxist sociologist Giovanni Arrighi suggests in *Adam Smith in Beijing* that Smith is not a free-market capitalist at all, but rather a proponent of a highly controlled state-regulated market.

4. This debate begins in Germany in the 1890s with August Oncken's "The Consistency of Adam Smith"—in which he terms this potential bifurcation "Das Adam Smith Problem"—and continues through the twentieth century. In the American context, Jacob Viner and Glenn Morrow elaborate the same bifurcation in Smith's thought; see Viner 216; Morrow 4. Keith Tribe provides an overview of the scholarship on this issue in "'Das Adam Smith Problem.'"

5. See Rothschild, ch. 5.

intends only his own gain; and he is in this, as in many other cases, led by an invisible hand to promote an end which was no part of his intention. Nor is it always the worse for the society that it was no part of it. By pursuing his own interest, he frequently promotes that of the society more effectually than when he really intends to promote it. I have never known much good done by those who affected to trade for the public good. (book 4, chapter 2)

Beyond discouraging government intervention in the market, Smith's metaphor implies an unsettling disjunction between intention and effect. The capitalist who pursues his own interests produces public good; the philanthropist who tries to improve society directly ends up failing.[6] The invisible hand establishes, as Eleanor Courtemanche puts it, a "veil of ignorance between economic cause and effect"; just as easily as private vice might lead to public good, "altruistic actions might also lead to disaster" ('Invisible Hand' 2, 6).[7]

Generations of readers have understood the invisible hand less as a metaphor than as a social and economic mechanism, arguing by its logic that governments and individuals can best act upon benevolent motives not by intervening to help those less fortunate but rather by *withdrawing* intervention. This principle was already being put to the test in the decades following Smith's death as the issue of poor relief came the fore. While Smith himself is relatively silent on the issue of poor relief, the next generations of political economists drew upon his concept of unintended consequences in their calls for abolishing the Poor Laws. In his criticism of the Speenhamland system (an amended form of poor relief instituted in 1795), David Ricardo doubles down on the disjunction between intention and effect highlighted by Smith: "The clear and direct tendency of the poor laws . . . is not, as the legislature benevolently intended, to amend the condition of the poor, but to deteriorate the condition of both poor and rich; instead of making the poor rich, they are calculated to make the rich poor" (105–6). For Ricardo, centralized attempts to improve the lives of the poor are not only futile but actively harmful.[8] The

---

6. In this sense, Smith's invisible hand is a sort of inversion of Frances Hutcheson's religious conception of "Moral Sense." Hutcheson suggests that this moral sense works in the opposite direction, turning altruistic intentions into personal good; when we act upon moral sense, "we are only intending the Good of others," but "we undesignedly promote our own greatest private Good" (83).

7. Courtemanche explores the invisible hand metaphor both within and beyond its economic context, demonstrating how it "suggests an ironic mode of social action in which the results of individual actions are displaced to some indefinite spatial and temporal distance, creating by implication an unimaginably complex and detailed web of moral causality" ('Invisible Hand' 1).

8. In The Great Transformation, Karl Polanyi provides useful background on the shifts in political economy at this historical moment, tracing how the specific failures of the Speenhamland system contributed to political economy's rejection of welfare programs.

principle of the invisible hand thus precipitates a moral paradox: benevolent intentions must be enacted through the *absence* of benevolent actions.

The Population Problem

The principle of noninterference that Smith and Ricardo champion sits uneasily alongside the ideas of the Reverend Thomas Robert Malthus, whose *Essay on the Principle of Population* became another famous touchstone for Victorian economic debates. In the essay, first published in 1798, Malthus asserts that "the power of population is indefinitely greater than the power in the earth to produce subsistence for man" (19). At the heart of Malthus's thinking is a deep pessimism about the perfectibility of human society. His essay responds to what he saw as the misguided optimism of his late eighteenth-century contemporaries, William Godwin and the Marquis de Condorcet, who imagined quasi-utopian futures based on intellectual progress and optimal technocratic management, respectively. For Malthus, the gap between projected population growth and food production will thwart any scheme to eliminate human misery. He argues that population, if unchecked, will grow geometrically, while food production will at best grow arithmetically; the means of subsistence will inevitably run out (19). Population growth must thus be managed, one way or another: if not by "preventative checks" (delayed marriage, abstinence)[9] then by epidemics, wars, and famines (*Essay* 43). Through Malthus's lens, periods of prosperity become harbingers of future suffering, because widespread prosperity leads to early marriage and population growth, which will inevitably lead to want and suffering when trade turns down, the subsistence limit is reached, and resources run out. Malthus is skeptical of any proposal to circumvent this problem by means of technology or social programming—in particular, by direct relief to the poor. As Malthus writes in the first version of the *Essay* and expands upon in subsequent versions, the Poor Laws are responsible for increasing poverty and distress in the long term by encouraging procreation among the poor. He advocates for the gradual but total abolition of these laws. The human drive to reproduce is for Malthus the ultimate factor that limits economic growth, obstructs social programs to mitigate the effects of poverty, and hinders any scheme toward the perfection of society. Procreation and population growth emerge not as signs of vitality but as

---

9. Malthus is uncompromising in his position that any form of birth control other than abstinence is a vice. His theories take a different turn in the hands of followers such as Francis Place and John Stuart Mill, who agree with Malthus on the need to limit population but see contraception as a valid and effective way to do so. For more on Mill's advocacy for birth control, see Himes; Langer; Schwartz 245–52.

checks upon human progress and harbingers of death. As Emily Steinlight puts it, "procreation is both systematically necessary to the continuation of the species and (in the absence of sufficient checks) inimical to its existence" (45).

Historically, this idea of population as a problem emerges alongside the idea of laissez-faire noninterference, but political economy is not a monolithic field of thought. While Malthus was influenced by Smith and Ricardo (and personal friends with the latter), their goals and positions do not always coincide. Most crucially, they differ on the valence they assign to population. The population growth that Malthus views as a cause of misery is for Smith a positive sign of national prosperity and an essential stimulus for increased labor specialization, which Smith views as an engine for economic growth.[10] Moreover, a Malthusian concern with the subsistence of the population does not always imply the same policy positions as a Smithian commitment to free trade. For example, Malthus's commitment to the development and maintenance of domestic agriculture set him at odds with his contemporary Ricardo. After agreeing in their support of the New Poor Law, the two political economists split on the issue of the Corn Laws. Ricardo took the side of free trade, supporting the repeal of tariffs on foreign corn in order to bring food prices down, while Malthus argued for the necessity of tariffs to protect domestic agriculture and maintain England's ability to produce its own food supply ("Observations").[11] While Malthus generally supported free trade policies, his concern that falling food prices would lead to disinvestment in agriculture and British dependence on foreign imports to feed its population led him to publish a pamphlet in support of the Corn Laws in 1814, which created a rift between him and Ricardo, McCulloch, and Mill.[12] Further, Malthus was characteristically concerned about the possibility that a sudden drop in food prices might lead to a boom in population growth.

Alternately condemned as basely sex-driven, reducing humanity to animalistic drives (by Godwin and Hazlitt), and as perversely asexual, reducing marriage to economic calculus (by Byron and Percy Shelley),[13] the mild-

10. For more on Adam Smith's views on population, see Spengler. For a recent analysis of the differences between Smith's and Malthus's positions, see Kreager.

11. The "Observations" pamphlet was initially published in spring of 1814; a second edition was published later in 1814 and an expanded third edition the following year.

12. See Winch, *Malthus* 68–74.

13. Percy Shelley describes Malthus's doctrines as "those of a eunuch and a tyrant" (51), while Byron takes a jab at Malthusian thought when he satirizes the prospect of "turning marriage into arithmetic" in Canto 15 of *Don Juan*. Hazlitt, in contrast, accuses Malthus of writing about human beings as if they are nothing more than "so many animals in season" (56). For more on the conflicting characterization of Malthus as alternately "an asexual or an over-fertile hypocrite" (43), see Steinlight 40–44. See also Gallagher, *Body Economic* 8–16.

mannered Reverend Malthus was an unlikely lightning rod for nineteenth-century anxieties about sex and death. In the hands of his critics, he becomes a sort of metonymic figurehead for the ravenous death drive of a new economic order that seeks to kill the poor. As I will discuss further in chapter 1, his name becomes so deeply connected with cold-blooded capitalist calculus that many working-class people come to believe that he proposed a program of mass infanticide. In fact, the real Malthus is more typical of Victorian culture than the caricature his critics presented. What Malthus wants is to minimize misery. His conundrum is that he believes that allowing a certain amount of death to occur, by withdrawing financial support from the poor, is a necessary step in preventing greater suffering in the long run. Like Smith and Ricardo, Malthus believes in the existence of immutable natural laws that human beings cannot circumvent. The most salient and immutable of these laws, for Malthus, is the paradox of population, according to which the "the reproducing body" must "eventually destroy the very prosperity that made it fecund" (Gallagher, *Body Economic* 37). This results in a deep ambivalence about life and death that I argue here is widely and characteristically Victorian. The Malthusian conundrum is at the heart of Victorian necroeconomics: At what point does the preservation of life become a threat to life itself? How much death must be allowed in order to preserve life?

It is the convergence of these two central economic ideas—nonintervention on the one hand, and population as peril on the other—that forms the Victorian necroeconomic imaginary at the heart of this book. When combined with Malthusian fear of the specter of excessive population, Smith's principle of nonintervention transforms into a mandate to let the poor die. I borrow the term "necroeconomics" from Mike Hill and Warren Montag, who use it to describe the particular necroeconomic innovation of laissez-faire capitalism. That is, they argue that the self-regulating economic system elaborated by eighteenth-century political economists and evangelized by early Victorian reformers not only posits an "immutable and immanent order of what would come to be called the market" but also advocates for the "legitimate power to expose [citizens] to death through hunger . . . in the name of the laws of [that] natural order" (263). In other words, in arguing for the primacy of the market as a self-governing mechanism that will bring about maximum prosperity when allowed to function without government intervention, these political economists are also arguing for the government's *right and responsibility* to abandon its citizens to death in order to preserve the market's freedom. Lethal nonintervention is not just permissible; it is morally necessary. This economic ideology is "necroeconomic" in that it requires *letting people die*—not in service of profit or sovereignty, but in service of market freedom and population control.

This is the form of necroeconomics that Dickens famously criticizes in *Oliver Twist*. In a paradigmatic passage, the "very sage, deep, philosophical men" who comprise the parish board make the strategic choice to let poor people die:

> They established the rule, that all poor people should have the alternative (for they would compel nobody, not they), of being starved by a gradual process in the house, or by a quick one out of it. With this view, they contracted with the water-works to lay on an unlimited supply of water; and with a corn-factor to supply periodically small quantities of oatmeal; and issued three meals of thin gruel a day, with an onion twice a week, and half a roll of Sundays. . . . For the first six months after Oliver Twist was removed, the system was in full operation. It was rather expensive at first, in consequence of the increase in the undertaker's bill, and the necessity of taking in the clothes of all the paupers, which fluttered loosely on their wasted, shrunken forms, after a week or two's gruel. But the number of workhouse inmates got thin as well as the paupers; and the board were in ecstasies. (14)

The board's system involves no compulsion, no active violence, but it is clearly designed to cull the population. The workhouse functions here as a bureaucratic mechanism for abandoning the indigent to their inevitable death by starvation. Dickens draws attention to this system as a kind of passive murder, characterized by strategic nonintervention and motivated by fear of an excessive population.

In this book, I am concerned with how these two interconnected ideas surface—sometimes overtly and sometimes subtly—in Victorian fiction. In the hands of literary writers who are not economists, the concepts undergo distortion, reframing, and transformation. As I explore these works, I am not writing a history of economic thought but rather contributing to the body of scholarly work called the "new economic criticism," which has worked for three decades to illuminate the complex and productive overlap between economic history and theory on the one hand and Victorian literature and culture on the other.[14] A range of scholars, including Catherine Gallagher, Mary Poovey, Philip Connell, Gordon Bigelow, Donald Winch, and Anna Kornbluh,

14. Other key work in this subfield includes Regenia Gagnier's *The Insatiability of Human Wants*, Mary Poovey's *The Financial System in Nineteenth-Century Britain*, and Martha Woodmansee and Mark Osteen's edited collection, *The New Economic Criticism*.

highlights a much more complicated engagement between economists and artists than the "two cultures" hypothesis might lead us to believe.[15] Gallagher's *The Body Economic* reveals, through detailed analyses of the dialectical interaction between political economists and Romanticists and early Victorian critics, the emergence of organic life itself as the primary measure and source of value in the nineteenth century—an insight that lays the groundwork for my own project. For Claudia Klaver, economic writing emerges as a "scientific" discipline in uneasy conversation with its own literary popularization; in a kind of reversal of these terms, Mary Poovey shows how the genre of literary writing itself is shaped in negotiation with the market.[16]

My own work here builds on this rich tradition of scholarly attention to the intersection between literature and economics to ask specifically how the Victorian novel confronts and is confronted by the *specter* of necroeconomics—not the economic theories themselves, but the moral and social questions that they raise. In this sense, I build methodologically upon the work of scholars who explore how Victorian literature deals, formally and imaginatively, with the problems raised by a dramatically evolving economic landscape. In particular, I build upon the work of Eleanor Courtemanche, who investigates the metaphor of the "invisible hand," and Emily Steinlight, who addresses the idea of the surplus population. This project brings these two powerful concepts together to explore their implications for novelists: how do narrative fictions struggle to address the passive killing of the surplus population by the invisible hand of the market?

Steinlight's work crucially reshapes our scholarly understanding of the Victorian novel's relationship to biopolitics. Victorian scholarship has built productively on Foucault's distinction between the premodern power of the sovereign, who is vested with the power to "let live or make die," and modern disciplinary power, which actively "makes live" through dispersed techniques of discipline and passively "lets die." Critics since D. A. Miller have argued that the rise of disciplinary power and the rise of the novel as genre bear a deeper connection than historical coincidence. Miller aligned the novel with the active "making live" techniques through which disciplinary power produces individual subjects; Miller sees, for example, a correspondence between the surveillance of modern disciplinary power and the panoptic eye of the omniscient narrative voice. Other critics, such as Nancy Armstrong and Mary Poovey, have similarly conceived of the novel as an "individualizing technolog[y]" (Poovey, *Making* 22). Lauren Goodlad's *Victorian Literature and*

15. In addition to works discussed in the text, see Bigelow; Connell; Kornbluh; Winch, *Riches and Poverty.*

16. See Klaver; Poovey, *Genres.*

the Victorian State evolved the conversation by shifting focus from Foucault's writing about panopticism to his later lectures on governmentality, which emphasize how liberalism works through a combination of disciplinary action and strategic inaction; I follow Goodlad in similarly focusing on Foucault's later lectures, published as *Security, Territory, Population* and *"Society Must Be Defended."* Emily Steinlight shifted the conversation even more fundamentally by challenging the idea that the novel is primarily concerned with the individual at all. In contrast, she argues that the Victorian novel formally represents human superfluity: a mass of life, devoid of any meaningful qualitative distinction between "fit and unfit organisms," (16) which necessarily "overruns and overwhelms the socioeconomic order" (15) designed to contain it. I agree with Steinlight that the world of the Victorian novel presents no stable difference between valuable individual and disposable surplus. However, I explore a different dynamic: instead of focusing on how the novel represents superfluity itself, I focus on what the novel can tell us about what happens when individuals are tasked with the micro-level work of disposing of that surplus. Even as the biopolitical imagination that Steinlight describes erodes the distinction between productive individual and disposable surplus, both the liberal state and the Victorian novel continue to enlist individual actors in the work of maintaining that untenable distinction. Thus, I see "individual" and "mass," "fit and unfit" not as stable categories that correspond with any real distinction, but rather as positions into which people are placed and between which they can move depending on circumstance. I focus on how the novel represents the interplay between these two contingent positions in the context of the passive violence of necroeconomics. In this sense, many of the narrators I write about are, in fact, aligned with the work of the biopolitical liberal state—but not in the way that Miller suggests. Rather than surveilling and disciplining—doing the work of "making live"—they are complicit in the strategic inaction of letting die.

In using the term "necroeconomics," Hill and Montag build on Achille Mbembe's foundational work on necropolitics as the corollary and necessary supplement to biopower. Elaborating upon and revising Foucault, Mbembe highlights how biopower functions not only through the management of life but also through the "controlled exposure [of populations] to want, dearth, and deprivation" (*Necropolitics* 263). Like Foucault, Mbembe sees racism as a central technology of necropower—one that "make[s] possible the murderous functions of the state" ("Necropolitics" 17). But Mbembe also enriches Foucault's brief analysis of biopower's death function by examining both its history and its continued life in the context of slavery, apartheid, and the colony.[17] In the space of colonial occupation, necropower operates not just as passive abandonment to death (the "letting die" of Foucauldian security) but also through technologies that straddle the line between passive "letting die" and active "making die," such as territorial fragmentation, infrastructural warfare, and the state of siege. Since Mbembe's coinage of the term in 2003, scholars have productively applied the rubric of necropolitics to a range of policies, systems, and modes of power. Focusing primarily on the Israeli-Palestinian conflict, for example, Jasbir Puar's *The Right to Maim* highlights necropower's investment in debility as well as death.[18] Scholars across various disciplines— geography scholar Ruth Gilmore, anthropologist Frédéric Le Marcis—have analyzed the necropolitics of prisons and the carceral state in terms in necropolitics. Others have argued that Foucault's original formulation of "making live and letting die" does not hold across contexts. Marina Gržinić and Šefik Tatlić point to the "pure necropolitics" that actively *makes die* in the Balkan wars of the 1990s, and Sayak Valencia's *Gore Capitalism* illuminates practices like kidnapping and contract murder in Tijuana, where the "destruction of the body becomes in itself the product or commodity" (20). Taken together, this work gives us a vocabulary for a range of ever-evolving forms of sovereignty that operates through "the generalized instrumentalization of human existence and the material destruction of human bodies and populations" (14).

The time and place where my own book begins—the late 1820s and early 1830s in Great Britain—is marked by its uniquely visible and deeply contradictory necroeconomic forms. Domestically, the first wave of national reforms initiated the shift toward the dominance of the free market: the New Poor Law, which signals a move toward government nonintervention; the repeal of the Corn Laws, which indicates an increasingly globalized market, beginning a trend toward market freedom that William Morris will suggest negates nationhood entirely by the end of the century. But it is also a period defined by imperial violence, justified in terms of national, racial, and religious difference, which operates according to a separate necroeconomic logic that is often at odds with the doctrine of the free market.[19] In these early years of Britain's imperial century, formal colonial occupation around the globe expanded

---

17. The sociologist Orlando Patterson, who describes the social death of the slave, is a forerunner for Mbembe's line of thought here. See Patterson.

18. Puar's work on queer necropolitics also explores the intersection between queer politics and Islamophobia. Jin Haritaworn, Adi Kunstman, and Silvia Posocco extend and proliferate this thinking in their collection on *Queer Necropolitics*.

19. In *The Economics of European Imperialism*, Alan Hodgart provides a comprehensive analysis of the complex relationship between market logic and nationalism in European imperialism.

alongside the development of Britain's informal imperial power in countries like China and Argentina.[20] Typified by the violent collaboration between the East India Company and the Royal Navy, Victorian colonial necroeconomic violence took place at sites where corporation and nation were fundamentally blurred.[21] Despite the often self-congratulatory national discourse surrounding the outlawing of the slave trade in 1807 and the belated abolition of slavery in the Caribbean in 1833, Britain remained financially invested in plantation slavery in the American South and continued to profit from slave labor in its non-Caribbean colonies.[22] It was a moment when Victorian publics—including literary writers—were asked to confront conflicting moral and social rationales for necroeconomic policies at home and overseas.

These different necroeconomic modes were at times pitted against each other; in abolition debates, for example, some working-class advocates such as William Cobbett doubled down on racial difference when they argued that the needs of white English paupers were more pressing than those of Black slaves,[23] while abolitionists like Harriet Martineau employed the logic of free-market evangelism in their arguments against the use of slave labor.[24] Christopher Taylor has shown how these ideas overlapped uncomfortably in the postabolition British West Indies, where colonial West Indians interpreted the early nineteenth-century shift toward economic liberalism as a form of state abandonment or neglect.[25] In other cases, the interests of imperial expansion and industrial free-market capitalism align and enable one another. For example, Hannah Arendt argues that "capitalist production" creates, as a "by-product," a "superfluous" working population, which in turn fuels imperialist expansion (150). Conversely, Ann Laura Stoler argues that the disciplinary techniques generally linked to the rise of European free-market capitalism were largely developed in the context of colonialism. Sven Beckert's study of the history of cotton production highlights the geopolitical entanglement of the plantations of the American South and the textile factories of Manchester and Liverpool, illuminating how cotton production simultaneously fueled

20. See Gallagher and Robinson. For an analysis of how the British position in Latin America paradoxically combined imperialism and anti-imperialism, see Reeder. For more on Britain's quasi-imperial involvement in China, see Bickers and Howlett; Dean.

21. See Keay for an analysis of the overlap between commercialism and imperialism, as well as a further account of British informal empire in China.

22. For a thorough analysis of how Britain continued to profit from slavery post-1807 and the loopholes of the British Emancipation Act, see Sherwood.

23. See Gallagher, *Industrial Reformation* 6–10.

24. See Martineau, *Writings*.

25. See Taylor.

the expansion of both slavery and the "free market." Free-market capitalism and imperialism arise in contentious but mutually constitutive entanglement. And yet, the novels that I examine in this book often occlude that relationship. The novels that I read—all written by white English authors—reflect upon the morally complex role of British citizens within an evolving domestic capitalist free market that often defined itself against a vaguely defined non-British other. Discussion of imperialism's spaces, actors, and techniques of power appear primarily as foils for domestic capitalism. Even the explicitly anti-imperialist Morris criticizes imperialist expansion largely in terms of its expansion of the global market for capitalist goods. In the chapters of this book, I seek to draw out moments in which the relationship between imperialism and free-market capitalism becomes visible; for example, in chapter 2, I investigate what *Bleak House* reveals about how the "letting die" of domestic free-market capitalism depends on affective relations more characteristic of the imperial situation. Yet I also recognize that there is much more to say about necroeconomics and imperialism in Victorian fiction that falls beyond the scope of this project, and I look forward to future scholarship that covers what my own book does not.

"FEELINGS"

I take as my premise that necroeconomic capitalism is not just imposed from the top down by bureaucrats, politicians, and oligarchs. Instead, it works in and through emotions and desires—the affective encounters among capitalists, consumers, and workers. Scholars of affect have been exploring the feelings of capitalism in a variety of ways. Kathleen Stewart writes experientially of the affective experience of living under capitalism, describing power as "a thing of the senses" (84); Dierdra Reber calls attention to the affective dimension of twenty-first-century marketing campaigns (e.g., "Love. It's what makes a Subaru, a Subaru."). Lauren Berlant tracks the "cruel optimism" of late capitalist subjects—the "affective attachment to what we call 'the good life,' which is for so many a bad life that wears out subjects who nonetheless, and at the same time, find their conditions of possibility within it" (97). For many of these scholars, capitalism's instrumentalization of affect has intensified and deepened in the late twentieth and early twenty-first centuries. Michael Hardt and Antonio Negri identify in the late twentieth century a shift from industrial labor to an "immaterial labor" that is irreducibly affective (108–9). Brian Massumi describes how new communication technologies facilitate "relational marketing" that "works by contagion rather than convincing, on affect rather than rational choice," capturing our "affective capacities" as a "capitalist tool" (25).

Victorianists such as Mary Poovey, Pamela Gilbert, Catherine Gallagher, Krista Lysack, and others have illuminated the various ways in which liberal capitalism requires and produces particular emotions and desires.[26] But perhaps more so than any other manifestation of capitalism, early nineteenth-century laissez-faire capitalism conspicuously positions itself as separate from emotional or affective concerns. Writers like Ricardo sought to subtract emotional and moral considerations from economics,[27] and political economists tried to rewrite passion as interest.[28] But laissez-faire capitalism always exceeded (and perhaps was never within) the bounds of cold scientific rationality. Indeed, Deirdre Reber pinpoints the "birth of free-market capitalism" in the late eighteenth century as the beginning of an "epistemic shift from reason to affect" (16). Capitalism, she claims, "constructs itself epistemologically" not on a model of transcendental rationality directed by the thinking head but rather "on the model of immanent and foundationally affective homeostasis" directed from within by the feeling body (16). She traces this shift to "affect-as-episteme" all the way back to Adam Smith and the "visceral logic of the invisible hand, which mindlessly, through somatic wisdom, achieves a perfect distribution of resources throughout the greater human body" (28). Her argument shares ground with Massumi, who (drawing in turn on Deleuze and Guattari) claims that "the concept of affectivity is more fundamental than rationality" for "the understanding of capitalism as a process" (90–91). I follow Reber and Massumi in attending to how capitalism *feels* as a primary way of understanding how it works. But while Reber's work focuses on affect-as-episteme's apogee in the post–Cold War era of "'one-world' capitalist globalization," I am interested in delving deeper into its nineteenth-century origins (16). When we look closely at the problem of necroeconomics in Victorian fiction, we see that capitalist affects are disturbed from the very beginning by the injunction to let die. Feeling emerges simultaneously as both the legitimating epistemic mode of capitalism and its most salient threat.

The Victorian novel, which has been cast as both textbook and laboratory of feelings, is thus a crucial archive for the excavation of nineteenth-century necroeconomics. A range of scholars have characterized the Victorian novel as a genre that is particularly invested in trying to teach people how to feel. Rachel Ablow has argued that experiencing the novel's emotional pedagogy

---

26. See also Kowaleski-Wallace.

27. See Klaver.

28. See Hirschman.

was in fact the "explicit goal of novel reading" for many Victorian readers ("Victorian Feelings" 201). Some, such as Martha Nussbaum, have argued for the prosocial value of this emotional pedagogy, viewing it as a means of producing ethical behavior among readers. Others have characterized this emotional training as complicit in capitalism. For scholars such as D. A. Miller, Mary Poovey, Nancy Armstrong, and Carolyn Betensky, the Victorian novel works upon the emotions in a way that helps to produce subjects who work *for capitalism*: as appropriately desiring consumers; as maximally productive, disciplined workers; and crucially, as emotionally active but politically passive middle-class bystanders who witness working-class suffering without interference. While these scholars take a wide variety of approaches, they agree that the Victorian novel, which appears to represent feeling in and for a private realm outside of capitalism, actually teaches feeling in a way that is particularly useful for capitalism. My own readings here suggest that Victorian fiction was neither categorically on the side of capitalism nor firmly against it; all the novels that I examine in this book both rehearse and undermine the premises of capitalist economics. What is most productive about the novel, I argue, is that it is an epistemological tool that shows how capitalism works, not only as an economic system but as an affective one. I follow Deleuze, Guattari, and Massumi in suggesting that "ideology works best when its structure of ideas is lived—acted out in the everyday" (Massumi 85). Novels provide iterative models of that everyday enactment, giving us insight into how capitalist ideology is lived.

In the conversation surrounding working-class precarity under capitalism in Victorian studies, the feeling that has most frequently been discussed is *sympathy*. This conversation is heavily inflected by the theory of sympathy put forth by Adam Smith in his *Theory of Moral Sentiments*. Following Smith, scholars such as Catherine Gallagher, Audrey Jaffe, and Rae Greiner[29] all characterize Victorian sympathy as an imaginative or specular encounter, reading the materiality of the body as a "barrier that constitutes an obstacle to sympathy" (Jaffe, *Scenes* 7).[30] While I build upon these scholars, I contend that literary scholarship in this area has been hemmed in by a tendency to rely upon a theory of interpersonal feeling that originates within laissez-faire capitalist ideology. While many have viewed Smith's theory of sympathy separately from his economic arguments for the free market, I follow Hill and Montag in viewing them as fundamentally linked. They read Smith's intervention in *The*

---

29. See Gallagher, *Nobody's Story*; Jaffe, *Scenes*; Greiner.

30. For Gallagher, fictional sympathy works differently than enacted sympathy; for Jaffe, fictional sympathy is consistent with enacted sympathy in that both involve the "[imaginative conversion of] other persons into [one's] own . . . 'impressions'" (*Scenes* 7, n. 12).

Theory of Moral Sentiments as a "translation" of sympathy from a "transindividual phenomenon," understood by prior theorists "as a 'communication' or 'transmission' of affect from one individual to another," into an "intraindividual" phenomenon—"nothing more than an exercise of the imagination that finally neither depends upon others nor even requires their existence" (110). By this means, Smith defangs affect—which he sees as both necessary for and threatening to a self-regulating economy—by imposing upon feelings the same logic of private property that underwrites his economic theory. In this book, I ask what we can see in the Victorian novel when we think outside of Smith's definition of sympathy.

In discussing feelings that exceed and disrupt the boundaries of rational individualism, I am entering into a discourse about affect. While affect is notoriously slippery to define,[31] I follow Deborah Gould in using the term "affects" to describe unnamed, unstructured "but nevertheless registered experiences of bodily energy and intensity that arise in response to stimuli impinging on the body" (19). I do not situate affect in a privileged, naturalized space outside of culture,[32] nor do I want to suggest that affects are "true" in a way that language or thought is not. Like Ben Anderson, I view affects as "an inescapable element within an expanded definition of the political, rather than a natural dimension of life to be recuperated and recovered or a secondary effect of the secret ideological workings of power" (164). Indeed, it is the very "illusion that affect is 'beyond debate'" that makes it so ripe for analysis (Jaffe, "Affect" 715). I agree here with Audrey Jaffe that the site "of what goes without saying because it simply feels true . . . is where ideology most comfortably resides" (715–16). Affects are central to the process by which *ideology becomes visceral,* causing commitments to be felt as attachments and political differences to be felt as physical aversions. Attending to these "gut feelings" affords an opportunity to understand how "systems of meaning" get "lodged in the gut" as well as how affect might be mobilized to change those systems of meaning (Holland, Ochoa, and Tompkins 395).

Throughout this book, I use "feelings" as a deliberately inclusive umbrella term to encompass the whole range of sensations that circulate in and around interpersonal encounters, from infracognitive intensities as they register on the body to the cognitive rationalizing of emotional response in relation to

---

31. For an account of this slipperiness as productive, see Gregg and Seigworth 1–4; for a more skeptical account of it, see Jaffe, "Affect" 714–15.

32. In doing so, I diverge somewhat from psychologist Silvan Tompkins, whose foundational work defines affects both categorically and biologically, and align more with literary and cultural critics such as Deleuze, Guattari, Massumi, and Negri (who, in turn, look back to Spinoza).

situated ideologies. Like the novelists I read, I am interested in this whole (nonchronological) circuit, including the body that feels, the mind that reflects, and the space between bodies in which feelings circulate. While these novelists come to different conclusions, they are all concerned with the circulation of feeling: how it *does* circulate, how it *should* circulate, and how it has *been prevented from* circulating. Examining a diverse archive of feelings—positive, negative, catastrophic, mundane, perverse—I suggest that we can learn as much from the pleasures of necroeconomics as we can from its more obvious pains. Influenced by Sara Ahmed, I am interested in the "sticky" properties of feelings. They can bind communities together, sticking body to body; they can make certain signs or ideas "stick" to certain objects or bodies (Ahmed 13). I posit that Victorian feelings get especially sticky around the problem of letting die. By excavating literary representations of necroeconomic feelings, this book seeks to illuminate what feelings *do* within a system of capitalism that operates through death—and what they might do differently.

SUMMARY OF ARGUMENT

The book begins at the moment of the New Poor Law in the early 1830s, with texts that treat the issue of "letting die" literally. It then moves chronologically forward and conceptually outward, exploring novels that treat the problem of necroeconomics in increasingly figurative ways. The organization of the book thus mimics the trend I see across the Victorian period as the problem of "letting die" diffuses outward, becoming less of an open debate and more of an anxious haunting. I begin in chapter 1 with Harriet Martineau's massively popular *Illustrations of Political Economy* (1832–34), which quite literally uses narrative to train a lay readership to think and, more importantly, to *feel* like political economists. In her didactic narratives, which are rooted in her readings of Smith, Malthus, and Ricardo, Martineau seeks to reeducate her audience's affective responses to make them less likely to disrupt the operation of the free market. Things get complicated, though, when she comes up against the problem of necroeconomics in her depiction of a country doctor who is led by his belief in laissez-faire economics to resign his medical position at local charitable institutions. In the Malthusian doctor's dilemma, Martineau reveals a conflict between an economic system that she considers eminently natural (which demands letting die) and a set of affective responses that she depicts as instinctive, laudable, and fundamentally "natural" as well (which make letting die feel troubling). It is this paradox that makes her illustrations necessary; the narratives act as affective retraining measures, teaching readers not to "trust their gut" and instead to feel like capitalists—in other words, to get comfortable with letting people die.

This tacit violence is made dramatically explicit during the Marcus pamphlet controversy at the end of the decade, when working-class journalists and activists accuse Martineau and her allies of mass murder. Following Gregory Vargo, I read the coverage of this controversy in the working-class radical press as a strategic response to the slow violence of necroeconomics, employing a combination of satirical text and serious response to bring embedded violence to the surface. Finally, I close the chapter by reading Martineau's novel *Deerbrook* (1838) as a revisionist redemption story for the Malthusian doctor. *Deerbrook* follows the undeserved trials and eventual vindication of the provincial Dr. Hope as he navigates a dangerous cholera epidemic and an even more dangerous small-town rumor mill, which unfairly casts him as necroeconomic villain. Exploring the echoes between the accusations of murderous experimentation upon the bodies of the poor against Dr. Hope and the similar accusations against Martineau herself during the Marcus scandal, I read *Deerbrook* as her displaced self-vindication narrative. In seeking to distance herself from the accusations of violence being leveled at her in the press, however, she ends up implicitly disavowing a central tenet of the laissez-faire ideology she sought to popularize: the noninterventionist mandate to let die. In this ambivalence, Martineau becomes an unlikely and perhaps uncomfortable forerunner of the trend I explore in this book: the Victorian novel's tendency to dwell on, highlight, criticize, and otherwise get stuck on the ethical problem of letting die at the heart of laissez-faire capitalism.

Elizabeth Gaskell kicks off this trend in earnest. Gaskell shares a key premise with Martineau—a recognition that affect has to be managed and manipulated in order to make capitalism work. But while Martineau saw such affective management as a necessary step to create a healthy social body under the immutable laws of political economy, Gaskell sees it as an unhealthy repression of the natural flow of sympathy on which a healthy social body should be founded. In *Mary Barton* (1848) and *North and South* (1854), Gaskell focuses on the pathological effects of this affective manipulation. Although Gaskell characterizes herself as an economic outsider, I argue that her industrial novels actually present an incisive critique of a necroeconomic system that must systematically repress natural sympathy in order to protect and empower itself. In doing so, she expands our understanding of necroeconomics, revealing something much more insidious than a passive commitment to "letting die." Through her description of the mill owners' management of their workers, she illuminates the workings of what I call "pathoeconomics"—that is, strategically making people ill and utilizing that ill health as a tool for maintaining class hierarchy and exploiting workers. Beyond this, she imagines what might happen if the affective management of capitalism were destroyed—that is, if affects were allowed to return to what she sees as their "natural" pathways. This has often been read as an apolitical infusion of sympathy into capitalism, designed to make relations between masters and workers more compassionate without altering any of the larger power structures that produce inequality, but it is a central premise of this book that affects *are* political and necessary to economic systems, and as such, have political and economic implications.

My reading hinges on a critical reinterpretation of what Gaskell means by sympathy. I argue that her definition is crucially different from the conditional, imaginative sympathy described by Adam Smith, whose work has often been taken as foundational for Victorian novelists. Gaskell's version aligns much more closely with the radically transindividual sympathy of Spinoza. That is, Gaskell presents sympathy as a mode of instinctive, embodied affiliation that is inherently disruptive to necroeconomic capitalism and that thus has been systematically repressed in order to bolster and protect that system. When she imagines a world in which those disruptive affects are restored to their natural pathways, she is removing a cornerstone from the foundation of that necroeconomic system. By the end of *North and South,* Gaskell ultimately imagines an alternative economic system, the radical strangeness of which, I argue, has been underappreciated by critics: that is, a not-for-profit capitalism made possible by putting the means of production into the hands of middle-class women, whose emotional training for that role is an accidental byproduct of the necroeconomic system Gaskell seeks to replace.

Chapters 1 and 2 explore the emotional management or training we need in order to be capable of letting others die in the service of market freedom. Chapter 3 pushes this question further: what forms of affective experience can make people not just *let* others die but actually *want* them to? What is the broader affective structure that enables people to think that others must be allowed to die in order for them to live most fully? And how do affective experiences constitute the boundary between those who must live and the "other" who can die? In this chapter, I read Dickens's *Bleak House* (1852–53) to reveal how specific affective structures and modes of circulation, which are primarily learned and performed in domestic spaces, make necroeconomics possible. Specifically, we see in this text how the performance of an inverse affective relation, wherein one person's negative affect generates positive affect in another, can instantiate boundaries or subdivisions within a population— boundaries that, under necroeconomics, become divisions between who must live and who can or should be allowed to die.

This mechanism of subdividing a population aligns closely with what Foucault describes as biopolitical racism and, along with other theorists, characterizes as a foundational technology of the modern biopolitical (and necropolitical) state. Seeing these barriers emerge in Dickens's serialized novel gives us a fuller picture of how the ideology of necroeconomics takes root. It is not mechanically imposed on citizens by robotic bureaucrats or a faceless government program; rather, it is continuously emerging through interpersonal interactions and affective practices that we see occurring over time in the serialized space of the novel. In fact, the principal actors of necroeconomics in *Bleak House,* from Mrs. Pardiggle to Skimpole to Inspector Bucket, seem to *enjoy* the practice of letting die. Martineau's cerebral political economists felt only sadness and regret as they reluctantly declined to provide aid to the unemployed; Dickens's necropolitical subjects relish their "letting die" function, actively prolonging the death of the other and seeking a front-row seat to their extended suffering. Dickens shows, in other words, that there is pleasure in necroeconomics. And it is this pleasure, which exceeds any rational justification for the efficacy of laissez-faire policy, that transforms necroeconomics from a coldly rational policy into a deeply felt compulsion that threatens to destroy the social body from within. Drawing on Roberto Esposito's concept of *immunitas,* I argue that Dickens represents necroeconomics as an autoimmune disease of the social body, causing it to compulsively build barriers to the point that it self-destructs. But because Dickens locates necroeconomics in everyday affective experiences, he also establishes a horizon of possibility for change by means of affective intervention. This shift reframes Esther Summerson, often seen as an apolitical angel in the house, as someone engaged in political action, working to break down necroeconomics by engaging in alternative affective practices.

Dickens and Gaskell both establish a mutually constitutive relationship between the material conditions of necroeconomics and its operative feelings—a cycle by which the structure of interpersonal interactions under industrial capitalism encourages affective relations that make people more comfortable enacting its ideology, which helps (re)entrench and justify material hierarchies, which then crystallize the affective relations, and so on. In the final chapter, I turn to two late-century authors—George Eliot and William Morris—who imagine two different ways of breaking that cycle. While Morris and Eliot are very different, generically and politically, I argue that they take parallel approaches to the problem of necroeconomics. Both authors go to the very root of necroeconomics, presenting the circulation of capital itself as fundamentally pathological and imagining what individuals would look like and what kind of communities they might create if emptied out of capitalist feelings. They approach the problem from opposite sides, however, both temporally and conceptually. Eliot's retrospective novels *Felix Holt* (1866) and *Middlemarch* (1871–72) approach the problem by looking backward in time to the years around the New Poor Law debates with which this book began. Through her depiction of disgust in *Middlemarch*, Eliot suggests that the feeling of letting die *travels* between individuals via the "sticky" vector of capital. To engage in the circulation of capital is thus to risk entering into a chain of metonymic connection that compromises not only bourgeois individualism but liberalism as a whole. Eliot imagines a solution to this problem in the form of characters defined by their total lack of affective investment in capital, which both obviates the need for the medium of the invisible hand and protects them from getting "stuck" to others. But when we place *Middlemarch* alongside *Felix Holt*, we see how easily critiques of capitalist feelings can get folded back into the ideology of capitalism itself, as the disavowal of financial self-interest that protects Caleb Garth from social contamination also functions to guard against any radical political action that would meaningfully alter existing economic hierarchies. Morris's solution is founded upon precisely such political action. In *News from Nowhere* (1890), he projects several generations into the future to imagine an agrarian anarcho-communist utopia that is entirely free of wage labor, private property, and money. Morris thus inverts Eliot's approach, starting by positing a massive overhaul of the global system of production and resource distribution writ large and then exploring how interpersonal feelings morph in response. In *News from Nowhere*, he suggests that communism deprivatizes not only property but also feeling. Morris's postrevolutionary society is peopled by characters who feel the pain and pleasure of others as their own and thus cannot engage in the quasi-sadistic pleasures of necroeconomics. Solving (with utopian ease) the problem of feelings under necroeconomics that the previous chapters highlight, Morris imagines a world in which letting die is impossible.

WEIRD FEELINGS

If, as Brian Massumi states, a "good problem" is one that "twists itself around its own loose ends to tie itself into an alluring knot," then the problem of letting die is a good problem in the Victorian novel (204). When we examine the intensification and multiplicity of feelings that circulate around this problem, we reveal that capitalist feelings are a lot weirder than we have given them credit for. The Victorian period is often understood to be defined by a constellation of normalizing drives, all of which work in service of liberal capitalism. Massumi assumes this as well, associating "normality" (20) with the Victorian period and suggesting that it only begins to "lose its hold" in the second half of the twentieth century. In this new late-capitalist landscape, "the oddest of affective tendencies are OK—as long as they pay. Capitalism starts intensifying or diversifying affect, but only in order to extract surplus value" (20). But Victorian literature tells a different story. The novels I examine in this book reveal the perverse, compulsive, anachronistic, and otherwise "weird" affective patterns that capitalism both produces and demands right from the beginning. From its ideological inception, the fiction of the "homo economicus" generates a range of affective byproducts, reactions, workarounds, and contradictions. These feelings proliferate with particular abundance around the concept of letting die. Examining how feelings circulate around this necroeconomic mandate helps us think beyond the binary of prosocial sympathy versus cold economic self-interest to see the diverse and sometimes surprising ways in which free-market capitalism is *felt*.

CHAPTER 1

How to Let Die

Malthusian Medicine in Martineau and Marcus

> Fellow-workmen . . . You well know that any truly honest and inde-
> pendent man that comes forward to advise or defend the mis-
> guided and degraded slaves of Britain, has all the thunders of
> the iniquitous and damnable laws that has [sic] been purposely
> framed to carry into effect the objects of the bloody trio—Mal-
> thus, Marcus, and Martineau—launched at his devoted head.
>
> —T. Higgins, "Stephens and Liberty," *The Champion,* 12 May 1839

The Victorian debate on the politics of letting die begins not in "expensive novels" but in the popular press (Haywood 141). The late 1820s and 1830s saw a polyvocal explosion of print media debating the poor's right to live. The Poor Law Commission, in cahoots with allied organizations like the Society for the Diffusion of Useful Knowledge (SDUK), published reams of reports, tracts, and narratives highlighting the "supposed abuses and corrupting effects of parish relief" in a propaganda campaign that Oz Frankel refers to as "print Statism" (Frankel 2, 39–40). At the same time, working-class radicals launched an almost equally prolific counterattack in the unstamped press. Often facing prison sentences for their publications, these radical authors not only weighed in on the Poor Law debate but sought to redefine its terms. This chapter exam-ines two sets of texts from opposite sides of that debate—Harriet Martineau's *Illustrations of Political Economy,* on the one hand, and the coverage of the "Marcus pamphlet" in the radical working-class press on the other—both of which make visible the necroeconomic stakes of Poor Law policy. In the didactic narratives that make up the *Illustrations,* Martineau sought to make the "utility and beauty" of political economy accessible to a layperson audi-ence (Preface ix).[1] Alongside their economic lessons, however, they also offer a

---

1. Citations of Martineau's preface to *Illustrations* refer to volume 1 of the original 25-volume set, published in 1832 by Charles Fox. Citations for *Cousin Marshall, A Manchester Strike,* and *Weal and Woe in Garveloch* refer to Deborah Anna Logan's 2004 scholarly edition of *Illustrations,* which includes those three tales along with *Sowers Not Reapers.*

disturbing affective education for middle-class readers. Presenting cross-class sympathy as a problem that interferes with the operation of a laissez-faire economy and encouraging middle-class readers to resist their sympathetic impulses to aid the poor, the *Illustrations* offer a shadow education in "how to let die." This implicit violence is made explicit during the controversy surrounding the mysterious "Marcus pamphlet" that circulated through the popular press from late 1838 into 1839. Riding the line between satire and forgery, the pseudonymous "Marcus" mimics the obtuse, bureaucratic style of a government report as he proposes a plan to systematically kill the infants of the poor. The working-class radical press—at times responding to the pamphlet as a genuine leaked proposal from the Poor Law Commissioners and at others appearing to be in on the satire—jumped at the opportunity "Marcus" presented to depict both the Poor Law Commissioners and Martineau herself as mass murderers.[2] Rewriting strategic nonintervention as active murder, this coverage transforms the passive middle-class bystander who looks on as the poor die into a diabolical conspirator in a national scheme of mass infanticide. In the final section of this chapter, I read Martineau's *Deerbrook* in the context of this debate, examining its revisionist echoes of key moments from *Illustrations* to highlight how the problem of "letting die" unsettles the ideology of even the most evangelical adherent of political economy.

LEARNING TO LET DIE:
ILLUSTRATIONS OF POLITICAL ECONOMY

In her autobiography, Harriet Martineau characterizes her whole life as a journey toward political economy. The daughter of a fabric manufacturer and Unitarian deacon, Martineau grew up in a financially comfortable middle-class home in Norwich. Her childhood, however, was defined largely by "wretchedness"; in addition to a strained relationship with her mother, Martineau was plagued by health problems from birth and was aware that she was becoming increasingly deaf (*Harriet Martineau's Autobiography* 53; henceforth abbreviated *AB*). Daily walks, incessant needlework, and the obligations of social visiting were a source of both physical and emotional pain. The highlight that stands out from this "depressed and wrangling life" is the "beloved hour" after dinner when she would sneak away from the family and read the *Globe* newspaper "in its best days, when, without ever mentioning Political Economy, it taught it, and viewed public affairs in its light" (*AB* 54). She acknowledges that

---

2. For a much more in-depth analysis of the Marcus pamphlet controversy specifically and anti–New Poor Law writing in the working-class press more broadly, see Vargo, ch. 2.

this was an unusual "indulgence" for a girl of twelve years old; indeed, her interest in political economy earned her the mockery of her brothers, "who would ask me with mock deference to inform them of the state of the Debt, or would set me, as a forfeit at Christmas Games, to make every person present understand the operation of the Sinking Fund" (*AB* 54). Recalling her youth, Martineau notes, "I was all the while becoming a political economist without knowing it" (*AB* 55).

The family's financial fortunes took a dramatic downturn beginning in 1827, when Martineau's father lost most of his wealth in the 1825–26 stock market crisis and, soon after, died. Martineau, along with her mother and sisters, lost the relatively small amount of money that was left to them when the Norwich manufactory in which the money was invested failed in 1829. Martineau refers to this apparent "calamity," however, as "one of the best things that ever happened" to her; the loss of "gentility" gave Martineau newfound "liberty to do [her] own work in [her] own way" (*AB* 108). She transformed a hobby into a job and began to publish her writing for profit (Logan 29). Soon afterward, she began the series of novellas that became known as *Illustrations of Political Economy*. Between 1832 and 1834, Martineau wrote twenty-five of these tales, first published individually and then republished in nine volumes in 1843. Her tales are essentially didactic novellas, meant to use narrative to illustrate certain tenets of political economy and thus educate the novel-reading populace about the ideas of thinkers like Smith, Malthus, and Ricardo. Just in case the lessons were not clear to readers, Martineau concludes each novella with a section titled "Summary of Principles illustrated in the volume," which lists the axioms that the narrative was supposed to teach. Although she initially struggled to find a publisher for the tales, they became an almost overnight success that made both her fame and her financial independence (Logan 30). Estimates of the readership of the initial serial numbers stand at about 144,000 (Webb 113), and the tales were consequently reprinted in volume form, translated into Dutch, German, Spanish, French, and Russian, and even adapted for use in French public schools (Logan 35). Reaching more readers than many of the political economists whose work formed her source materials, Martineau's narratives played a crucial role in shaping the way Victorian culture digested political economy.

Influenced by her Necessarian religious beliefs, Martineau is more optimistic than the political economists she idolized, ascribing almost utopian transformative power to popular understanding of political economy.[3] If the

---

3. Elaine Freedgood provides an extensive explanation of how Martineau is more optimistic than her sources in "Banishing Panic." Gallagher notes how Martineau's providential optimism was influenced by her reading of Joseph Priestly and John McCulloch (*Industrial Reformation* 60). See also Blaug 123.

people understood the "utility and beauty of the science," they would see that it is "at least their duty, should it not be their pleasure, to listen to those who have observed and compared and reflected and come to a certain knowledge of a *few grand principles, which, if generally understood, would gradually remove all the obstructions, and remedy the distresses, and equalize the lot of the population*" (Preface ix, emphasis added). Learning the lessons of political economy is, for Martineau, an absolute "moral imperative" (Klaver 56). She claims that this all-important education has been hampered, however, by the abstract, scientific style in which treatises of political economy have been written. While criticizing British readers for neglecting this key to social melioration, she also admits that political economy's foundational texts are "very long, in some parts exceedingly difficult," and "not fitted nor designed to teach the science to the great mass of the people" (Preface x). While these books are invaluable, they "do not give us what we want—the science in a familiar, practical form. They give us its history; they give us its philosophy; but we want its *picture*" (Preface xi). Seeing no reason why "an explanation of the principles which regulate society should not be made more clear and interesting at the same time by pictures of what those principles are actually doing in communities," Martineau thus seeks to combine "truth and its application" in her *Illustrations*. In doing so, she hopes to "[get] rid of the excuse that these subjects cannot be understood" by all (Preface xv).

Martineau's transplantation of the self-consciously scientific discourse of political economy into the medium of fiction produces a bidirectional channel of influence that changes both. Several scholars have illuminated how her fusion of the political tract or treatise with the fictional story helps lay the groundwork for a half-century of what would come to be called "social-problem" novels, ranging from Elizabeth Gaskell's *Mary Barton* (which I analyze in the next chapter) to George Eliot's *Felix Holt* (which I analyze at the end of this study).[4] Inversely, Martineau's narrative form also shapes (or, according to some critics, misshapes) the economic principles she seeks to instill in her audience. While she is influenced by Ricardo, who sought to establish political economy as a scientifically rigorous discourse by stripping it of all ethical or moral concerns, her narrative writing turns his purportedly amoral discourse into the "groundwork of the new moral system" (Klaver 55).

---

4. See Logan 41. See Courtemanche, "'Naked Truth'" for an excellent explanation of Martineau's influence on both Dickens specifically and the development of Victorian realism broadly. For more on Martineau's influence on other novelists, including Charles Dickens, Benjamin Disraeli, Elizabeth Gaskell, and Charles Kingsley, see Cazamian 51–54; for her influence on Frances Trollope, Charlotte Elizabeth Donna, and Elizabeth Stone, see Fryckstedt 12–13, 16; for her influence on Harriet Beecher Stowe, see Midgley 97; for her influence on the Brontës and George Eliot, see V. Sanders 195.

In her analysis of the tensions and paradoxes within the *Illustrations*, Claudia Klaver argues that Martineau's attempt to "synthesize such divergent modes of discourse" produces a range of "disjunctive effects" (58–59). Form reshapes content: the "narrative conventions . . . show themselves to have the power to determine and disrupt the economic ideas they were meant to merely 'enliven' or serve" (Klaver 77; see also Vargo 64–65).

This self-undermining nature is a common thread in critical treatments of Martineau. Perhaps surprisingly due to her evangelical support of laissez-faire ideology, Martineau was somewhat of an ambiguous political figure in her own lifetime; while many working-class activists saw her as their committed enemy, other critics of industrialism picked up on her tragic depiction of working-class suffering as a critique of the industrialism with which she explicitly affiliated herself (Webb 122–23). Recent Victorian critics have been similarly attentive to what Gregory Vargo calls the "divided nature" of Martineau's tales[5]—the way in which they seem to contain their own critique—but have attributed this internal conflict to different causes (Vargo 55). For Klaver, this conflict stems from the narrative form itself. Catherine Gallagher attributes it to Martineau's "peculiar blend of optimistic, providential beliefs and pessimistic, mechanical doctrines" (*Industrial Reformation* 55). Vargo also reminds readers that Martineau was not "writing from a position of undisputed ideological dominance" and argues that many of the tensions within her writing stem from her attempts to "contend with working-class radicalism, which presented alternative explanations and solutions to the social problems she addressed" (55). Like these critics, I am interested in the complicated ideological knots Martineau ties herself into as she tries to square her evangelical allegiance to an amoral, laissez-faire economic system with her moral commitment to working-class well-being. In my view, however, this internal conflict centers on and stems from necroeconomics. Martineau writes these novellas because she wants to produce the healthiest possible social body, but in doing so, she finds herself in the position of trying to persuade her readers of the ethical value of withdrawing aid and letting people die. Even Martineau, propelled by her quasi-religious belief in the social good of laissez-faire, comes up against the problem of "laissez-mourir." In this sense, Martineau lays the foundation not only for the Victorian social-problem novel but also for that novel's struggle to deal with necroeconomics—the struggle that this book will trace.

---

5. See Mike Sanders on Martineau's equivocation about the necessity of class conflict (193); Courtemanche on her conflicted representation of whether strikes are justified ("Naked Truth" 393); and Linda Peterson on Martineau's ambivalent use of religious didacticism to share a secular gospel of political economy. See also Gallagher, *Industrial Reformation*; Vargo; and Klaver.

Martineau draws upon her extensive reading of a range of economic theorists—most notably Adam Smith, David Ricardo, Jeremy Bentham, and Thomas Malthus, as well as popular writers John McCulloch and Jane Marcet[6]—in the *Illustrations*. In several tales, she illustrates specific principles and policy positions: Ricardian rent theory in *Ella of Garveloch*, emigration as a solution to poverty in *Homes Abroad*, the futility of strikes in *A Manchester Strike*, opposition to the Corn Laws in *Sowers Not Reapers*. At a more foundational level, she draws on Adam Smith and the earlier physiocrats in imagining the capitalist economy as a kind of organic body, governed by predictable, immutable natural laws. At the same time, she depicts England's population as a body—the "body of the people," which she exhorts to "understand those natural laws" by which the economic body works (Preface xi, 115).[7] These two bodies are adjacent to each other and interact with one another, but they are decidedly nonidentical.[8] The economic body both supersedes and supports the social body; the social body is both subject to the economic body and is that body's raison d'être. What makes Martineau's goal so complicated is that she is trying to make both bodies healthy at the same time. The paradoxical nature of this goal—of making necroeconomics healthy—becomes most evident in the two tales in which she seeks to illustrate the theories of Thomas Malthus: *Weal and Woe in Garveloch*, which illustrates Malthus's principle of population, and *Cousin Marshall*, which makes an argument against parish relief.[9]

The first of these stories, *Weal and Woe in Garveloch*, recounts the fortunes of a small Scottish fishing community over the course of several years. In times of plenty, many young couples marry and have children; when poor seasons return, they find themselves with too many mouths to feed. Even the provident Murdoch family faces near-starvation and is forced to make sacrifices: unable to find work on the island, the cherished eldest son Kenneth joins the army and leaves his family behind, while the long-suffering Robert decides

---

6. For comparison between Marcet and Martineau, see Klaver 54–55.

7. She is also drawing on Smith in using this phrase; Smith repeatedly describes the population as "the great body of the people" in *The Wealth of Nations*.

8. Martineau's depiction of the British worker's two bodies parallels, in this way, the medieval political theory that Kantorowicz details in *The King's Two Bodies*. While the historical context and political thrust of the two theories are, of course, quite different, both posit deeply paradoxical versions of bodily duplicity in order to solve an ideological problem. Indeed, several scholars have read the theory of sovereign incorporation that Kantorowicz illuminates in terms of premodern proto-biopolitics. Agamben refers to it in *Homo Sacer* (92); Eric Santner provides a detailed account of the afterlife of "carnal" kingship in modern secular citizenship in *The Royal Remains* (xvii). See also Malabou; Biddick.

9. For a thorough analysis of the precise relationship between Malthus's ideas and Martineau's interpretation of them in the *Illustrations* (as well as an elaboration of the critical and popular response to Martineau's writing), see Huzel, ch. 2.

against marrying his beloved Katie because he does not want to add to an already excessive population. The story is meant to illustrate Malthus's principle of population, which Martineau articulates both within the tale itself and in the "summary of principles" that follows it. The magistrate Mr. Mackenzie explains to Ella and Angus Murdoch that, regardless of agricultural improvements, "the people must increase faster than the produce" and "the produce will fall behind more and more, as every improvement, every outlay of capital yields a less return" (81, 85). Soon, he claims, Garveloch "will be in the condition of an old country like England, where many are but half fed, where many prudent determine not to marry, and where the imprudent must see their children pine in hunger, or waste under disease" (85). The Murdochs are convinced "that there must be some check to the increase of the people, and that the prudential check is infinitely preferable to those of vice and misery" (116).

Like Malthus, Martineau both raises and subsequently others the specter of maternal violence. Malthus states that the "positive check to population, by which I mean, *the check that represses an increase which is already begun,* is confined chiefly, though not perhaps solely, to the lowest orders of society" (*Essay* 23, emphasis added). Conflating abortion and infanticide through his euphemistic turn of phrase, Malthus associates "positive checks" on population with poverty. Martineau is more overt in her discussion of infanticide, although she shifts the blame away from the British poor and toward racial others. In an unusually frank discussion, Ella tells Katie about "mothers in China" who kill their infants during times of famine (*Weal and Woe* 114). Ella claims that in China's "great cities, newborn babes are nightly laid in the streets to perish, and many more are thrown into the river," while Katie claims that "the same thing is done in India" (114). After linking this behavior with an ethnic other, Martineau raises the possibility that Britain might become like that other through imprudent reproduction. Ella "shudder[s]" to imagine that "such should be the lot of our native kingdom" but acknowledges that "such is the natural course of things when a nation multiplies its numbers without a corresponding increase of food" (115). She blames people like her improvident neighbor Noreen, who continues to have children despite lacking the means to feed them adequately, for being "little better than the mothers in China" (114). Martineau suggests that reproduction *itself,* under the conditions of poverty, is akin to violence.

Martineau thus, like Malthus, constructs an oppositional relationship between healthy working-class bodies and the overall health of the social body. Catherine Gallagher sums up Malthus's crucial reimagining of the economic value of population in the claim that "healthy bodies eventually generate a feeble social organism" ("Body versus Social Body" 83). Rather than viewing human reproduction as an "index of a healthy state" like his predecessors and contemporaries, Malthus recasts human vigor and fecundity as the source of future suffering and death (Gallagher, "Body" 83). Martineau follows and extends Malthus's depiction of the threat of the healthy body when she writes, in *Weal and Woe,* that "every one that is born must help to starve the living" (111). She ascribes violence not only to the overly reproductive mother like Noreen, who essentially commits infanticide by giving birth, but also to the healthy infant, who essentially commits murder by being born. Even as she states that her goal is to ensure that all of the "many millions of our population" are "temperately fed with wholesome food, instead of some being pampered above-stairs while others are starving below" (Preface v–vi), her tales focus much less on equitable resource distribution and more on reducing those many millions to a more manageable population that will be more easily fed. The healthy body may be the goal, but it is also the problem. It is not surprising, then, that this understanding of human population leads to and legitimates an overtly "necro" version of economics.[10] If healthy, virile bodies necessarily produce an unhealthy social body, then death becomes both necessary and defensible to maintain a healthy social organism.

In *Cousin Marshall,* Martineau reveals the implications of this Malthusian view for both public policy and personal morality. Written in the years leading up to the New Poor Law's framing and passage in 1834, this tale is part of a massive campaign[11] of "print Statism" to turn public opinion against the old system of parish relief (Frankel 39). *Cousin Marshall* follows the struggles of a poor family dealing with a series of misfortunes: first, the father dies, then a fire destroys their home, and shortly thereafter, the mother dies, leaving behind four young children, one of whom is blind. A kind but poor cousin (the titular Cousin Marshall) takes in the two younger children, but the elder

---

10. In his analysis of surplus population, Marx inverts the direction of causality that Martineau imagines here; he argues that surplus population is both a result and a technology of capitalist production. The "varying phases of the industrial cycle" create a "disposable industrial reserve army" that "belongs to capital just as absolutely as if the latter had bred it at its own cost" and that serves the goal of capital accumulation (784–85). While Malthus sees population increase as an immutable natural law, Marx focuses on its historically specific amplification through capitalism: "Capitalist production can by no means content itself with the quantity of disposable labour-power which the natural increase of population yields. It requires for its unrestricted activity an industrial reserve army which is independent of these natural limits" (788).

11. Martineau participated even more directly in this campaign when Lord Brougham, MP and leader of the Society for the Diffusion of Useful Knowledge, commissioned her to write *Poor Laws and Paupers Illustrated* in 1833 to illustrate the findings of the Poor Law Commission for a popular audience (Frankel 39–40). Unlike *Illustrations,* the series was a massive financial flop, and Martineau came to regret affiliating herself with Brougham (See *AB* 177, Vargo 56–57).

two are forced to go to the dreaded workhouse. The tale contains some unsurprising (and not-so-subtle) encouragement to working-class readers to avoid charity, rely upon their own industry, restrict reproduction, and take care of their own families. But it is in her advice to the middle classes—not the people who are dying, but the people who are witnessing death—that necroeconomics most disturbingly rises to the surface. The novella is interwoven with the perspectives of a thoughtful country doctor named Burke and his philanthropically minded sister Louisa, who spend a lot of time talking about how to best live according to their principles. During one of these conversations, Burke states that he wishes that he weren't a doctor. When his sister guesses why, he rejects her guesses, claiming that "is a deeper matter than any of" the objections she imagines. The following conversation ensues:

> "The greatest question now moving in the world is, 'What is charity?' . . . A clergyman, Louisa . . . may set many right; and God knows how many need it! . . . He will not suppose because charity once meant alms-giving that it means it still; or that a kind-hearted man must be right in thinking kindness of heart all-sufficient, whether its manifestation be injurious or beneficial. He will not recommend keeping the heart soft by giving green gooseberries to a griped child,—as he might fairly do if he carried out Paley's principle to its extent."
>
> "A professional illustration," replied Louisa. "You want me to carry it on unto the better charity of giving the child bitter medicine. But, brother, let the clergyman preach as wisely and benignantly as he may, why should you envy him? Cannot you, do not you, preach as eloquently by example?"
>
> "That is the very thing," replied her brother. "I am afraid my example preaches against my principles.—O, dear, if it was but as easy to know how to do right as to do it!" (238–39)

What he means by "his example" is his position at various charity hospitals—the dispensary, which provides free medical care for the poor, and the lying-in hospital, which provides free care to pregnant women. As the medical officer for these institutions, Dr. Burke is tasked with providing potentially life-saving care to patients who cannot pay for his services—a task that he claims conflicts with his "principles."

Those principles are, of course, the same principles of political economy that informed the passage of the New Poor Law of 1834 and that, conveniently, are also listed at the end of the tale. Martineau takes a firm stance against both private charity and public relief, claiming that "all arbitrary distribution of the necessities of life is injurious to society, whether in the form of private almsgiving, public charitable institutions, or a legal pauper-system" (293). According to Martineau, these "modes of distribution" are an "evil to society" for several reasons: they "[render] consumption unproductive, and [encourage] a multiplication of consumers, [do] not meet the difficulty aris-ing from a disproportion of numbers to the means of subsistence," "encour-age improvidence with all its attendant evils," "injure the good while relieving the bad," "extinguish the spirit of independence on one side,—and of charity on the other," and "increase perpetually the evil they are meant to remedy" (293–94). A committed Malthusian, Martineau accepts the premise that the fundamental problem is a mismatch between the number of mouths to feed and the quantity of resources available with which to feed them. The only true solution, then, is to either increase the quantity of resources or decrease the number of people trying to subsist on them. With this in mind, Martin-eau's argument against poor relief is overtly twofold but implicitly threefold: (1) relief consumes capital that could otherwise be invested toward economic growth, (2) relief incentivizes or at least makes possible procreation among the poor, increasing the number of mouths to feed, and implicitly (3) relief increases the number of the poor by keeping alive people who would other-wise die. Instead, she argues for the strategic withdrawal of aid: "Capital and labour [must] be allowed to take their natural course; i.e. the pauper system must, by some means or other, be extinguished" (294). Sounding very Malthu-sian indeed, she states that "the number of consumers must be proportioned to the subsistence-fund. To this end, all encouragements to the increase of population should be withdrawn, and every sanction given to the preventive check" (294). As a believer in Martineau's gospel of laissez-faire, Dr. Burke should not intervene on behalf of the poor in any way that would increase their numbers—including saving their lives.

Obviously anxious about the appearance of hard-heartedness in advo-cating for a withdrawal of care, Dr. Burke offers a medical metaphor: giving charity to the poor is like "giving green gooseberries to a griped child." The problem, though, with applying this individual medical metaphor to a collec-tive social problem is that the acute suffering and the long-term payoff become severed from one another. In the case of the griped child, the same child who swallows the bitter medicine is the child who is cured. The experience of tem-porary suffering is directly, viscerally connected to the benefit of the perma-nent cure. When this medical metaphor gets expanded and transposed onto the social body, such a connection no longer holds. The "bitter medicine" that Dr. Burke (and Martineau) wants to apply to the social body is the abolition of all charitable institutions that tend to "lessen capital" or "increase population," including dispensaries, lying-in hospitals, foundling hospitals, workhouses, and almshouses for the aged (242). To remove those institutions "intrepidly, steadily, and at a gradually increasing rate" (242) would of course cause acute suffering. It would leave orphaned children, unmarried or widowed pregnant women, and disabled elderly people who lacked benevolent neighbors or extended family totally unprovided for, and although Martineau tiptoes around explicitly saying so, many of these people would die. Perhaps she is correct that the abolition of the foundling hospital would discourage "excessive" reproduction among the poor in the long term, but it would certainly leave infants to suffer and die in the short term—bitter medicine, indeed.

Unlike in the case of the "griped child," though, the short-term suffering and long-term cure do not take place within the same body. The long-term cure that Martineau imagines—a reduction or even elimination of both poor rates and indigence—happens on the level of the social body as a whole. The short-term suffering, on the other hand, happens to the physical bodies of individual poor people, many of whom will not survive to become part of the "healed" social body that arises as a result of the "bitter medicine" they take on its behalf. Martineau conflates social problems with physical maladies in such a way as to rewrite the death of paupers as the temporary discomfort of swallowing unpleasant medicine en route to health. By using this analogy, she instructs her readers to register the death of paupers and their children due to hunger, exposure, or disease as discomfort and not as death. She wants to rewrite death as not-death. In order for this slippage to work, readers have to imagine paupers not as independent human bodies but rather as diseased and disposable parts of the social body—parts that, like a gangrenous limb or a diseased appendix, must be excised in order to protect the whole.

What Martineau "half conceals and half reveals" in this scale-shifting medical metaphor is the "necro" function of laissez-faire capitalism. As much as she wants to draw attention to "preemptive checks" like delayed marriages and away from mass famine and death, her focus on Dr. Burke highlights that her ideology makes "letting people die" compulsory. This necroeconomic dictate puts the Malthusian doctor in a bind. Martineau's political economy sets up a conflict of interest between caring for the individual bodies of poor patients and caring for the biologized social body as a whole. The metaphorical "bitter medicine" that Dr. Burke thinks the social body needs is, quite literally, the withdrawal of actual medicine from the poor. From the perspective of the indigent, this measure is not "medicine" at all; it is indirect violence, a willing and intentional abandonment to death. The withdrawal of care Dr. Burke calls for extends beyond traditional medical care to include the material resources necessary for good health, like food and coals. When he explains to his sister that many of his patients need "rest and warmth" or "better food" more than medicine, Louisa responds, "How you must wish sometimes that your surgery was stocked with coals and butcher's meat!" (241). But Dr. Burke disagrees, claiming that "the evil would only be increased, provided this sort of medicine were given gratis, like my drugs" (241). Inasmuch as Dr. Burke imagines himself as a doctor of the social body, a practitioner of "public health," he is compelled to refuse medical care to those patients who cannot pay for it. In Martineau's clearly problematic scheme, to be a good social doctor is to refuse to act as a medical doctor for certain populations.

In order to be able to do this, he has to resist his own gut feelings, the tenderness of sensibility that impels him to want to care for the poor. In *Cousin Marshall* and throughout the *Illustrations,* Martineau takes for granted that middle-class British people do feel sympathy when they witness working-class suffering. Even the capitalists who appear hard-hearted based upon their actions almost universally feel sympathy for their suffering employees and wish they could provide higher wages. The mill owner Mr. Wentworth in *A Manchester Strike,* for example, has "a heart to feel for the poor" and "regard[s] their distresses with compassion," explaining to his striking workers that he would "make [wages] higher if [he] could" (171–73). Dr. Burke accepts as fact that it would "make [Louisa's] heart ache" to see the "children born puny from the destitution of their parents, or weakly boys and girls, stunted by bad nursing, or women who want rest and warmth more than medicine" among his dispensary patients (241). Moreover, Martineau depicts Louisa's ready sympathy in the face of suffering as characteristic of middle-class Britons more generally. Dr. Burke, whose dialogue in the novella reads as a narrative exposition of Martineau's own views on political economy, states that "British benevolence" is "vast . . . in amount" (242).

But both Dr. Burke and Martineau claim that this "tenderness of sensibility" is a problem because it leads people to support charitable institutions like the dispensary and the lying-in hospital. She claims that these institutions in fact increase the "misery" they seek to remedy; while the "charitable fund" grows in size every year, fueled by misguided benevolence, "distress [grows] more prevalent than ever" (242). In contrast to many of her contemporaries, Martineau does not identify the indifference or cruelty of the middle and upper classes as a cause of working-class suffering; instead, the problem is their excessive but misguided sympathy. In Martineau's construction, the British middle class is like a kindly but uneducated nurse, indulging the sick child with gooseberries and thereby making the illness worse rather than administering the bitter medicine that will lead to a long-term cure. "Kindness of heart" is, in other words, the very root of what Martineau describes as "an evil to society" (239). While Victorian literary critics have often read sympathy as a replacement for action—an interpersonal acknowledgment of shared humanity that assuages the guilt of the dominant party and assures social harmony without changing material hierarchies in any real way[12]—Martineau asserts a direct and immediate connection between sympathetic feeling and benevolent action. The "heart ache" that arises in the breast of the benevolent middle-class Briton when looking upon the suffering poor is a problem precisely because it is too readily converted into action: people "look no farther than the immediate relief of distress, and [think] the reality of the misery a sufficient warrant for alms-giving" (241). Only the "wisdom" of political economy can teach these over-benevolent Britons to reject the immediacy of sympathy and see that the "bitter medicine" of withdrawing aid is ultimately the "better charity" (239). In this way, Martineau explicitly encourages middle-class readers to adopt a delayed relation to their own affective responses. Audrey Jaffe identifies that very delay between affect and reaction as a foundational element of Victorian class distinction; "middle-class identity," she claims, "includes a capacity for self-knowledge defined as the ability to distance the self from primitive or innate affects, and hence to overcome or at least compensate for them" ("Affect" 717). But the "immediate, instinctive responses" (717) that characters distinguish themselves by resisting in Jaffe's argument are primarily antisocial, "bad" feelings: repulsion, disgust, shame, anger, animalistic drives, and so forth. This rubric for assessing class identity becomes much weirder in Martineau's hands, where the apparently dangerous affect that the middle class needs to learn to resist is *instinctive cross-class sympathy*. Martineau essentially says to those who want to help the poor, "Don't trust your gut": resist the sympathetic impulse you feel when you come into contact with suffering others.

Martineau acknowledges that this will be seen as unnatural—and in fact, it feels unnatural, even for Burke and his sister, characters who are hardly more than walking, talking principles of political economy. Both Burke and his sister worry about being viewed as "hard-hearted." As a woman, Louisa experiences more "little trials" on her mission to behave according to the principles of political economy; in addition to "abuse from beggars" to whom she has refused to give alms, she endures "the astonishment of her fellow-members of the school committee at her refusing to sanction large gifts of clothing to the children; the glances of the visitors of the soup and blanket charities, when she decline[s] subscribing and yielding her services; and above all, the observations of relatives whom she respected, and old friends whom she loved, on the hardness of heart" she shows in her refusal to support charity toward the

---

12. For a thorough articulation of this position, see Carolyn Betensky's *Feeling for the Poor.*

poor (244). Through Louisa's example, Martineau attempts to teach middle-class readers to feel more comfortable making the apparently heartless choice to eliminate parish relief that is desperately needed in the short term in order to "reduce the number of indigent" in the long term—that is, how to feel more comfortable letting people die. In a move that sets her apart from both the sentimental mode upon which she draws as well as the social-problem novel for which she has been credited with laying the groundwork, Martineau encourages middle-class readers to actively stifle their sympathy for the poor.

Martineau's negative orientation toward affect gives her characters a peculiar emotional flatness. Valerie Pichanick crystallizes the scholarly consensus on Martineau's characters in the *Illustrations* when she describes them as "two-dimensional" and "wooden" (53). Catherine Gallagher attributes it to the deterministic nature of Martineau's ideology (providential political economy) as well as her chosen form (didactic stories illustrating predetermined lessons) (*Industrial Reformation* 59). Martineau's "didactic determinism . . . flattens the tale's emotional course" (60) for both character and reader: even a tragic hero like doomed strike-leader William Allen in *A Manchester Strike* is "rendered affectively neutral, and the reader experiences a similar emotional blankness and distance from the represented suffering" (58). The affective flatness is particularly evident among the middle-class characters who act as Martineau's "ideological mouthpieces"; as Gregory Vargo notes, these characters, like Dr. Burke, "lack defining habits and emotional quirks and speak a monotone language" (59). It is, however, "too simple to call them flat. Though drained of personality, they are surprisingly dynamic, because the positions they advocate differentiate them. They change and develop, have conflicts and crises, but all in the realm of ideas" (59). While most critics (as well as contemporary readers) view this lack of emotional richness as a weakness of Martineau's writing, I argue that it is a necessary result of her ideological project. As a proponent of an inherently necroeconomic ideology, Martineau wants middle-class people to witness working-class suffering differently: to flatten their affective response to the spectacle of suffering, subjugating their gut sympathy response to their "rational" belief in the greater good of laissez-faire. The project of necroeconomics requires and actively encourages affective flatness in the face of working-class suffering and death.

Crucially, Martineau directs this call for affective suppression toward her middle- and upper-class readers only. She draws a firm distinction between middle-class affect and working-class affect: while the privileged classes express a surplus of (mismanaged) benevolence, she criticizes the poor for an alleged dearth of "tenderness of sensibility" in response to the suffering of their peers. Dr. Burke claims that if charitable institutions like almshouses for the elderly were abolished, "we might see some revival of that genial spirit of charity and social duty among the poor, whose extinction we are apt to mourn, without reflecting that we ourselves have caused it by the injudicious direction of our own benevolence" (243). Martineau suggests, in other words, that misdirected middle-class benevolence has flooded the affective marketplace, leaving no need for working-class benevolence. Withdrawing that surplus affect, then, will create a demand for and thus stimulate working-class benevolence. She essentially proposes a national affect management scheme, which will force the poor to become more affectively similar to middle-class people by suppressing those same feelings among the middle-class population. Paradoxically, Martineau's purportedly noninterventionist economic ideology demands unprecedented regulation of the British marketplace of feelings, stopping them up where there is a surplus in order to solicit them elsewhere.[13]

While Martineau offers extensive affect management advice to middle-class readers, she ultimately has little to offer to the working-class readers to whom the tales are purportedly addressed. The tales include a few suggestions for how workers can modify their behaviors to better accord with the immutable economic laws "under which and by which they subsist" (*Weal and Woe* 115): she suggests that factory workers should contribute to communal "mutual relief" funds designed to help families survive periods of low wages or unemployment due to downturns in trade and should collectively place their children in occupations "least likely to be overstocked" in order to avoid an oversupply of labor in any one industry (*Manchester Strike* 197). She warns workers against hoarding through the example of Angus in *Weal and Woe in Garveloch,* who refuses to buy more food than he needs when supplies finally arrive to the famished island even though he has plenty of savings and a large family nearing starvation. Angus, who acts as a sort of working-class mouthpiece for Martineau's ideas in the story, states, "We have enough for the present, and I will neither take what others want more than we, nor raise the price by increasing the demand" (119). But none of these suggestions even approaches the level of social melioration that Martineau promises in the preface, in which she claims that political economy, "if generally understood, would gradually remove all the obstructions, and remedy the distresses, and equalize the lot of the population" (viii). Even the working-class characters who most fully internalize the lessons of political economy meet tragic endings: Cousin Marshall dies impoverished and alone, isolated

---

13. Although she does not say so explicitly, one can imagine that Martineau also sees working-class sympathy as less of a problem for a free market because, unlike middle-class feeling, it is not connected to the redistribution of material resources to prolong the lives of "surplus" people.

from her community because of her refusal to accept charitable relief; William Allen loses his factory job after the strike and is forced to eke out a living selling water from a street cart. Her working-class characters seem, as Catherine Gallagher puts it, "doomed to struggle, doomed to lose" (*Industrial Reformation* 53). The only form of "heroic self-determination" that a character like Allen can achieve is in manfully submitting to his fate (58).

This tragic fatedness stems from Martineau's zero-sum understanding of working-class subsistence: wage laborers, she argues, must subsist on a finite "fund" comprised of the difference between revenue and the cost of production, minus "profit enough to make it worth [the owner's] while to invest his capital" (*Manchester Strike* 216).[14] As Martineau emphatically summarizes at the conclusion of *A Manchester Strike*, "THE PROPORTION OF THIS FUND RECEIVED BY INDIVIDUALS MUST MAINLY DEPEND ON THE NUMBER AMONG WHOM THE FUND IS DIVIDED" (215). The only effective means of improving the condition of the poor, then, are to increase the "fund" of capital that they divide among them (through increased top-down investment and effective management) or to decrease the number of people among whom it is divided (through birth control and delayed marriages or through death). Just as charity is futile because it reduces the all-important "fund," removing from the economy money that could be invested as capital, Martineau vehemently opposes strikes as "worse than in vain" (197). Not only does the strike fail to accomplish either of the only two goals Martineau deems effective—increasing capital or decreasing the number of workers—but it also occasions "wasting capital" (216). Martineau's argument here is more than just a reactionary admonition against unruly or disruptive working-class organizing; it is a denial of the possibility of any working-class political action whatsoever. Martineau only allows for two avenues of action for shaping wealth distribution and quality of life across one's population: increasing capital and decreasing population. She concedes that workers are not in a position to increase capital, and thus, the worker's only available interventions are to *not strike* and to *not have children*. Martineau's working class can find power only in their scarcity, not in action or collectivism. Only when "there are permanently fewer workmen than are wanted" can "the men hold the power"; as long as there are "more than are wanted, . . . the power is in the masters'

---

14. Notably, Martineau does not address the appropriate division of total profit between the investor's private share and the fund that will support the workers through wages. How much profit is required to "make it worth his while to invest" is left conspicuously unstated. Based on the number of capital-owning characters who are making just enough to provide for themselves and cover costs in Martineau's fiction, I think it is fair to speculate that her opinions on the capitalist's appropriate share of profit differ from those of contemporary Wall Street executives.

hands" (196). According to Martineau, the working class's only real means of improving their lot is to *exist less*.

MAKING VIOLENCE VISIBLE:
THE MARCUS PAMPHLET CONTROVERSY

In retrospectively pointing out the necroeconomic undercurrent of Martineau's *Illustrations*, I am in fact echoing the response of many working-class advocates at the time of their publication. While Martineau's didactic fiction earned her many powerful admirers, including parliamentary leader Lord Brougham and even Queen Victoria herself, it also earned her some (at times, vitriolic) criticism in the working-class radical press. This criticism came to a head in the late 1830s during the Marcus pamphlet controversy. Beginning in the fall of 1838, popular newspapers began to report on a scandalous pamphlet, authored by an unknown "Marcus" and printed by John Hill, that included a detailed plan for the mass murder of all third-born and subsequent infants born to poor families. Writing in the euphemistic idiom of bureaucracy, Marcus recommends the "painless extinction" of these superfluous newborns by carbonic acid gas. The pamphlet mimics the style of government publications so effectively as to be almost unreadably dull; casual readers would be forgiven if they did not register that this plodding essay on population is in fact calling for a national program of infanticide.

The conversation surrounding this mystery pamphlet in the working-class press, on the other hand, was anything but dull and plodding. Although the pamphlet was almost certainly a work of satire (in the tradition of Swift's *A Modest Proposal*) written to undermine the Poor Law Commission and their allies,[15] working-class radicals reported on it as a genuine leaked government document and responded with a mixture of righteous outrage and darkly humorous takedowns of the infanticidal authors. Leading the outraged response was the Reverend Joseph Rayner Stephens, a radical preacher and activist who spoke of the Marcus pamphlet in speeches given around the country that were subsequently printed in newspapers such as the *Northern Star*

---

15. The original authorship and intent of the pamphlet have never been clearly established. The general scholarly consensus, however, is that it was a deliberate ruse, written by an opponent of the New Poor Law and given life by the working-class press who covered it as genuine. See Vargo 80–87; McDonagh 102; Hadley, *Melodramatic Tactics* 253, n. 101; Clark 190. There are a few dissenting voices, however, such as Gertrude Himmelfarb, who assumes the pamphlet to have been written by a "fanatical Malthusian" (125–26).

and *Northern Liberator.*[16] These publications were at the forefront of a "textual explosion" that "gather[ed] its own momentum" and eventually forced chief Poor Law Commissioner Edwin Chadwick as well as Assistant Commissioner Power to release statements denying authorship of the pamphlet and reassuring the public that they had no plans to murder any children (McDonagh 105; see also Vargo 81). These awkward public denials only added fuel to the fire, providing new material for critics like Stephens and inadvertently extending the lifespan of what Gregory Vargo calls "one of literary history's most successful pranks" (68). The *Northern Star* produced and sold a "People's Edition" of the pamphlet; radical publisher and pornographer William Dugdale capitalized on the scandal by publishing *The Book of Murder,* which includes an "exact reprint" of the Marcus essay along with a "refutation of the Malthusian Doctrine" (Marcus, title page); books of anti–Poor Law poetry were advertised as "Anti-Marcus"[17] (see McDonagh 106; Vargo 68).

These newspapers also ran a series of works that were essentially anti-Marcus fanfiction, depicting a series of imagined meetings between the main players in the larger Marcus universe. The following poem, put forth as a "stray valentine" from Peter Thimble (an unfriendly nickname for noted Malthusian and pioneer of contraception Francis Place) to Whig politician Lord Durham that was lost in the post, was printed in the *Northern Liberator* on February 16, 1839, and then reprinted in the following week's edition of the *Northern Star.* In addition to lampooning the fictional Marcus in order to highlight the real violence implicit in Malthusian policies, the poem advertises an upcoming lecture by Marcus at Hertford College and names Martineau as an expected guest:

> Your Lordship is, I know, too transcendental,
> Not unto Malthus to have given great heed,
> And see that soon there'll be an end to rental,
> If the pauper people be allowed to breed.
> But now, my Lord, we've fall'n upon a fellow
> Who beats both Malthus and his "checks" dead hollow.
>
> Malthus might prate of prudence and restraint,
> But what's restraint when men see girls have charms?
> Or who, unless it be some Popish saint
> Can keep them out of one another's arms?

---

16. See Faulkner 94–95 and Gammage 55–59.
17. *Northern Liberator,* Saturday 2 November 1839.

Love says to Malthus, 'tis in vain your gull to try;
And married once, by jingo they *will* multiply!

This was our case, as well your Lordship knows;
And hence came many a most superfluous carcase;
When fortune in our way a God-send throws
A prime philosopher! His name is "Marcus."
And he exclaims "now by the holy poker,
I'll give their surplus progeny a choker!"

In short, my Lord, we find that our salvation
Rests solely in carbonic acid "GAS;"
And to our doctrine to convert the nation
Is all we now need bring to come to pass:
To put the matter out of all conjecture,
"Marcus," next week, my Lord, intends to lecture!

The lecture to take place at Hertford College,
In the same room where Malthus once held forth;
And to drink up this new found spring of knowledge
Come all the dilettanti, south and north;
May we not hope your Lordship will be there
To meet Miss Martineau? Brougham takes the chair.

Creating friction between the euphemistic language of the Marcus pamphlet ("convert the nation," "surplus progeny") and bold-faced descriptions of direct violence (giving children a "choker"), the poem depicts advocates of the New Poor Law as sadists who not only allow but actually revel in murder. The *Liberator* then follows up on March 2 with an almost Dickensian satire, titled "Marcus Unveiled," that purports to give an account of that very lecture, paired with an illustration depicting "Marcus" and his allies gathered ominously around an infant sleeping in a bassinet. Written in the voice of an enthusiastic Marcus supporter, the story describes Marcus's demonstration of his method for "the 'painless extinction' of an infant, with which he had been kindly furnished, through the seal of one of the members of the Society for Promoting the Happiness of the Offspring of the Poor." His "enlightened audience" watches with "breathless excitement" as Marcus places the sleeping baby into a "transparent cradle" and gasses it to death. While the author performatively redacts the names of the audience members, readers would easily recognize the "Lord ———" and "Miss ———" noted as present as the same Lord Brougham and Miss Martineau mentioned in the lecture's poetic advertisement.[18] Martineau in particular is singled out as a rapt observer of the baby's death: "'Exquisite!' whispered Miss ——, as she watched eagerly the pulses of the beautiful babe—'exquisite!'"

From the beginning of the Marcus scandal, Martineau is viewed as a sympathizer if not an active co-conspirator. In the months and years following the controversy, the names "Marcus, Malthus, and Martineau" frequently come up together in the radical press, even in articles on other topics: a *Northern Star* article about the Corn Laws mentions the "anti-population doctrines" of "Malthus, and Marcus, and Harriet Martineau";[19] a writer for the *Northern Liberator* proclaims, "We will have no Malthusian Marcus to poison the minds of the people by incitements to child-murder! We will have no Broughams and Martineaus to stigmatize marriage as a crime, and charity as a folly!"[20] The Rev. Stephens actually names Martineau as a possible author of the pamphlet after Chadwick denies that it was penned by the Poor Law Commissioners.[21] Given the seriousness of the accusations being leveled against her, Martineau is surprisingly silent on the matter. While she does admit some regret about working with Lord Brougham, describing their connection as a "detriment to my usefulness and my influence," she does not directly mention the Marcus scandal, nor does she ever issue a public denunciation of the pamphlet like Chadwick (*AB* 167). Her autobiography offers some evidence, however, that the criticism in the radical press made its way to her ears; she mentions that it was a "distasteful task" to read the newspaper, not only because the opposition to the New Poor Law was "so venomous, so unscrupulous, so pertinacious, so mischievous in intention, and so vicious in principle" but also because she was met with "every sort of personal insult which could make a woman recoil" (*AB* 170, 447–48). Ironically, the press is accusing her of encouraging the same act—infanticide—that she herself described as most "horrible" and "corrupt" in *Weal and Woe* (*Illustrations* 114). In the wake of the Marcus scandal, Martineau finds herself involved in an intertextual argument about who is responsible for violence against children. Martineau equates irresponsible reproduction with violence, comparing improvident parents like Noreen to baby killers. Meanwhile, the radical press equates the New Poor Law with violence, accusing its framers of mass infanticide.

Of course, Martineau did not have a hand in writing the Marcus pamphlet, nor did she (or anyone else) reverently look on while a Malthusian

18. Vargo (83) and McDonagh (103–4) also identify them in this way.
19. *Northern Star and Leeds General Advertiser,* Saturday 15 August 1840.
20. *Northern Liberator,* Saturday 27 April 1839.
21. *The Champion,* Sunday 20 January 1839.

mad scientist murdered a baby. Her name becomes associated with this scandal because an oppositional press is leveraging the rhetorical horror of infanticide to demonize Martineau and thus discredit her pro–political economy popular writing. Much of the criticism that she endures is shaped by her position as a nonnormative woman, both professionally and personally: as a woman writing about economics as a science, she is criticized as overstepping her feminine role; as a single, childless woman, she is attacked as a sort of perverse Malthusian mother, ominously cooing over the incubator of a dead infant.[22] Beneath the misogynistic attacks and outlandish satire, however, is a serious critique of the passive violence of political economy. In an open letter addressed to Lord John Russell, the authors of the *Liberator* note that the Marcus "agitation" reflects not only working people's concern about the pamphlet itself but also their larger belief that the New Poor Law "actually *does* (though by worse means) that which Marcus *recommends*."[23] They argue for a fundamental continuity between passive policies that kill the poor by withdrawing aid and active policies that kill the poor by gassing infants: "The people begin to think his scheme only a probable consequence of the scheme of a 'rural police'—and ask themselves it if be *right* to kill people by slow starvations in bastiles, why it should be *wrong* to 'hocus' superfluous infants with 'gas' in a 'rural police station'?"[24] By asserting this continuity, these authors collapse the difference between "letting die" and "making die." This elision represents, as Gregory Vargo has argued, a strategic response to the "representational challenge" of what Rob Nixon calls "slow violence" (69). Through the Marcus controversy, radical writers use satire to make the slow, passive killing of nonintervention legible as state-sanctioned violence. By depicting Martineau as an accessory to murder, eagerly looking on as Marcus gasses an infant, these authors bring necro-economics to the surface, making the argument that political economy not only condones but demands death.

REVISIONIST REDEMPTION:
DEERBROOK

In the same year when the working-class radical press was lambasting Martineau for her advocacy of what they saw as murderous economic policy,

---

22. For more on the gendered attacks on Martineau in response to *Illustrations,* see Huzel 74–89.

23. *Northern Liberator,* Saturday 26 January 1839.

24. *Northern Liberator,* Saturday 26 January 1839.

she was writing a novel that shows a lot more ambivalence toward the moral acceptability of letting die. An early example of domestic realism that influenced works such as Gaskell's *Cranford* and Eliot's *Middlemarch* (V. Sanders xiv–xv), *Deerbrook* (1838) tells a story of provincial life, small-town scandal, and ill-advised marriage in the village of Deerbrook following the arrival of the newly orphaned Ibbotson sisters, Hester and Margaret. The novel centers on the country surgeon Edward Hope, a doctor protagonist in a very similar position and with very similar political commitments to Dr. Burke in *Cousin Marshall*. Like Dr. Burke, he is appointed medical provider for the parish's almshouses, paid by the municipal government to provide free care to the indigent poor. He does not, however, undergo the same crisis of economic conscience that leads Dr. Burke to resign his position. Martineau's *Illustrations,* in which she characterizes the withdrawal of aid from the suffering poor as a moral imperative, predate Victoria's reign by five years. When Martineau writes *Deerbrook* in 1838, just after attending Victoria's coronation, she seems unwilling to depict protagonists who submit to this Malthusian imperative. It is in this ambivalence that Martineau becomes most Victorian: after playing a central role in popularizing a necroeconomic model of noninterventionist ethics, she shifts gears and sets the stage for Victorian literature's obsession with the ethical problem of letting die.

Martineau signals this problem primarily through narrative evasion; Dr. Hope does not have a crisis of conscience about providing free medical care because he is not given a chance to have it. Before a period of scarcity (similar to the one Dr. Burke labors under) arrives in Deerbrook, the poor themselves have already rejected Dr. Hope's care of their own accord. Due to a series of malicious rumors, the almshouse inhabitants become convinced that Dr. Hope is their enemy. They throw stones at him from the hedges as he travels to the almshouse (343), prevent him from approaching the bedsides of his patients (344), and undo any measures he does manage to take as soon as he departs from the establishment (345). Despite this "unpleasantness" and against the warnings of the town patron, Sir William Hunter, who advises Dr. Hope to "stay away" and warns that the "consequences may be serious" if he continues to attempt to provide care at the almshouses, Hope persists in attending to his poor patients (349). Sir William Hunter's warnings turn out to be all too prescient when a mob of the Deerbrook poor attack Hope's home that same night, breaking windows, destroying his surgery, and burning him in effigy on a bonfire in the backyard (368–69). Unsurprisingly, Hope soon finds himself relieved of his almshouse duties by Sir William Hunter and replaced by a newly arrived rival physician, Dr. Walcot. Hope is not given the option of withdrawing care from the poor; they withdraw themselves from his care, against his will and to his great displeasure.

The rumors that derail Hope's career in Deerbrook center around the fear that he does not value the lives of the poor. The primary accusation against him is that he is a "Burker"—that is, that he is stealing dead bodies from graveyards (or perhaps even killing patients on purpose) in order to use the corpses for dissection.[25] The term "Burker" derives from the Burke and Hare scandal of 1828, in which William Burke was convicted of murdering sixteen people and selling their bodies to Edinburgh doctor Robert Knox for dissection. (Hare avoided prosecution by turning king's evidence and providing testimony against Burke [Burrell and Gill].) Although the Burke and Hare case gained notoriety because the men were not just digging up already-deceased corpses but were actually murdering people, the term "Burker" came to be identified with all extralegal practices of acquiring bodies for medical dissection and research. This scientifically motivated grave robbery is what the Deerbrook mob is accusing Dr. Hope of when they make "jokes about churchyards" (345), suggesting that he is digging up bodies for dissection. Such accusations of "Burking" were not uncommon during the 1820s and '30s: fears of Burking were at the root of several riots, including one in Aberdeen in 1831 in which a mob of twenty thousand attacked an anatomical theater.[26] While the passage of the controversial Anatomy Act in 1832 (which gave doctors the legal right to claim for dissection the corpses of poor people who died in prisons and workhouses) largely ended the black-market traffic in bodies, it only reinforced fears among the poor that the medical establishment might capitalize upon their deaths.[27] The Deerbrook poor take action to protect themselves from a doctor they fear views their bodies as more valuable dead than alive; after a young girl dies at the almshouse, her neighbors set up a nightly vigil in the graveyard to watch out for Hope coming to dig up her body, which they maintain until "the want of their regular sleep" compels them give it up (347). Along the same lines, they circulate the rumor that Dr. Hope has "cut off a sound limb for the sake of practice and amusement"—that is, they accuse him of using their bodies as raw material for profit and professionalization (355). Later, when the mob attacks the Hopes' house, they target his surgery because it is "the place where the people expected to find the greatest number of dead bodies" (368). Of course, they find none.

25. Dr. Lydgate of *Middlemarch* is similarly accused of Burking and loses business and social standing as a result.

26. *Liverpool Journal,* 31 December 1831.

27. See Richardson.

Implied in these rumors is the possibility that Dr. Hope is like another Burke—Martineau's own model Malthusian doctor from *Cousin Marshall*.[28] The almshouse inhabitants accuse Dr. Hope of doing exactly what Dr. Burke insisted to be a doctor's moral imperative under political economy: denying adequate medical care to the poor on the basis of their class status. During Hope's final trip to the almshouse, an elderly man "growls" at him about not having fixed his failing eyesight: "Not a bit better could he see now than he could a year ago, with all the doctoring he had had: and now the gentleman would not try anything more! A pretty doctor indeed! But it would not be long before there would be another who would cure poor people's eyes as if they were rich: and poor people's eyes were as precious to them as rich people's" (344). The patient suggests that Dr. Hope does not care about his poor patients—that their bodies are less precious to him, less valuable than those of wealthy people—and thus provides them with a lower quality of care. Hope is unfairly accused of being like Dr. Burke from *Cousin Marshall,* and as a result, he is spared from making the choice that would reveal whether he is indeed like Burke or not. Through this somewhat frustrating narrative evasion, Martineau prevents Dr. Hope from weighing in on the Malthusian doctor's dilemma—the choice between either providing care or upholding the principles of political economy.

The novel enters its most didactic phase in the wake of these rumors, as the loss of Hope's position at the almshouse along with the majority of his private patients leaves the family with almost no income. The Hope family is forced to subsist on the small inheritances of Hester (Hope's wife) and Margaret (Hester's unmarried younger sister), which "can hardly be called sufficient" even for "mere bread" (387–88). Over the subsequent months, they are compelled to give up many of the markers of gentility: they dismiss all their servants, including their beloved housekeeper Morris; Hope sells his horse and travels to see his remaining patients on foot; they give up purchasing meat, leading the local butcher to think he must have offended them (502); they no longer host friends for tea, much to the consternation of their biggest supporters in Deerbrook, the Greys (435). In their sudden poverty, the Hope

---

28. I have no evidence to suggest that Martineau deliberately named Dr. Burke after the notorious murderer—it seems unlikely she would do so, given that Dr. Burke is a protagonist and a mouthpiece for her own views—but I do find the resonance striking. Martineau wrote *Cousin Marshall* in 1832, just a few years after the Burke and Hare scandal hit the news and right at the peak of the debates about the Anatomy Act, during a time when the term "Burker" was certainly in wide circulation. She was certainly aware of the scandal, briefly mentioning the "special horror" of the Burke and Hare murders in her autobiography (*AB* 295). Martineau even "followed Bentham's example" by leaving her body for dissection in her will, although she later changed this provision after the passage of the Anatomy Act.

family becomes a model of the habits of domestic political economy that Mar-tineau marketed to the poor in her *Illustrations*. They moderate their spending to match their means, cutting back on everything they can: "One superfluity after another vanished from the table; every day something which had always been a want was discovered to be a fancy; and with every new act of frugality, each fresh exertion of industry, their spirits rose with a sense of achievement" (420). With the "nicest management and the most strenuous domestic indus-try," they manage to live on their small means. They bear it all with a sense of "cheerful sacrifice" (420), enjoying every "little extra comfort" that comes to them when Hope is able to obtain a small payment from a patient—"the din-ner of meat," the "fire in the evening," or the "sack of apples" from a country patient with no money to spare who pays for Hope's services with the pro-duce of his thriving orchard (491). Most importantly, they refuse to become dependent upon or indebted to anyone. Unlike Eliot's similarly struggling Dr. Lydgate in *Middlemarch,* Hope refuses to purchase anything for which he is "not certainly able to pay" and rejects the penitential offers of charity from Mr. Rowland, husband of the originator of the damaging rumors (491). Freed from the responsibility of providing care to actual paupers, Hope instead becomes a living illustration of *how not to become a pauper.* Showing by example that it is "always possible for able and industrious people, in health, to obtain bread . . . provided that they can cast pride behind them" (387), the Hopes demon-strate that pauperism need not exist (at least among the able-bodied) if people conform to appropriate habits of spending, saving, and industry. This is still an attempt to eliminate the category of pauperism from the social body, but it is certainly a gentler physic than Dr. Burke's "bitter medicine."

But ultimately, it is not in Dr. Burke's analogue but his sister's that we see the biggest ideological shift from *Illustrations* to *Deerbrook.* In place of Louisa, patiently accepting the criticism of her friends as she withdraws aid from the poor, we get Margaret, Dr. Hope's sister-in-law, who flatly refuses to let her indigent neighbors die when a cholera epidemic strikes Deerbrook. As the feared contagion reaches and spreads through the town, Deerbrook's inhab-itants—from the poorest almshouse inhabitants to the wealthiest family in Deerbrook, Sir William and Lady Hunter—begin to isolate and protect them-selves, to the point of denying emotional and material aid to their neighbors. Hope is "disappointed" to find that the poor show "so little disposition to help each other," succumbing instead to either "apathy" or "selfish terrors" that he finds to be "worse to witness than the disease itself" (546). The behavior of the poor cannot be wondered at, Hope suggests, when the wealthy Hunter family sets such a bad example by "shutting themselves up," leading the Hope house-hold to wonder "what sort of a heart" (575) the Hunters have:

> They keep their outer gates locked, lest any one from the village should set foot within their grounds; every article left at the lodge for the use of the family is fumigated before it is admitted into the house: and it is generally understood that neither the gentleman nor the lady will leave the estate, in any emergency whatever, till the disease has entirely passed away. (546)

Many of Deerbrook's middle-class residents follow suit, doing all they can to avoid contact with their ailing neighbors. The shopkeeper Miss Miskin refuses to visit her lifelong best friend Mrs. Howell's sickbed until the dying woman sends a "message threatening to haunt [Miss Miskin] if she did not," at which point the reluctant Miss Miskin still "would not approach nearer than the door-way" (586). For her intense aversion to coming into contact with the potentially contagious, Miss Miskin is criticized as a "selfish wretch" (586). Even the Hopes' closest friends, the Greys, leave Deerbrook to take refuge in Brighton, hoping to escape the epidemic (553).

Margaret, Hester, and Dr. Hope show none of this reluctance to come into contact with the sick. Dr. Hope, of course, attends to the sick (including those who burned him in effigy a few months prior), and the Hope family appears to share none of Sophia Grey's concern about "how very dangerous it must be" for medical men who must always be "going among so many people who are ill" (539). But this commitment to care for their neighbors extends beyond Hope's professional obligations; Margaret also demonstrates this commitment by spending multiple nights in a squalid cottage caring for the poor Platt family, all of whom have been struck with cholera (539). Margaret's entry into the filthy cottage is not just symbolic. Martineau goes into almost graphic detail about how Margaret "conveyed pailful after pailful of the noisome shavings to the dunghill at the back of the cottage"—that is, she removes bedding that is covered in human excrement with her own hands and then washes the bed and the sick woman's body (549–50). She holds the dying child, with "black blood which was still oozing from his nose, ears, and mouth," in her lap until he breathes his last (548). She does all this despite being met with hostility and threats of violence from the only inhabitants of the cottage who are strong enough to make any kind of protest; despite the fact that Mr. Platt turns out to be the masked housebreaker who stole Hester's watch and Margaret's prized turquoise ring; and despite the fact that the Platts have all the improvident "pauper" habits that Martineau criticizes both in *Illustrations* and, tacitly, in contrast with the prudent economy of the Hope household. Even though the Platt family would without question be categorized as undeserving paupers by Dr. Burke in *Illustrations,* Margaret cannot abandon them to death. The gangrenous limb of the social body that Dr. Burke felt ethically compelled to cut off has now become worth saving.

Ultimately, *Deerbrook* is a story of redemption. Dr. Hope's career is nearly ruined by rumors that he was killing the poor or amputating their healthy limbs for sport; only after he shows himself willing to venture into a space of contagion to try to save the poor, the metaphorical gangrenous limb, is Hope redeemed in the eyes of the town. But the accusations against Dr. Hope are so clearly unjustified that his redemption rings a bit hollow. Hope is so unfailingly upright that he even endures some friendly mockery from his closest friends for his excess of moral "'enthusiasm,' as Mr. Grey called what some others would have named virtue" (554). While his long-awaited vindication is satisfying, the "redemption" takes place entirely within the hearts and minds of his appraisers. His redemption story has almost nothing to do with him. Read alongside the *Illustrations* and the criticism of Martineau in the popular press that followed their publication, however, Hope's story becomes more compelling as the displaced redemption of Martineau herself. The rumors that circulate about Hope imagine him as a sort of Marcus: the Malthusian doctor who turns medicine into murder. He becomes the embodiment of a perverse version of medicine that takes the tenets of political economy to their logical extreme—that is, a version of medicine that not only passively kills by looking on as the poor suffer and die but that actively hastens and profits from their deaths. Readers of *Deerbrook* are forced to agree that Dr. Hope does not deserve these accusations, but writers at the *Northern Liberator* and the *Champion* would argue that Martineau does.

When her name appeared in the radical press's criticism of the New Poor Law, Martineau saw the criticism as undeserved: "My share in the punishment I could never understand" (*AB* 170). She seems to imagine herself in a similar position to Dr. Hope, pilloried and abused by a misguided working class for crimes she did not commit. But if Dr. Hope's story is a displaced redemption for Martineau herself, it is one that ends up admitting more guilt than she might be comfortable with, because it hinges upon a fundamental change in her ideology. Dr. Hope is not a revival but rather a reversal of his literary predecessor, Dr. Burke. Burke clearly espoused and acted upon a "laissez-mourir" ideology that compelled him to abandon the poor to death. Hope, on the other hand, fought tooth and nail to continue providing aid to a working-class population that kept rebuffing him based on the mistaken assumption that he was like Dr. Burke. Like a Malthusian Christ figure, Dr. Hope suffers on behalf of an ideology whose "sins" he does not share. In redeeming Dr. Hope of the accusations of violence being leveled at her in the press, Martineau gives up a fundamental element of her philosophy: the imperative to "let die." In doing so, she lays the groundwork for both the narrative tradition and the ideological problem that this book investigates. Eleanor Courtemanche notes that while future writers of social-problem novels rejected Martineau's politics, "they inherited both her belief that fiction could serve as a broadly galvanizing political force and her assertion that fiction was a form of moral science, a laboratory in which to gauge the human effects of social policy" ("'Naked Truth'" 387). They also inherited, I argue, complicated feelings about letting die. As it is for Martineau, the imperative to "let die" becomes for these authors a sticking point, a wrench in the gears of capitalist ideology that threatens to break the whole machine.

CHAPTER 2

Making III

Pathoeconomics in Gaskell's Industrial Novels

> All along it came natural to love folk, though now
> I am what I am. I think one time I could e'en have
> loved the masters if they'd ha' letten me.
>
> —John Barton in *Mary Barton*, Elizabeth Gaskell

At the climax of *Mary Barton*, the mill owner Mr. Carson cries out for sympathy to the murderer of his only son, "Oh, my God! comfort me, comfort me!" (353). John Barton, who killed Carson's son in retribution for his treatment of striking workers, answers the appeal; tears fill his eyes, sympathy fills his heart, and he collapses in anguish at the pain he caused. Soon after, Barton dies in the arms of his enemy, who speaks words of forgiveness over his corpse. In that moment, "rich and poor, masters and men, were then brothers in the deep suffering of the heart" (353). Many literary critics have seen this turn to cross-class sympathy in Gaskell's industrial novels as a half-hearted remedy for the abuses of capitalism at best, if not an endorsement of and contribution to capitalism's most insidious disciplinary mechanisms. For these scholars, Gaskell's emphasis on sympathy speaks either to political quietism (Gaskell encourages feeling *in place of* structural change) or complicity with capitalism (Gaskell "deploys sympathy . . . as a tool to discipline both the workers in her novels and the workers who read her novels") (Schaub 15).

I aim to reveal the radical potential of Gaskell's depiction of sympathy. For Gaskell, sympathy is not capitalism's handmaiden, but rather its kryptonite. In this chapter, I take seriously Gaskell's claim that sympathy is a problem for capitalism—specifically, a necroeconomic capitalism that produces and instrumentalizes death. In doing so, she is making a major theoretical statement that cuts against the economic theories of Adam Smith that comfortably fold sympathy into the logic of capital. In contrast to Smith, who defines sympathy in terms of cognitive projection, Gaskell understands sympathy as a natural impulse that resides in the body and compels action. Such sympathy threatens to interfere with a necroeconomic system that not only "lets die" but also strategically produces a vulnerably embodied work force. Over the course of *Mary Barton* and *North and South,* Gaskell shows how capitalism has solved this problem by systematically repressing the natural circulation of sympathy while simultaneously producing a private stock of emotional labor in the person of the bourgeois woman.

Beyond setting necroeconomic capitalism against sympathy, Gaskell's novels show us how staggeringly different the world would have to be if we really took sympathy—as Gaskell understood it—deadly seriously. For Gaskell, sympathy is a radical force of connection that, if unleashed, would disrupt the very foundations of necroeconomics. Her turn to sympathy, then, is not a facile call for civility on both sides or an apolitical plea for moral improvement. It is a step-by-step analysis, revealed through a narrative series of interpersonal interactions, of the systemic manipulation of feeling that has to take place to make necroeconomics work. This analysis leads Gaskell to a place where the only solution she can imagine is to hand over management of modern industrial capitalism to middle-class women, who she imagines will comprise a new class of sympathy-driven investors. If this seems like an odd turn of events, that is because Gaskell's novels are particularly good at unearthing the strange contortions that happen when we reconsider not only the feelings upon which an economy is based but also those that have been squashed in service of that economy. Ultimately, her industrial novels contain a sort of shadow argument for the value of narrative in economic critique. When economic exploitation depends upon the long-term management and sedimentation of feelings, the Victorian novel becomes a crucial tool of economic analysis, modeling a temporal sequence of interpersonal interactions iterated over time in a way that economic theory cannot.

INDUSTRIAL CAPITALISM AS NECROECONOMICS

In her depiction of the Milton labor strike in *North and South,* Gaskell reprises a theme that Martineau explored in *Cousin Marshall*: the relationship of the medical professional to the laws of the capitalist marketplace. During the days of the strike, Mr. Thornton and Dr. Donaldson bump into one another on the street and discuss how their respective businesses affect one another. The doctor says to the mill owner, "Your bad weather, and your bad times, are my

good ones. When trade is bad, there's more undermining of health, and prepa-
ration for death, going on among you Milton men than you're aware of" (210).
For readers who have just learned about the dire effects of factory work on
Bessy's health and the "clemming," or starvation, of unemployed workers and
their families, this comes as no surprise. Prolonged unemployment, whether
the result of a downturn in trade or necessitated by a strike, will of course produce suffering, illness, and death in the already undernourished bodies of the
Milton workers—and a lot of business for the wry town doctor. Unlike Martineau's Dr. Burke, Dr. Donaldson experiences no crisis of conscience about
providing care to the poor; he is not a publicly employed parish doctor, nor is
he, like Burke, a fictionalized mouthpiece for the tenets of political economy.
We only see him providing medical care to middle-class characters who can
pay for his services, so we never see him pressed to choose between providing
care and upholding the principles of political economy. But his reminder of
capitalism's death toll sets up the problem of letting die, which both Thornton
(as capitalist) and the Hales (as middle-class bystanders) will face.

Mr. Thornton, however, seems to misunderstand and reroute Dr. Donaldson's comments. He assumes that the doctor is concerned about the health of
the mill *owners* and responds by assuring the doctor of his own hardiness and
ability to withstand the anxiety of the strike: "I'm made of iron. The news of
the worst bad debt I ever had, never made my pulse vary. This strike, which
affects me more than any one else in Milton,—more than Hamper,—never
comes near my appetite. You must go elsewhere for a patient, Doctor" (210).
Thornton fails to recognize the irony of assuring the doctor that his appetite
is still healthy during the strike while his workers are dying because they lack
food to satiate their own appetites. Even as he offers to buy anything that
could aid the dying Mrs. Hale because he knows that "money is not very plen-
tiful" in the Hale household, he does not seem to consider for a moment the
wider effects of money's scarcity on the health of the workers of Milton. Crucially, this is Thornton at his least composed. Having proposed to and been
rejected by Margaret the previous day, he has kept his mind off his heartbreak
by throwing himself into the trial of the rioters. After the trial, his stoic self-
control finally breaks down, and he lets his mind do what it will: "It seemed
as though he gave way all at once; he was so languid that he could not control
his thoughts" (210). It is at this moment that Thornton is surprised by the
greeting of Dr. Donaldson. Thus, I do not read his response as the conscious
rhetorical move of a capitalist who does not want to acknowledge the suffering
of his employees and thus pretends to misunderstand the doctor's statement
about ill health. I read it, rather, as a demonstration of the mental gymnas-
tics required to perform the business of letting die. As a mill owner engaged

in a labor dispute with his employees, Thornton's leverage depends upon his willingness to witness the slow starvation and potential death of his striking employees (both by waiting them out and by bringing in nonunion workers from Ireland to break the strike, as Thornton ultimately does). His tolerance of letting die seems to depend upon a kind of selective failure of apprehension—a deeply engrained redirection of attention away from the reality of his workers' suffering that does not fail him even in his most unguarded moments.

It is not so engrained, however, for the Hales, who are stymied by the problem of letting die. Their confusion comes to a head when Margaret witnesses the distress of the starving Boucher family and sends them a basket of food. The Hale family then proceeds to deliberate about whether they acted rightly in providing food to the family of the striking worker. They know where Mr. Thornton stands on the issue; earlier in the narrative, Thornton attempts to dissuade the Hales from helping the "turn-outs," claiming that doing so would only "prolong the struggle" (157). In doing so, he is echoing the eighteenth-century founders of political economy[1] (and indeed will be echoed by the twentieth-century founders of neoliberalism),[2] who claimed with varying degrees of bluntness that both the state and private citizens not only can but must allow "those who without state intervention will starve to do so" in order to protect the freedom of the market and maximize the overall production of the economy (Hill and Montag 273). In this case, the conflict that Martineau's Dr. Burke faced is displaced onto the middle-class woman who must similarly decide whether to let die or provide care.

When pressed to arbitrate between Thornton's laws of political economy and his wife and daughter's act of charity, Mr. Hale can only come to an "unsatisfactory" and logically inconsistent compromise. He claims that Margaret and Mrs. Hale have "done quite right" in helping Boucher and "could [not] have done otherwise" under the circumstances (157). At the same time, he claims that what Thornton said about how the economy worked was "very true" and that it was therefore "clear enough that the kindest thing was to refuse all help which might bolster" the workers in what he characterizes as

---

1. Adam Smith himself skirts around the issue in *The Wealth of Nations* by making the (either naïve or deceitful) claim that real starvation will not occur in a true free-market economy, even in a year of the "scantiest crop" (493). But the message is the same: the state must not intervene by regulating prices or distributing food. In fact, the state should only intervene to protect the private property of merchants against any potential looting or riots (527).

2. Neoliberal thinkers like Ludwig von Mises and Friedrich Hayek are considerably more blunt; they acknowledge that famine and want might occur but argue that the state must not intervene to alleviate it, flatly rejecting any "enforceable human right to subsistence" (von Mises 839). Instead, the state must "be prepared to crush the onslaughts of peace-breakers" who will inevitably rise up in response to their suffering (149).

misguided efforts to obtain higher wages by striking (157). Mr. Hale finds himself at an impasse: it is right to feed the starving and, simultaneously, it is
wrong to feed the starving. Hale's reasoning breaks down as the unspoken
premise of political economy rises briefly to the surface—that establishing
a truly "free" market requires the creation of a "juridico-economic category
of those who, while they cannot be killed by the state, may be allowed by it
to die" (Hill and Montag 313). Mr. Hale's illogical compromise highlights his
inability to square his ethical commitments with his belief in the laws of a
free-market economy. He experiences a feeling of being at sea that I would
identify as characteristic of middle-class Victorian bystanders who witness
the "laissez-mourir" side of a laissez-faire economy. Following in the spirit of
Sianne Ngai's neologism "stuplimity" to name the twentieth-century feeling of
boredom combined with astonishment,[3] we might say these Victorian characters are feeling "impuzzled"—confused and unsure how to act in response
to finding oneself at an impasse. The Hales have "done quite right" by doing
what "may have been doing wrong"; they "could not have done otherwise"
than what they ought not to have done; what is "very true" is false in this case;
what is "clear enough" is opaque in this case (157). When faced with the reality
of letting die, the Hales are profoundly impuzzled.

But Gaskell shows that free-market capitalism's necroeconomic tendencies go beyond a purportedly passive "letting die" of starving turn-outs. In
her descriptions of strike-breaking tactics and factory conditions, she shows
that capitalism's strategic repertoire also includes a systematic "making ill"
of workers' bodies. That is to say that industrial capitalism in Milton both
creates and *instrumentalizes* the bodily vulnerability of the mill workers. We
can see how the workers' poor health is used as an instrument of the capitalist owners during the strike. Thornton's success in his conflict with the
workers actually depends on their bodily vulnerability in comparison to his
"iron strength." He feels confident that he can prevail and prevent the success
of the strikers precisely because he can essentially starve them out—or perhaps more accurately, he can out-starve them. That is, he can last longer than
they can without work because their bodies are closer to starvation than his
body is. The same problem that leads the workers to strike—wages that are
too low to support healthy bodies or to accrue any savings—prevents their
success, because their bodies are already weak and starving before the strike
begins, and they do not have savings with which to buy food when they are
not receiving wages. A healthy body can negotiate—can hold out for a better offer, can weigh options, can think a proposal through—in a way that a

---

3. See Ngai, ch. 6.

starving body cannot. Mr. Thornton's well-fed, steady, powerful body exists in a different, slower, less urgent temporality than that of the workers' starving bodies, and this gives him leverage in their conflict. The poor person is thus denied economic negotiating power by the very bodily vulnerability poverty produces.[4] Necroeconomics thus operates well before the absolute threshold of death, as mill owners utilize their workers' relative *proximity* to death as a bargaining chip.

Further, the hunger of the workers becomes an instrument of the capitalists' power because it turns vulnerable laborers into advocates for their own unhealthy working conditions. Just after this exchange between Thornton and Dr. Donaldson, Margaret learns that her working-class friend Bessy Higgins has died. The young woman finally succumbed to her long, factory-borne illness in the morning, perhaps at the same time that Thornton was discussing the strike's impact on health in Milton with Dr. Donaldson. Bessy's fatal illness originated during her time working in a "carding-room" in a textile factory, where raw cotton is prepared for spinning. In these carding rooms, bits of material "fly off fro' the cotton . . . and fill the air till it looks all fine white dust" (102). This "fluff got into [Bessy's] lungs" and made her ill. According to Bessy, this is a common plight of carding-room workers; she tells Margaret, "There's many a one as works in a carding-room, that falls into a waste, coughing and spitting blood, because they're just poisoned by the fluff" (102). This health hazard can be easily prevented by installing a "great wheel at one end o' [the] carding-rooms to make a draught, and carry off th' dust," but Bessy explains that "between [the objections of both] masters and men," these wheels have not been successfully implemented (102–3). Masters object to installing a wheel, unsurprisingly, because it "costs a deal o' money—five or six hundred pound, maybe, and brings in no profit" (102). Seeing as masters have no trouble procuring willing workers in their mills, it is no surprise that they do not choose to take several hundred pounds out of their profits to pay for machinery that will improve working conditions.

More surprising, though, is the fact that the workers themselves object to the installation of the wheels. The bodily vulnerability brought on by prolonged poverty and undernourishment makes them not only unable but also unwilling to negotiate with the masters for safer working conditions. Bessy explains their objections: "I've heard tell o' men who didn't like working in

---

4. Indeed, Adam Smith very nearly acknowledges this in *Wealth of Nations* when he notes that masters will always have the advantage in wage disputes because they have resources to "live a year or two" without employing labor, while workers generally only have enough savings to last a few days without earning wages (83).

places where there was a wheel, because they said as how it made 'em hungry, at after they'd been long used to swallowing fluff, to go without it, and their wage ought to be raised if they were to work in such places" (102–3). The half-starving workers depend on having their stomachs artificially filled up by the unhealthy byproducts of their labor. The factory air, contaminated by the raw material of industry, is yet another numbing drug (like alcohol, tobacco, or opium) that helps the workers forget their hunger, their pain, and their poverty. It is, from the perspective of the factory owners, the perfect drug: it weakens their bodies, thus reducing the threat of revolt; it numbs their hunger without making them unruly; it makes them dependent on factory labor to get their fix; it makes the ill-treated workers into advocates for their own poor working conditions; and rather than costing the masters anything, it excuses them from the cost of buying new equipment. As was the case in Thornton's strike negotiations, it is in the interest of the masters to keep the bodies of their laborers starving and vulnerable. They are able to avoid cutting into their profits to purchase equipment that will improve working conditions and prevent Bessy's lung disease precisely because their workers are perpetually hungry and cannot bear to go without the cotton fluff filling their empty bellies.

For mill owners like Thornton, the body of the perfect laborer is not robust and strong; it is hovering above the threshold of starvation, addicted to harmful substances, and dying of industrial diseases. Gaskell echoes Engels as she shows that industrial capitalism "undermines the vital force of these workers gradually, little by little, and so hurries them to the grave before their time" (Engels 96). In highlighting the systemic ill health of the industrial laboring class, Gaskell joins a chorus of concerned commentators raising the alarm about the "general enfeeblement" of the working class during the early Victorian period (Engels 105). This chorus included voices representing a wide range of political affiliations and goals, from wholesale critics of capitalism like Engels to liberal reformers like James Kay-Shuttleworth, from philanthropic ladies' organizations to Benthamite pioneers of bureaucratized public health like Edwin Chadwick and Southwood Smith.[5] Perhaps surprisingly, though, Gaskell's critique shares more with that of the revolutionary socialist Engels than with liberal reformers like Chadwick in that she presents working-class debility as an *operative technology,* not an accidental byproduct, of industrial capitalism.

---

5. See Engels; Kay-Shuttleworth; Chadwick. For more on Victorian concern about the health, cleanliness, and sanitary habits of working-class bodies, see also Poovey, *Making*; Gilbert, *Citizen's Body.*

In Gaskell's depiction, Thornton's free-market capitalism is a system that depends not only on the willful abandonment of citizens to death by starvation but also on the production and instrumentalization of vulnerable, suffering bodies. Gaskell thus extends Hill and Montag's critique of political economy's necroeconomic character, showing that necroeconomics operates not just at the threshold of death but across death's proximate zone. In a strategy that could perhaps more accurately be called "pathoeconomics," the mill owners benefit from keeping the bodies of their workers close to death. In this production of endemic debility, to use Jasbir Puar's term, the necroeconomics of market freedom overlaps with other contemporaneous necroeconomic forms, such as imperial violence. Puar highlights debilitation—the "practice of rendering populations available for statistically likely injury"—as a key technology of settler colonial rule (xviii). Of course, debilitation does not operate in the same way in these two cases; for one thing, the very proliferation of writing from dominant-class authors like Gaskell that laments the debilitation of English workers speaks to the racial, ethnic, and religious privilege that makes their situation distinct from people displaced by Western imperialism. But the parallel applications of a rubric of debility in these two disparate cases highlight the "centrality of debilitation to the workings of capitalism" (Puar 78).

CAPITALISM'S PROBLEM WITH SYMPATHY

But this pathoeconomic tendency to produce vulnerable, suffering bodies creates a problem for capitalism: sympathy. Critics have often viewed the turn to sympathy in response to the pathologies of capitalism with a skeptical eye—and with good reason. The production of cross-class sympathy or pity does not necessarily lead to compassionate action, let alone to the kind of systemic change required to eliminate nationwide poverty. Proposing interpersonal sympathy as a catch-all solution for the harm caused by industrial capitalism can very easily function as an act of reactionary misdirection that distracts from material inequality and discredits the political activism of the working class. Carolyn Betensky and Melissa Schaub in particular have shown how sympathy-as-solution can not only fail to bring about material change in the living conditions of the poor but can actually further entrench capitalism's inequalities. Sympathy can be used, as Schaub explains, to discipline working-class characters, limiting their willingness to rise up against oppressive systems because of their attachment to the masters who benefit from those systems. Indeed, we see this happening in both *Mary Barton* and *North and South*: Gaskell depicts a rowdy working-class boy on the street disciplined by sympathy for the wealthy young girl he accidentally injures; she shows how sympathy for Thornton leads his factory hands to work unpaid overtime to try to keep his factory afloat; she suggests that sympathy for the mill owners would prevent workers from rising up in violence against them. And sympathy can also redirect attention away from the material causes of working-class suffering and toward the feelings of middle-class witnesses to that suffering. For Betensky, the effect of Gaskell's novels is not to produce social activism or material change, but rather to produce bourgeois feeling as an end in itself, collapsing the differences between working-class sufferer and middle-class observer through imaginative identification and allowing bourgeois readers to understand themselves as both sympathizing and deserving of sympathy. The novels, in this light, are not really about their working-class characters but the formation of proper bourgeois subjectivity in their readers.

Betensky and Schaub highlight important ways in which sympathy can become complicit in an oppressive system of capitalism—and yet, I argue that Gaskell presents sympathy as fundamentally opposed to free-market capitalism as a necroeconomic system. My divergence from these other scholars stems from a difference in how I view Gaskell to be theorizing sympathy. To attend to her depiction of scenes of sympathy, I argue, is to reveal that she is using a very different definition of sympathy from the Smithian sympathy that scholars such as Rae Greiner have positioned as foundational to Victorian literature. The sympathy that Gaskell presents is not an autonomous, willed, cognitive act of imagining that takes place in the bounded and rational mind of the individual. Gaskell's sympathy begins with an instinctual, embodied response to proximity with the suffering or vulnerable body of another and ends with compassionate action. It is *impulsive,* happening before, below, or against cognition, and it is *compulsive,* compelling the sympathizer to act for the suffering other. This sympathy is a problem for capitalism—and in particular, it is a problem for a pathoeconomic capitalism that produces vulnerable, suffering bodies and is invested in keeping them that way.

We see this sympathy in action in both *Mary Barton* and *North and South* as Gaskell depicts characters who come into close contact with suffering others with whom they are not inclined to sympathize, who experience an affective response that disrupts their predispositions, and who then find themselves acting on behalf of the sufferer against their plans or self-interest. In *North and South,* for example, a reluctant Mrs. Thornton visits the dying Mrs. Hale strongly disinclined to sympathize. She "doubt[s] the reality of Mrs.

Hale's illness" and only submits to her son's entreaty that she go with "as bad a grace as she could," full of "contempt for Mr. and Mrs. Hale, and positive dislike to Margaret" (236). As soon as she arrives and comes into close proximity with the dying Mrs. Hale, however, her resentment is interrupted and nullified by her experience of the intensity of her encounter. Mrs. Thornton is "softened all at once," and her dislike is "struck into nothingness before the dark shadow of the wings of the angel of death" (236). No cognition or rational thought seems to take place; she responds immediately, without reflection, to Mrs. Hale's vulnerable, suffering body: the "heavy moisture of tears . . . on the eyelashes," the "hand groping feebly over the bedclothes" (236). Moreover, she responds *with* her body. She does not think, speak, or even feel; she *softens*. In this scene, Gaskell depicts sympathy not as imaginative projection but as affective encounter, originating in the "intensities that pass body to body" (Gregg and Seigworth 1). This intensity compels action, as Mrs. Thornton submits to Mrs. Hale's request to care for the soon-to-be-motherless Margaret. Sympathy here occurs as an impulsive response of one body to another body that disrupts and supersedes Mrs. Thornton's thoughts and feelings about the Hales and compels her to action on their behalf. This phenomenon occurs more dramatically in *Mary Barton* when the boatman Sturgis is impelled to care for a lost, completely vulnerable Mary, "interested in her in spite of himself, and his scoldings of himself" (290). He takes her home with him to safety, "swearing at himself while he did so for an old fool" (290). Mary's vulnerability paradoxically keeps her safe in Liverpool, because it instigates a sympathy response in Sturgis that leads to compassionate care. The boatman and his wife experience sympathy for Mary, a total stranger to them, in response to her physical weakness—how her "cheek flushed, and then blanched to a dead whiteness; a film came over her eyes, and catching at the dresser for support in that hot whirling room, she fell in a heap on the floor" (301). Mary fades in and out of consciousness, unable to speak in her "stupor." While she does eventually explain her situation to them, they experience sympathy for her and act in response to that sympathy well before they have any understanding of her identity or the cause of her difficulties. Mrs. Sturgis feels the impulse to "pity and to help" Mary without knowing anything about her, deciding that the strange girl "shanna leave the house to-night, choose who she is,—worst woman in Liverpool, she shanna" (303). Sympathy occurs before knowledge, as a visceral response to a vulnerable and suffering body.

A similar process occurs in the famous scene near the end of *Mary Barton,* when the elder Mr. Carson feels sympathy for his son's dying murderer, John Barton. Only in the presence of the total bodily vulnerability of John

Barton (as well as his daughter) does Mr. Carson begin to feel sympathy for his enemy. Mr. Carson returns to the Barton home to find John Barton "fallen across the bed," unable to move and barely able to breathe, and an exhausted Mary struggling "in vain" to "raise him" (358). Both John (literally) and Mary (symbolically) are at the very brink of death: John dies and Mary falls unconscious just minutes after Mr. Carson arrives. John Barton is almost like a representative of bodily vulnerability itself, clinging to life by a thread. He is as close to death as possible without actually being dead, merely able to look "with gratitude" at the man who raises him up and holds him before dying in his arms (358). Only in the close physical presence of this extreme bodily vulnerability does Mr. Carson begin to feel sympathy for the man who killed his only son. Even in this extreme case, the visceral impulse to sympathize with a vulnerable, suffering body is stronger than the cognitive predisposition against sympathy.

In addition to being aroused by the body of the other, Gaskell's form of sympathy also seems to be best expressed through and by the body rather than with words. We can see this in Mr. Carson's sympathy toward John Barton, which is first expressed through the physical action of lifting the dying man and holding him. Gaskell depicts Mary's sympathy toward Mrs. Wilson when Jem is wrongly imprisoned in a similarly physicalized way. Mary speaks comforting words to Jem's mother, but the real communication of sympathy happens through Mary's bodily presence and actions, not through her words:

> She spoke in a low gentle tone the loving sentences, which sound so broken and powerless in repetition, and which yet have so much power, when accompanied with caressing looks and actions, fresh from the heart; and the old woman insensibly gave herself up to the influence of those sweet, loving blue eyes, those tears of sympathy, those words of love and hope, and was lulled into a less morbid state of mind. (244)

It is not Mary's words but rather her affectively expressive body—her eyes, her tears, her looks and actions, the tone of her voice—that conveys sympathy to Mrs. Wilson. For Gaskell, sympathy is a visceral response felt by one embodied being in the physical presence of another embodied being, so it makes sense that she also depicts the expression of that response as primarily embodied. In a way that parallels Gregg and Seigworth's definition of affect, Gaskell roots sympathy in "a body's *capacity* to affect and to be affected" (Gregg and Seigworth 2). For Gaskell, provoking sympathy and experiencing sympathy *is* (to borrow Deleuze's paraphrase of Spinoza) "what a body can do" (Deleuze 217).

The kind of sympathy that Gaskell is depicting here is, importantly, *not* the sympathy that Adam Smith describes in his *Theory of Moral Sentiments*— a phenomenon that takes place within the imagination of the bounded individual, through that individual's willed cognitive act of imagining themselves experiencing what they see someone else experiencing and thinking about how they would feel in that situation. Smith's sympathy is not immediate or instinctive; it requires us to "take time" to "picture out in our imagination" what another person is experiencing and "consider his situation, fully and in all its parts" (18). Nor is it rooted in the body; it happens exclusively in the mind, a space that Smith imagines can be independent from the body through stoical "self-command" (206). The version of sympathy that Smith imagines is based on the premise that any genuine transmission of affect or feeling between individuals is impossible; our senses "never did, and never can, carry us beyond our own person" (9). For Smith, sympathizing with another is really just a cognitive process of relating to oneself, entirely contained within the impenetrable refuge of one's own person. What Smith describes as sympathy is fundamentally different from the sympathy Gaskell is imagining—immediate, instinctive, embodied, and involving real affective permeability between individuals. In making this claim, I am diverging from a critical trend of taking Adam Smith's depiction of sympathy as the primary lens through which to view Victorian novelists' engagement with sympathy.

In this shift, Gaskell draws upon a theory of sympathy that precedes Smith and that threatens capitalism in way that Smith's does not—a version of sympathy, in fact, that Mike Hill and Warren Montag have suggested Smith deliberately tries to efface and render unthinkable *because* it threatens capitalism. In *The Other Adam Smith,* Hill and Montag juxtapose Smith with Spinoza, showing how Smith radically redefines sympathy in a way that empties it of what, for Spinoza, *made it sympathy*: the "'communication' or 'transmission' of affect from one individual to another" (Hill and Montag 110). Smith's argument in *The Theory of Moral Sentiments* is "constituted by a double gesture that preserves the idea, or perhaps merely the term 'sympathy,' only to the extent that it empties it of any content or significance that would exceed the boundary of the individual" (108). This transformation of sympathy is instrumental to capitalism. It configures the kind of individual necessary for the success of a free-market capitalism that depends on the transformation of rational self-interest into social good via the action of an invisible hand. In order for that self-interest to be unassailable, "the individual must be made separate and solitary, impervious to the affects and desires of others . . . immune to the affective contagion whose effects other authors so feared" (144). "Our own

person" must be, as Smith suggests it is, "an absolute horizon" (112). Moreover, by transforming sympathy from an immediate instinctive response into
a cognitive act that takes both effort and time, Smith introduces a whole series
of obstacles to sympathizing. The imaginative process of sympathizing might
be interrupted by our "disgust" for excessively "clamorous" suffering (*Theory*
24), our "contempt" for the beggar (144), or our belief that we would avoid
suffering in the same circumstances—indeed, Smith claims that "poverty may
be easily avoided" in "civilized nations" (297). (He also categorically writes off
the possibility of real deprivation among the working poor, confidently asserting that the "wages of the meanest laborer" in England are always enough for
"the necessities of nature" [50].) Finally, his flat rejection of the transindividual
dimension works to render unintelligible the possibility of collectives with
shared affects and desires—groups that both arise as a result of and threaten
industrial capitalism (117–28, 146). Smith's is a form of sympathy that does not
threaten and in fact ideologically enables capitalism.

I see Gaskell as trying to recover or revitalize a form of sympathy that
does threaten capitalism—an impulsive sympathy that, like Spinoza's, emerges
without will or cognition in the productive space between vulnerable bodies
and compels compassionate action. This is fundamentally unlike the spectatorial sympathy of Smith or Hume, which centers on a sympathizer *looking at* an object of sympathy. David Marshall notes the visuality of Smith's
model, while Laura Hinton investigates how Hume describes sympathy as "a
voyeuristic-fetishistic medium" (23). Gaskell's sympathy, in contrast, hardly
seems to involve spectatorship at all. John Barton acts upon sympathy with
the Davenports before even seeing them; moreover, when Mr. Carson sympathizes with the dying John Barton, the language of visuality is only applied
to Barton himself: "Mr. Carson stood in the door-way. In one instant he com-
prehended the case. He raised up the powerless frame; and the departing soul
looked out of the eyes with gratitude. He held the dying man propped in his
arms" (358, emphasis added). Barton, the object of sympathy, looks; Carson,
the sympathizer, comprehends and acts. In this sense, the embodied sympathy
that Gaskell depicts in *Mary Barton* is fundamentally unlike the perverse voyeurism of Lovelace, peering through the keyhole to witness the distress that
he caused to Clarissa—an example that Hinton uses to illustrate the "moral-
representational paradoxes" (36) of the Enlightenment sympathy of Hume and
Smith. Despite its centrality to the plot, this moment of sympathetic connection between Carson and Barton is barely narrated. The time during which
Carson could be said to be "watching" is reduced to "one instant." This is
not the drawn-out voyeurism of Lovelace that fuels Richardson's famously

lengthy novel and that Hinton takes as paradigmatic. Hinton claims Richardson's novel shows sympathy to be "not regulated by reason but stimulated by visual pleasure" (36). Carson's sympathy in this moment, though, barely involves either. Carson's role as sympathizer is not characterized by thinking *or* by seeing but by physical presence and impulsive compassionate action. In this sense, Gaskell's sympathy resembles what Saint Augustine, writing in the wake of the sack of Rome in 410 CE, calls "compassion": "a fellow-feeling in our hearts for another's misery, which compels us to come to his help by every means in our power" (349).

This is not to say that Gaskell never presents moments in which sympathetic feeling is mediated via imagination or that these moments are necessarily politically inert. Jon Singleton persuasively argues, for example, that Gaskell (a devout Unitarian and wife of a minister)[6] presents a kind of Unitarian revision of Smithian imaginative sympathy, in which the Smithian "third position" is identified with an all-seeing God (922). I differ somewhat from Singleton's interpretation of Gaskell's sympathy for two reasons (beyond my focus on capitalism and his on religion). First, we interpret Smith somewhat differently; he sees in Smith's imaginative model of sympathy the potential for a much more meaningful "exchange of feelings" than I do (921). Second, we investigate somewhat different forms of narrative sympathy. While he focuses mostly on moments in which characters *think* about other characters (or a third-person narrator asks readers to think about characters), I look at scenes in which characters interact directly with one another, unmediated by imagination. I agree, though, with his conclusion that Gaskell envisions an "active sympathy," not based on the "fundamental principle of self-interest," "that causes people to act outside of their own interests" (922). However, I see this form of sympathy emerge not in moments of imaginative projection but in moments of impulsive, compulsive sympathetic embodiment. In this sense, Augustine's premodern model of sympathy is a more apt forerunner

6. A range of scholarly work has explored the religious context of Gaskell's "social-problem" novels. Amy Coté, for example, illuminates how Gaskell navigates contemporary political problems through the religious medium of the parable in *Mary Barton*. Rebecca Soares argues that Gaskell (along with Elizabeth Stuart Phelps) investigates the complexities of a modern industrial world by combining realist narratives with spiritual motifs in a generic innovation that she calls "spiritual realism." Jon Singleton examines how Gaskell challenges "the boundaries of her readers' political sympathies" (917) through the recontextualization of Biblical quotation. Coté, Soares, and Singleton all challenge a critical trend that Singleton identifies of associating Gaskell's religious faith with her ultimate alignment with middle-class interests or her failure to imagine meaningful political change (920–21). For these three scholars, religion is not a tool for papering over the complexities of class conflict but rather an apparatus for investigating those very complexities.

than Smith's of the form of sympathy that Gaskell presents as sociopoliti-
cally transformative in *Mary Barton* and *North and South*. Gaskell's impulsive
sympathy is more similar to what Smith describes as women's humanity: "the
exquisite fellow-feeling" women have for others that leads them to "grieve
from their sufferings, to resent their injuries, and to rejoice at their good fortune" and that prompts women to "humane action" without the intervention
of any "self-command" (*Theory* 274). But while Smith discredits this form of
sympathy as lesser than the cognitively mediated sympathy that he credits
primarily to men, Gaskell flips the script, presenting impulsive sympathy as
a powerful challenge to necroeconomics. Further, her emphasis on embodiment as a crucial element of transformative sympathy challenges the critical
understanding of Gaskell as someone who encourages abstract middle-class
feeling in place of direct political engagement. Ultimately, Gaskell's depiction
of sympathy suggests that it is not enough to "transport middle-class readers into the homes and minds of the poor" through the medium of the novel
(Poovey, *Social Body* 143); real change requires physical presence.

SYMPATHY UNDER NECROECONOMICS: MANUFACTURED BARRIERS

Gaskell alerts readers to the fact that Mr. Thornton's capacity for this kind of
sympathy is inhibited through his denial of his own embodiment in the conversation with Dr. Donaldson in *North and South* to which I referred above.
Mr. Thornton claims that he is not vulnerable to suffering from ill health as a
result of the strike, stating, "I am made of iron" (210). Thornton seems to be
insisting that he is outside of the realm of bodily vulnerability in which sympathy circulates. He essentially asserts that he is not a human body. Instead
of vulnerable human flesh, he is made of iron. His pulse does not vary; his
appetite does not alter. Mr. Thornton asserts this physical invulnerability as a
positive personal attribute, but in light of Gaskell's depiction of sympathy as
rooted in shared bodily vulnerability, we can see this claim as a character flaw
in Mr. Thornton and a problem that the novel needs to solve. To see oneself
as physically invulnerable and ironclad is to be cut off from the circulation
of sympathy. As Gaskell shows in both novels, however, this belief of Thornton's is not just an individual failing or an isolated character flaw. Rather, it is
evidence of the problematic way in which capitalism disciplines subjects into
repressing their own sympathy, thus interfering with natural human communal relations. In both *Mary Barton* and *North and South*, Gaskell shows how

the success of capitalism depends on the artificial withholding of this natural sympathy. In the case of the strike, Mr. Thornton's success in outlasting the striking workers depends on his withholding of sympathy for their starving families. In the case of poor working conditions, the mill owners' success in accruing the most profit depends on their lack of sympathy for both illness and hunger among their workers. Their power as capitalist owners requires the suppression of their natural sympathy. If they were to feel sympathy for the workers and provide food for the children who are dying of starvation, they would undermine their own power over their workers. Gaskell reveals several mechanisms by which industrial capitalism systematically interferes with the natural flow of sympathy between embodied human beings.

The simplest but perhaps most crucial mechanism is by restricting contact between masters and men. As shown above, the sympathetic response is aroused by intimate, close contact between bodies, and the system of industrial capitalism shown in *Mary Barton* and *North and South* structurally limits such contact between masters and workers through the employment of middle management intermediaries. Gaskell illuminates the effects of this practice in *Mary Barton* when George Wilson speaks to the elder Mr. Carson in hopes of obtaining an infirmary order for the gravely ill Mr. Davenport. When Wilson tells the mill owner that his employee is very ill, Carson responds with confusion: "Davenport—Davenport; who is the fellow? I don't know the name" (68). After Wilson assures Mr. Carson that Davenport has "worked in your factory better nor three years," Carson responds, "Very likely; I don't pretend to know the names of the men I employ; that I leave to the overlooker" (68). By employing "overlookers" to stand between themselves and the laborers, the mill owners are able to avoid the close contact with their men that would stimulate the sympathy that would pose problems for them as capitalists.

Perhaps less obviously, Gaskell also shows how the illusion of merit-based social mobility also functions to limit cross-class sympathy. As he reveals in a conversation with the Hales, Mr. Thornton espouses a deep belief in merit-based upward mobility, essentially claiming that anyone who "deserves" to be part of the middle class *will* become part of the middle class. He states that any working-class person who lives with "decency and sobriety of conduct, and attention to his duties," with "self-denial," despising any "indulgences not thoroughly earned" will be able to raise himself up and "come over to our ranks . . . on the side of authority and order" (84–85). In his view, the suffering of the poor laborer is the "natural punishment of dishonestly-enjoyed pleasure"—the fitting reward for "self-indulgent, sensual people" who deserve his "contempt for their poorness of character" (85). He is essentially making an argument that capitalism is a merit-based system, wherein merit is judged by how well an individual conforms to the standards of bourgeois morality. Anyone who acts like a proper bourgeois subject will rise financially and become part of the capital-owning or managerial class; those who do not embody those values and habits deserve their inferior economic position and their suffering and do not earn any sympathy from Thornton. His belief that industrial capitalism ultimately rewards merit justifies his lack of sympathy for his workers; his experience of raising himself from the position of worker to master justifies his feeling of contempt for any worker who has not been able to do the same.

Gaskell suggests, however, that merit-based upward mobility in industrial capitalism is actually an illusion, in two ways. First, she draws attention to the external influences and elements of privilege that contribute to determining an individual's professional success. After Mr. Thornton tells the story of his own rise from rags to riches, Mr. Hale gently questions whether his success was solely due to merit by drawing attention to Thornton's privilege. Mr. Hale believes that Thornton was aided in his professional success by "the rudiments of a good education," even though Thornton denies that his early education helped him at all as a manufacturer (85). After Mr. Thornton leaves, Margaret also asserts the importance of his privilege, claiming that he "owes his position" to the "training which his mother gave him" (87). While they acknowledge that Mr. Thornton is a "remarkable man," (88) both Margaret and Mr. Hale doubt that his rise to the position of mill owner is really the result of pure merit even as he understands it, bringing attention to other factors such as early education and the influences of family.

Second, and more important, Gaskell throws Mr. Thornton's definition of "merit" into question. Nothing is more important to Thornton's version of bourgeois merit than financial prudence. He locates his own worth as a man in his history of financial planning and self-denial. After his father's death, leaving the Thorntons in poverty, John worked in a draper's shop at a salary of fifteen shillings a week. He was able to provide for his mother and sister and still "put by three out of these fifteen shillings regularly" (85). This careful, prudent saving allowed him to accrue the capital that would eventually lead to the ownership of his own mill. Thornton certainly sees his careful husbanding of resources in order to accrue more resources as meritorious and morally right, but I argue that Gaskell suggests that financial improvidence among the poor is often not a vice but actually a sign of their merit. Throughout *Mary Barton* and *North and South,* Gaskell repeatedly highlights the moral value of improvidence and recklessness in service of hospitality, selfless care, and communal bonds.

Mary Barton opens with a scene of financial extravagance enacted for the sake of sympathy, friendship, and community. The Bartons, who are grieving after the disappearance of Mrs. Barton's sister Esther, invite the Wilsons over for an impromptu tea party. Mary is sent to buy eggs, ham, milk, a loaf of bread, and a bit of rum to share with the visitors. Spending this money is an "extravagance" with real financial consequences for the Bartons—when Mrs. Barton dies the following night, the tea-party expenditure leaves them "short of money" for funeral expenses (22). To spend money on a tea party[7] instead of saving it for necessities seems improvident, unless you think of communal bonds as the necessities of life, as Gaskell's working poor do. These moments of extravagant hospitality build up the culture of sympathy and communal care that John Barton believes is unique to the poor community. He complains to George Wilson that the rich do nothing to help the poor. They do not bring food to the starving or ill, share their plenty with the freezing, hungry man who is out of work in the winter, or comfort the grieving when their family members die—"No, I tell you, it's the poor, and the poor only, as does such things for the poor" (11). The extravagance of hospitality that the Bartons show, and that Alice Wilson shows later when she invites Mary and Margaret for tea and spends her morning's wages on "half an ounce of tea and a quarter of a pound of butter," is part of the same ethos that values communion and sympathy over personal property (29).

As we see later in *Mary Barton,* the development of a culture of sympathy among the poor is actually a matter of life and death, because the kindness of neighbors is the only safety net for those who fall on hard times. This is best demonstrated after the fire at the Carson mill, which puts many men out of work, including George Wilson and Ben Davenport. Wilson gets by on the

---

7. In both *Mary Barton* and *North and South,* we see the wealthy mill owners throw extravagant parties for their friends during times of downturn in trade. In *Mary Barton,* an out-of-work John Barton sees the wife of his former boss buying delicacies for a party while Barton's son is dying at home for want of "good nourishment" (24). And in *North and South,* the Thorntons throw an extravagant dinner party during the strike, while the children of many workers are starving. Bessy Higgins questions, "Suppose Thorntons sent 'em their dinner out,—th' same money, spent on potatoes and meal, would keep many a crying babby quiet, and hush up its mother's heart for a bit!" (149). While the celebration of financial extravagance for the sake of throwing a party as a merit in the poor paired with its criticism as a vice in the rich may seem like a contradiction, the difference here comes down to the emotional or affective function of the spending. In the case of the Bartons' little tea party, financial expenditure facilitates prosocial emotional circulation that binds a community together and accords with Adela Pinch's description of "emotional extravagance" in *Strange Fits of Passion* (3–4). In contrast, the money that funds the Thorntons' dinner party is spent in service of conspicuous consumption that shores up barriers between the rich and the poor—financial extravagance that inhibits, rather than facilitates, the general circulation of prosocial emotion.

wages of his son Jem, but Ben Davenport comes "down wi' the fever" (57) and has several children who are all too young to work. When George Wilson and John Barton go to help the Davenports, the two men reveal what we might call a proletarian morality that differs from bourgeois morality in its profound commitment to selflessness and sympathy, even when practicing such sympathy requires financial improvidence or even recklessness. After seeing the situation at the Davenports' cellar, John Barton pawns his only good coat and handkerchief to buy food, candles, matches, and coal for the family. In an unquestionably improvident act, Barton essentially gives up all of his savings, everything that he could sell for food if he were starving in the future, to provide for the immediate needs of a family he does not even know except through the connection of George Wilson. Throughout the novel, working-class sympathy impels characters to sacrifice their own future security for the immediate needs of the other. Gaskell presents these acts of financial improvidence for the sake of communal bonds and well-being as signs of Barton's merit and moral goodness. Thus, she throws into question Mr. Thornton's bourgeois belief in the correlation between financial prudence and merit.

In these ways, Gaskell suggests that Thornton's rise is not attributable to pure merit but rather is the result of the combination of privilege and a morally questionable ethos of financial prudence. But his mistaken belief in the structuring myth of capitalism, that the deserving will inevitably rise to the top, works to prevent his sympathizing with those at the bottom. Margaret's objections to Mr. Thornton early in the novel seem to arise from her objection to his complicity and investment in this myth. She criticizes him for thinking that the poor are "out of the pale of his sympathies because they had not his iron nature, and the capabilities that it gives him for being rich" (88). She recasts the qualities that have enabled Thornton to become rich as his "iron nature." This phrase implies that he is strong and steadfast, and indeed he is, but it also suggests that he lacks the embodied vulnerability that facilitates sympathetic communion. Margaret thus suggests that the qualities that make him capable of rising to a high position in industrial capitalism and differentiate him from his working-class associates—qualities that he sees as his virtues—are actually his flaws.

Margaret's criticism implies that this capitalist myth—which categorizes any qualities that allow a man to succeed as a capitalist as "virtues" and any that prevent his success as "vices"—allows Thornton to avoid sympathizing with his workers because of the very qualities that make them morally superior to him. It is their lack of an "iron nature" that justifies his contempt for them. It is their softness, their embodied humanness, their physical vulnerability that differentiates them from Thornton and inhibits their ability to rise in social class. While Mr. Thornton is physically invulnerable and financially prudent, the poor are physically vulnerable and generously improvident. As shown above, these qualities in working-class people are linked to their readiness to sympathize with their fellows: sympathy arises from close contact between vulnerable bodies, and it often prompts financial improvidence in service of communal care. But it is these very qualities that Thornton uses as reasons not to sympathize with the poor. In other words, Thornton refuses to sympathize with the poor because the poor are too inclined to show sympathy to one another. Gaskell reveals the problematic capitalist logic behind Thornton's views about the poor early in the novel: through the myth of merit-based class mobility, their working-class ethos of communal care, resource-sharing, and radical sympathy becomes the justification for why they do not deserve the sympathy of the wealthy.

Some of the mill owners go further than Thornton: instead of just passively disparaging the intraclass sympathy of their workers, they actively try to police it. We see this when Hamper (another mill owner) tries to forbid his workers from sympathizing with their unemployed peers. After the strike, Hamper requires all of his hands to pledge that "they'll not give a penny to help th' Union or keep turn-outs fro' clemming" (285). In order to gain access to the profits of capitalism, even at the lowest level, individuals have to forswear sympathy for their fellows and promise to let the turn-outs starve. Nicholas Higgins does not believe that such pledges actually produce the kinds of subjects that the mill owners hope to produce: subjects who obey authority, keep their earnings to themselves and do not share, and repress sympathy for the other members of their communities. Instead, Higgins claims that forcing workers to take the pledges just produces "liars and hypocrites" who will say anything the masters ask of them and then act differently when the masters are not around—a result that he believes is bad, but not as bad as "making men's hearts so hard that they'll not do a kindness to them as needs it, or help on the right and just cause, though it goes again the strong hand" (285–86). But Nicholas will not be hypocritical or hard-hearted, and so refuses to take the pledge and thus is left out of work. He encapsulates the problem when he describes his plight to Margaret: "I've been a turn-out, and known what it were to clem; so if I get a shilling, sixpence shall go to them if they axe it from me. Consequence is, I dunnot see where I'm to get a shilling" (286). Nicholas insists on maintaining his commitment to sympathy, generosity, and sharing his personal wealth, and as a result, he cannot get any wealth to share. Hamper's antiunion policy makes explicit what for Thornton was only implicit logic: that those who participate in unsanctioned sympathizing with their fellows ought to be excluded from the profits of capitalism.[8]

Gaskell later aims the same criticism in the opposite direction when she suggests that unions ape the tactics of the mill owners by similarly restricting the natural sympathy of their members. As Higgins explains to Margaret, the union gets reluctant workers to join by denying them any sympathy or fellowship in the workplace until they do:

> If a man doesn't belong to th' Union, them as works next looms has orders not to speak to him—if he's sorry or ill it's a' the same; he's out o' bounds; he's none o' us. I' some places them's fined who speaks to him. Yo' try that miss; try living a year or two among them as looks away if yo' look at 'em; try working within two yards o' crowds o' men, who, yo' know, have a grinding grudge at yo' in their hearts—to whom if yo' say yo'r glad, not an eye brightens, nor a lip moves,—to whom if your heart's heavy, yo' can never say nought, because they'll ne'er take notice on your signs or sad looks . . . just yo' try that, miss—ten hours for three hundred days, and yo'll know a bit what th' Union is. (228–29)

---

8. Somewhat hypocritically, the masters also punish the workers when they feel that they do not sympathize *enough* with their fellow workers, as when the striking workers gravely injure the "knobstick" coming for work in *Mary Barton*. The masters are

> indignant, and justly so, at the merciless manner in which the poor fellow had been treated; and their indignation at wrong, took (as it often does) the extreme form of revenge. They felt as if, rather than yield to the body of men who were resorting to such cruel measures towards their fellow-workmen, they, the masters, would sooner relinquish all the benefits to be derived from the fulfillment of the commission, in order that the workmen might suffer keenly. (176)

Some of the mill owners claim that the workers' violence toward the knobsticks is the primary reason not to acquiesce to their demands, saying that "if it were only for" their treatment of the knobstick, they would "stand out against them" (177). Another claims, "Ay, I for one won't yield one farthing to the cruel brutes; they're more like wild beasts than human beings," to which Gaskell adds, "(Well, who might have made them different?)" (177). Based on the rest of the book, she really does not go far enough in her reproach of the masters here, because it is not just that the masters could have made them different but that they actually made regulations and policies that contributed to giving the workers the very characteristics to which they are objecting. Or perhaps more accurately, the masters profit from a system that functions to discipline sympathy out of both masters and men, and therefore, it is hypocritical to punish the workers for failing to sympathize with their fellows without attempting to also change the system that creates and incentivizes such behavior.

In Gaskell's depiction, the union commits the same crime that the mill owners commit: it forces its members to deny sympathy to outsiders. Higgins believes that the ends justify the means in this case: "It may be like war; along wi' it come crimes; but I think it were a greater crime to let it alone. Our only chance is binding men together in one common interest" (229). For Higgins, it is worth committing the "crime" of withholding sympathy with nonunion workers so as to create a unified working class that can effectively engage in collective bargaining with the mill owners. But Mr. Hale and Margaret disagree with Higgins, condemning the "tyranny" of the union and the "slow, lingering torture" of nonunion workers as equivalent to the actions of mill owners like Hamper (229).

Framing the Hales' criticism in this way allows Gaskell to suggest that they object to the union not so much because it disrupts capitalism, but rather because it is *too much like* capitalism. Not only does the union similarly rely on the artificial suppression of natural sympathy, but it also (at least according to Boucher) demands that its members let their families die of starvation in the service of class goals in a way that directly parallels the actions of the masters. When Boucher is in the depths of despair, unable to feed his family during the strike, Higgins encourages him to take heart and hold out against the "tyrant" masters. Boucher responds by accusing the union of an even worse tyranny: "Yo' know well, that a worser tyrant than e'er th' masters were says, 'Clem to death, and see 'em a' clem to death, ere yo' dare go again th' Union.' Yo' know it well, Nicholas, for a' yo're one on e'm. Yo' may be kind hearts, each separate; but once banded together, yo've no more pity for a man than a wild hunger-maddened wolf" (154). Boucher suggests here that the union not only apes but actually outdoes necrocapitalism; while necrocapitalism demands that masters let workers die in service of market freedom, the union demands that men let their children die in service of collective bargaining. Even though it is voiced by an unreliable character in Boucher, the fact that Gaskell raises the specter of such a fundamental criticism of unions speaks to her deep skepticism of working-class collective action. The distinction she makes between individuals as "kind hearts" and the collective as a "wild hunger-maddened wolf" is characteristic of Gaskell's (unsatisfactory for many contemporary readers) endeavor to position herself as simultaneously pro-worker and anti-working-class political action.

Mr. Hale reinforces this assessment when he criticizes the union because it preserves the paradigm of oppositional class interests, within which one class gains only at the expense of the other. Hale claims that the union would be "beautiful, glorious,—it would be Christianity itself—if it were but for an end which affected the good of all, instead of that of merely one class as opposed to another" (229). In this statement, Mr. Hale (and, by extension, Gaskell) seems to be conflating what he *wishes* to occur with what currently exists. Mr. Hale conjures up the promise of a world in which class conflict has been eliminated and everyone can unite in "glorious" service of a universal good—but this transformation clearly has not occurred in Gaskell's contemporary England nor in the world of the novel. Gaskell's position here involves a temporal sleight of hand, as she demands that workers feel and act according to events that have not yet and may never occur. She shows the interests of workers and capitalists to be opposed in real time in both *Mary Barton* and *North and South* but then expects the working class to behave as if a radical restructuring of society that would eliminate the inherent conflict between the interests of wage-laborers and capitalists has already taken place.

It is an odd moment from a novelist who I have argued is highly attuned to the ways in which economic systems shape the formation and circulation of feelings and reveals, perhaps, a discomfort with working-class political power.[9] While Gaskell demonstrates how various feelings emerge in response to historically specific social and economic arrangements, she simultaneously seems to require that working-class political feeling be anachronistic, shaped by the conditions of a future that may someday exist. Gaskell condemns union organizers for being too firmly situated within their own historical moment—that is, for using the tools currently available to them to advocate for themselves within industrial capitalism as it exists. This view brings Gaskell into unexpected proximity with Martineau, despite their opposing views on the economic efficacy of middle-class sympathy. Martineau's condemnation of working-class organizing combined with her belief in the ameliorative power of limiting population left laborers with little agency to improve their lives except by existing less. Gaskell's condemnation of working-class organizing combined with her belief in the transformative power of cross-class sympathy leaves workers with no option but to wait for capitalists and middle-class women to come together to reroute sympathetic feeling and thus reshape industrial capitalism—which, conveniently for the residents of the fictional Milton (though not for those of its real-world analogue in Manchester) is precisely what will occur at the end of *North and South*.

9. Several scholars have characterized Gaskell's depiction of unions as conservative or reactionary: see Lucas xiv; Minogue; Carnall. Patrick Brantlinger makes a more complex argument about Gaskell's depiction of unions in "The Case against Trade Unions in Early Victorian Fiction" but ultimately comes to the conclusion that Gaskell believes in the laws of political economy and thinks that strikes cannot be successful in raising wages.

SYMPATHY UNDER NECROECONOMICS:
MANUFACTURED RISKS

I have argued that Gaskell shows how capitalism systematically interferes with the circulation of embodied sympathy. I am, of course, not arguing that the characters in Gaskell's novels never feel or act upon such sympathy. Far from it—Gaskell's novels are filled with characters who show sympathy to their fellows, often against the disciplining mechanisms of industrial capitalism and their own self-interest. In both *Mary Barton* and *North and South*, Gaskell shows that this work of sympathy is overwhelmingly performed by two groups of people—middle-class women and the poor. Middle-class women—and unmarried women in particular—function as a sort of sympathy labor force within the structure of the bourgeois family, filling the gap created by capitalism's strategic repression of sympathy. The poor, who are further away from the center of capitalist power, sympathize in spite of the systematic repression of sympathy, sacrificing their own needs in order to care for their neighbors. The people who engage in this marginalized sympathy work, however, are still negatively influenced by capitalism's restriction on sympathy. The capitalist suppression of sympathy imposes physical risks and psychological burdens upon such sympathizing. This short-circuiting of sympathy not only forces the greatest burden of emotional labor onto society's most vulnerable populations, but it also imperils sympathy, making unhealthy and vulnerable people even more unhealthy and vulnerable.

In *North and South*, Gaskell shows how unmarried middle-class women[10] function as supplemental sympathy generators for bourgeois communities, supplying sympathy in contexts where it has been systematically stamped out. Margaret is a prime example of this, functioning in all the domestic situations into which she is placed as a sort of sympathy mill, from which other characters can draw emotional support. She fills this role most often in her own family. For example, instead of telling Mrs. Hale himself, Margaret's father asks her to tell her mother about his decision to leave the church and move to Milton as a private tutor. Margaret spends the whole day engaged in the exhausting labor of calming and comforting her mother, "bending her whole soul to sympathize in all the various turns [Mrs. Hale's] feelings took," before she can finally let out her own sorrow in bed at night (47). Once in Milton, both Mr. and Mrs. Hale are "equally out of spirits, and equally [come] upon Margaret for sympathy" (67). Hardt and Negri refer to this kind of work as "affective labor"—that is, "labor that produces or manipulates affects such as a feeling of ease, well-

---

10. Working-class unmarried women (as well working-class married women) of course also do enormous amounts of emotional and affective labor, but their sympathy is not funded by and rerouted into a capitalist economy in the same way.

being, satisfaction, excitement, or passion" (108). Margaret labors throughout the novel to produce "good feelings" both in each of her parents individually and in the relationship between them. This labor becomes even more strenuous when her mother is dying, and her father draws heavily on her emotional resources: "Poor Margaret! All afternoon she had to act the part of a Roman daughter, and give strength out of her own scanty stock to her father" (238).

When Margaret joins the Shaw-Lennox household after the death of her parents, her value as an emotional support machine becomes even more apparent—and what's more, it becomes clear that her "stock" of sympathy has been funded by capital investment. Her move into their home is a sort of business arrangement in the guise of familial, emotional connection. The Shaws have a "claim upon" Margaret because they "brought her up," and this gives them the "right" to claim her, in Mr. Bell's words, "as if she were a lap-dog belonging to them" (350). In the most unromantic terms, the Shaws invested materially in Margaret, providing for her when she was young, and now they expect to receive her affection and emotional labor in return. Margaret's role in the Shaw-Lennox household is that of an unpaid emotional laborer, providing the same kind of sympathetic support to those around her that she provided to her parents when they were living:

> The course of Margaret's day was this; a quiet hour or two before a late breakfast; an unpunctual meal, lazily eaten by weary and half-awake people, but yet at which, in all its dragged-out length, she was expected to be present, because, directly afterwards, came a discussion of plans, at which, *although they none of them concerned her, she was expected to give her sympathy,* if she could not assist with her advice; an endless number of notes to write, which Edith invariably left to her, with many caressing compliments as to her eloquence du billet; a little play with Sholto as he returned from his morning's walk; besides the care of the children during the servants' dinner; a drive or callers; and some dinner or morning engagement for her aunt and cousins, which left Margaret free, it is true, but rather wearied with the inactivity of the day, coming upon depressed spirits and delicate health. (364–65, emphasis added)

The Shaws treat Margaret reasonably well—but Margaret is expected to perform an enormous amount of emotional labor in this household. Not unlike the flight attendants Arlie Hochschild studies in her work on emotional labor in the twentieth-century service sector, Margaret must manage her own emotions (by suppressing her grief and performing positivity) while also managing other people's emotions (by providing kindness, sympathy, and care).[11] Her status as

---

11. See Hochschild.

an emotional worker is underlined by the fact that her sympathy is not recip-
rocated in any meaningful way by her needy cousin or her prim aunt. Mr.
Hale reveals the inequality of the emotional exchange when he tells Mr. Bell
that "Margaret loves [Edith] with all her heart, and Edith with as much of her
heart as she can spare" (341). Edith receives Margaret's full love, and Margaret
receives only the surplus love that is left over after Edith attends to her primary
relations. Mr. Bell's offer to pay 250 pounds per year to the Shaw-Lennoxes for
Margaret's keep is an only somewhat successful attempt to lessen the strength
of this tacit obligation to perform affective and emotional labor.[12]

Mr. Bell may be criticizing Edith's superficiality or selfishness, but his
comment also speaks to the two women's different roles in the bourgeois family structure. Margaret can give Edith all her heart because she is unmarried.
As a married woman with children, Edith is already putting her sympathy to
the purpose for which it was produced. Taken together, these scenes depict
bourgeois womanhood as a means of privatizing sympathy via the mechanism
of the family. Capital is funneled into bringing up the bourgeois woman in a
particular way. Money is spent on educating her, but much more crucially,
it is both spent and forgone in order to keep her out of the workplace—the
space of capitalism that squashes sympathy. That investment is expected to
pay off later, when she reaches maturity and becomes an emotional laborer
within the family.[13] As an unmarried, nonworking, nonprocreative woman,
Margaret's emotional resources are her "stock"—the good that she can offer

---

12. I use both "affective laborer" and "emotional laborer" to describe Margaret for two
reasons. First, I do not see a sharp distinction between the kinds of work that Hardt and Negri
describe as "affective labor" and the work that Hochschild describes as "emotional labor." Both
use flight attendants as a primary example, and Hardt and Negri cite Hochschild's work without drawing any distinction between her description of emotional labor and the phenomenon
they describe (111, 375 n. 14). It seems to me that these authors are using different methods and
theoretical approaches to describe similar phenomena. Second, I think that the work Margaret
does is engaged with *both* affects and emotions. Especially in her interaction with her mother,
she is laboring to produce ease and well-being on the embodied, transindividual, infracognitive (to use Brian Massumi's formulation) level of affect. At the same time, she is managing her
own emotions as a thinking subject and helping her father, as well as Edith, process their own
emotions as thinking subjects.

13. I am influenced here by the work of Leonore Davidoff and Catherine Hall, who both
illuminate the emergence of this domestic ideology in the context of the economic, political,
scientific, and religious shifts taking place in the late eighteenth and early nineteenth centuries.
In "The Early Formation of Victorian Domestic Ideology," Catherine Hall provides background
on how the joint historical forces of the Evangelical movement and the formation of the industrial bourgeoisie interacted to produce the "Victorian middle-class ideal of womanhood" that
shapes Margaret's role in this novel (15). Crucially, Hall's work shows how this cultural ideal
is historically situated within and *produced by* the development of industrial capitalism. More
recently, Rachel Ablow's *The Marriage of Minds* sheds new light on women's roles as sympathizers within the context of marriage and explores the connection between "marital and readerly
sympathy" (14).

to the capitalist community. Gaskell thus shows how the bourgeois woman functions as a necessary supplement to necroeconomics, filling up the vacuum created by the systemic repression of sympathy under capitalism. The unmarried bourgeois woman is in a peculiar position here. In the absence of a husband's indisputable claim, the ownership of her sympathy is uncertain, and various parties make claims upon it as they would upon the assets of a wealthy bachelor. This makes her valuable, but it also makes her dangerous. While Margaret's sympathy certainly flows amply in socially acceptable directions (toward her immediate and extended family), it also threatens to burst out of the confines of the bourgeois family to become a public good—for example, when it compels her to step into the riot to try to prevent violence between Thornton and the workers. The community's assumption that this was an act of love for Thornton is a stabilizing interpretation of the incident—her sympathy must have gone toward a man with whom she wants to be married—but it is an interpretation that Margaret vehemently resists. If we dare to take a woman at her word, we end up with a much more threatening possibility: that the privately funded sympathy of bourgeois women, designed to supplement and stabilize necroeconomic capitalism, might by those women's own volition become public property.[14]

Margaret does her job as an emotional laborer well, producing an enormous amount of sympathy for others, within her family and outside of it, throughout her life. Because of the manufactured shortage of sympathy under necroeconomics, however, she is forced to produce and distribute an unnatural amount of sympathy while receiving very little in return, and she suffers as a result. Margaret undergoes great personal sorrow and stress over the course of the novel—the removal from her beloved home, the violence enacted upon her during the riot at Thornton's mill, the deaths of her mother, her father, her friend Bessy, and her friend and guardian Mr. Bell, the threat of death to and the reality of separation from her brother Frederick, and so on. And yet, she spends most of her time comforting others and is given almost no time to deal with her own anxiety and grief. It is only when she is left completely alone (during her father's trip to Oxford, where he unexpectedly dies) that she can indulge her own feelings instead of laboring to ease the feelings of others:

---

14. Indeed, the depth of shame and concern about her "maiden pride" (188) that Margaret experiences after the incident but *before* she learns that Thornton believes she is in love with him seems to indicate a concern about making herself inappropriately public. Before Thornton visits and confesses his love under the assumption that she reciprocates, she feels a "deep sense of shame that she should thus be the object of universal regard—a sense of shame so acute that it seemed as if she would fain have burrowed into the earth to hide herself." Her sense of shame over being "universally regarded" seems almost to echo the shame of the prostitute—that is, the woman who takes something that is supposed to remain a private good within the bourgeois family and makes it public (189).

> When her father had driven off on his way to the railroad, Margaret felt how great and long had been the pressure on her time and her spirits. It was astonishing, almost stunning, to feel herself so much at liberty; no one depending on her for cheering care, if not for positive happiness; no invalid to plan and think for; she might be idle, and silent, and forgetful,—and what seemed worth more than all the other privileges—she might be unhappy if she liked. For months past, all her own personal cares and troubles had had to be stuffed away into a dark cupboard; but now she had leisure to take them out, and mourn over them, and study their nature, and seek the true method of subduing them into the elements of peace. (336)

Margaret's emotional "stock" is not her own to spend as she pleases. Though bourgeois women's feelings are rhetorically placed outside of the marketplace, Gaskell allows us to see that Margaret's sympathy is a capitalist good, and like any laborer, Margaret produces but does not own it. She owes it to the family and friends who funded its development and production. Only in a rare moment of private leisure is she able to "spend" a bit of her stock on herself. Gaskell depicts here the exploitative circulation of sympathy within the structure of the bourgeois family, as women do emotional labor to fill the gaps created by capitalism and then are alienated from the products of that labor.

Notably, this dynamic changes when Margaret enters into the working-class world through her friendship with Bessy and Nicholas. Despite the difference in economic standing, the relationship between Margaret and the Higgins family is much more sympathetically reciprocal than any of Margaret's relationships within the bourgeois family structure. For example, Margaret notes that Bessy has made her feel better just as she was making Bessy feel better (138), and when Mrs. Hale dies, Nicholas goes to Mrs. Hale's funeral and won't accept pay for Mary's service. He also does Margaret the great (though perhaps accidental) service of explaining to Mr. Thornton what really happened with Frederick and restoring Thornton's belief in Margaret's chastity and virtue. This nonmonetary relationship is reinforced when they part, as Higgins refuses to take Margaret's money: "I'm not going for to take yo'r brass, so dunnot think it. We've been great friends, 'bout the sound o' money passing between us" (362). Margaret tells him that the money is for Boucher's children and reassures Higgins, "I would not give you a penny" (362). Unlike Margaret's relationship with the Shaws, this relationship is represented as materially and rhetorically separate from the capitalist marketplace. No money passes between them; they exchange heart-service for heart-service, love-works for love-works.

Indeed, throughout *Mary Barton* and *North and South,* Gaskell depicts working-class characters as models of natural, immediate, and often uncon-ditional sympathy for their fellows. This is, perhaps, unsurprising. As I have argued above, industrial capitalism incentivizes the repression of natural sym-pathy. Those incentives hold less force, however, over those people who are furthest away from capitalism's power and profits. The laboring poor, who gain little from capitalist production and often define themselves in opposition to the owners of capital, have less to lose (both psychologically and materially) by ignoring or resisting capitalism's decrees against sympathizing. Unlike the sympathy of bourgeois women, which is produced by capitalism to fill up the emotional vacuum it itself creates, the sympathy of the poor is outside of and against necroeconomics. Gaskell reveals an inverse relationship between characters' social class and their readiness to experience this kind of unsanc-tioned sympathy; those characters who are furthest from the center of capital-ist power sympathize most unconditionally.[15]

Gaskell highlights this inverse relationship between class and sympathetic capacity in the scene in which George Wilson attempts to obtain care for the ailing Ben Davenport. The underfed John Barton sympathizes immediately, before he even physically sees the sick man and his starving family. George Wilson's description of the Davenports' suffering is enough to spark his sym-pathy; compassionate concern spreads from one man to the next like a virtu-ous virus. Barton's sympathy is immediate and his generosity total; he gives them nearly all of his very small stock of food and money, going hungry so that the Davenport children can eat. But sympathy does not spread so easily when George Wilson brings his concern to the Carson household. The family's servants, who are a socioeconomic step above Barton and Wilson, sympathize only belatedly and in moderation. As they prepare the family's meal, they fail to notice that George Wilson, the "gaunt, pale, unwashed, unshaven weaver" waiting to speak with their master, is sick with hunger (68). Gaskell states, "They were like the rest of us, and not feeling hunger themselves, forgot it was possible another might" (66). However, the cook does eventually recognize his hunger and gives him some food: "When she had had time to think, after breakfast was sent in, [she] had noticed his paleness . . . [and] had meat and bread ready to put in his hand when he came out of the parlour" (69). This cook is able to sympathize with Wilson, but in a much more tempered fashion

15. In this way, Gaskell cuts against a trend illuminated by Kyla Schuller of assigning greater emotional sensibility to higher-status individuals. Schuller describes this production of "hierarchies of somatic capacity" as "central to the materialization of modern ideas of race and sexual difference" (12).

than that of John Barton's sympathy with the Davenports. Her sympathy with the suffering man does not impose itself upon her with the immediacy that Barton's does; she only feels sympathy once she has a bit of leisure time to think. Nor does her sympathy require her to sacrifice her own wants or needs: instead of giving up her own dinner and going hungry, she merely gives away surplus food.

The wealthy mill owner Mr. Carson shows even less sympathy for the sick man—and for George Wilson, who has come to advocate on his behalf. He does not provide the inpatient order Wilson asks for because he "doubt[s] if [he has one] to spare" (68). He refuses the request, willing to give only what he knows he can "spare," only the surplus that he will not feel the loss of—and indeed, maybe not even that. Neither Carson nor his son are at all emotionally affected by the hardship brought before them; the younger Mr. Carson leaves the house "gaily" to seek out "a smile from the lovely Mary Barton" (69). In contrast to the poor John Barton, who cannot resist getting emotionally invested in the well-being of the Davenports and gives what he *cannot* spare without risking death, the Carson men retain their emotional equanimity and give only what they will not miss. In light of Gaskell's critique of capitalism for its systematic repression of natural sympathy, this inverse relationship between social class and sympathetic response is not surprising. As mill owners, the Carsons are much more invested in the perpetuation of the economic status quo than laborers like John Barton, who exist in an ambivalent state of both dependence upon and opposition to industrial capitalism. As a result, the burden of sympathy work falls primarily upon the poorest and most vulnerable sectors of society.

For Gaskell, the capacity for and the practice of sympathy is an unquestionable moral good. When the poor practice sympathy in the problematic socioeconomic paradigm that Gaskell describes, however, it makes them vulnerable to increased physical harm. This is because sympathy involves exposure: it involves physical closeness and thus creates exposure to physiological disease; it involves emotional and psychological openness and thus creates exposure to negative affects. I have argued above that Gaskell presents such exposure as natural and necessary for moral conduct. To prevent such exposure to the bodies and affects of others is to repress one's natural ethical responsiveness, to become less human—to become "made of iron." This openness to exposure is what creates the possibility for friendship, love, and communal bonds. However, in a socioeconomic system in which capitalism is actively creating unhealthy bodies, those who open up their physical and affective boundaries enough to perform sympathy are also at risk of being exposed to disease. Gaskell emphasizes in her depiction of typhus in *Mary Barton,* though, that the problem is not the boundary-compromising practice of sympathy itself, but rather the creation of unhealthy bodies by an antisympathy system of capitalism.

When John Barton and George Wilson provide care for the Davenports, they make themselves vulnerable to physical harm in a variety of ways. First of all, John Barton sells his small stock of valuables to pay for food, candles, and coal for the family, leaving himself without any savings for the future and thus more vulnerable to starvation and want in the case of future unemployment. More urgently, by going into Davenport's home and caring for him and his family, both men expose themselves to the "virulent, malignant, and highly infectious" fever that eventually kills him (59). Wilson also exposes the rest of his family to the contagious illness by bringing two of the Davenport children back to his home to be cared for by his wife, and indeed, the Wilson family pays dearly for their kindness. Although the Davenport children do not catch their father's disease, the "ghoul-like fever was not to be braved with impunity, and baulked of its prey" (72), and soon after Davenport's widow is back on her feet, she finds out that George Wilson's youngest sons have come down with the same fever. They die shortly afterward. Although Gaskell does not explicitly state that Wilson's children catch the fever from the Davenports, it is strongly implied. Gaskell takes pains, however, to show that despite the spread of the illness through sympathetic care, the sympathy is not to blame and should not be regretted.

First of all, Gaskell very explicitly states that this disease is caused by poverty, unhealthy social conditions, and fluctuations in trade. She notes that it is "brought on by miserable living, filthy neighborhood, and great depression of mind and body" (59). Davenport was employed at the Carson mill and has been out of work since the mill fire. All of the risk factors that Gaskell notes for this disease, later referred to as typhus, are caused by the disruption of trade and the factory's failure to provide any kind of safety net for the workers while the equipment is replaced. As Gaskell shows earlier in the chapter, the Carsons actually prolong the shutdown of the factory, enjoying their newfound leisure time and using insurance money to renovate the factory with up-to-date equipment without the "weekly drain of wages given for labour" (56). Without those weekly wages, Davenport is forced to relocate to a damp cellar in a filthy slum, to go without food and warmth, and to endure the psychological and emotional toll of being unable to provide for his hungry, crying children. Gaskell emphasizes that Davenport's disease is generated by the social conditions created by an economic system that produces unhealthiness and represses sympathy. In other words, Barton and Wilson are only exposed to disease through their sympathy because the system of industrial capitalism created that disease in the first place.

Moreover, neither the narrator nor the characters express any regret over the choice to enter the Davenport home and care for the family, even after it leads to the death of the young Wilson twins. This stands in contrast to a novel like *Bleak House,* in which several characters regret Esther's show of sympathy toward the ailing Jo and subsequently blame Jo for spreading his illness to his caregivers and in which Esther quarantines herself in order to prevent the further spread of the disease. In *Mary Barton,* nobody blames the Davenports for the death of the Wilson twins, nor does anyone seek to isolate the twins once they fall ill. Hearing of their illness, both Alice and Mary Barton immediately go to the Wilson home to help care for the twins. Only once does Gaskell's narrator address the etiology of the disease, when the two men first enter the Davenport home; she notes, "The poor are fatalists with regard to infection; and well for them it is so, for in their crowded dwellings no invalid can be isolated. Wilson asked Barton if he thought he should catch it, and was laughed at for his idea" (59). The men laugh at the idea of trying to prevent exposure to contagion, and even after the disease spreads to Wilson's own family, they (like others in their community) continue to willingly expose themselves to contagious diseases in order to provide sympathetic care.

Here Gaskell evokes a common lament of public health reformers, who often complained that the poor believed that they could not alter the course of a disease and thus did not follow the instructions of doctors and sanitary officials. This misguided fatalism was often cited as a reason for the failure of various public health initiatives.[16] But Gaskell presents their response to contagious disease in a different light. She agrees that the poor ignore the possibility of disease transmission via close physical contact, but she does not present their fatalist approach as regrettable, mistaken, or ignorant. Instead, she suggests that the poor community's approach to disease is a strategic and morally laudable response to the material conditions of poverty created by a pathological system of capitalism. George Wilson and John Barton are not ignorant of the possibility that disease might spread through physical contact; Wilson brings up the risk of contagion as they enter the Davenport home. However, viewing disease as a physical entity spread through close contact is not a tenable position for the poor under their current material conditions. They cannot quarantine sick individuals because they do not have space; they cannot avoid coming into contact with sick family members, neighbors, and

---

16. See, for example, Hardy 274; Gilbert, *Cholera and Nation* 35, 51.

coworkers; they cannot hire sick nurses or get their loved ones into fever wards, so they must either directly care for the ailing or else abandon the sick to suffer and die alone. Thus, they participate in a community-wide strategic choice to ignore the possibility of contagion and to explain disease through fate rather than etiology. This choice of fatalism allows them to preserve both sanity and communal sympathy under social conditions that preclude the isolation of contagious individuals.[17]

By refusing to focus on the moments of contact that led to the death of the Wilson twins, Gaskell shifts attention away from the pathways of contagion and toward the root causes of disease. She is concerned about filthy living conditions and diseases of poverty, but she is not focused on changing the social norms of working-class communities to better align with the recommendations of public health officials. Instead, she is addressing a pathological system of capitalism, which is systematically creating unhealthy bodies. By refusing to express regret for the sympathetic care that led to the spread of typhus or to place blame on the men for being ignorant about the spread of infection, Gaskell is emphasizing that the pathology lies in capitalism, not sympathy. Sympathy is not in itself dangerous or disease inducing; it is made dangerous by a system of capitalism that creates social conditions that lead to disease. The danger involved in sympathizing is a side product of this system of capitalism. The solution, then, is not to limit or alter working-class practices of sympathetic care but rather to alter the system of capitalism that is making those practices of sympathy dangerous. She wants to replace a necroeconomic system that generates both disease and profit with a new vital economic system of capitalism that generates health.

GASKELL'S SYMPATHETIC CAPITALISM

We can see the beginnings of such a system in Thornton's "experiments" at the end of *North and South*. For example, his "dinner-scheme" helps workers gain access to better quality food by creating a communal kitchen; Thornton takes dues from the workers and uses it to buy food in bulk and provide a cook in order to maximize their spending power. As he takes on these projects, we see Thornton shifting from an agent of "letting die" to one of "making live." His communal kitchen represents an attempt to move away from a pathoeconomic system that thrived upon workers' bodily vulnerability and

---

17. There were certainly concerns as well among medical professionals and public health officials about the ethical implications of contagionism; see Gilbert, *Cholera and Nation* 95.

proximity to starvation. Importantly, this dining room project is not a charity; Thornton is not engaging in philanthropic work outside of his role as a mill owner. Rather, it represents a shift in how he sees his own role as a capitalist. Instead of systematically creating unhealthy bodies and instrumentalizing their vulnerability, as we have seen the Milton mill owners do previously, Thornton is trying to orient capitalism toward the systematic production of healthy worker bodies. This is, of course, a shift within rather than a step outside of political economy. In this shift, he has become both more "Malthusian" and less "Smithian." As Catherine Gallagher has explained, Adam Smith and Malthus (particularly in the first version of his *Essay on the Principle of Population*) disagreed about how to measure a nation's wealth. Malthus accused Smith of valuing all economic growth equally without attending to the difference between "the produce of the land," which directly supports worker health, and mere commodities such as "silks, laces, trinkets, and expensive furniture" (*Essay* 112). For Malthus, a nation's true wealth is measured by how many healthy worker bodies it can support. By the time Thornton starts his dinner scheme (and claims that "money" in the abstract is "not what [he] strive[s] for" [325]) at the end of *North and South*, he seems to have shifted from a Smithian focus on "exchangeable value in the abstract" to a Malthusian focus on what Gallagher calls "bioeconomic value"—that is, measuring the value of economic enterprise by its ability to support the "vital needs of human groups" (*Body Economic* 43, 50). Thornton is still engaged in what Malthus would call "unproductive labor," in that his mill produces goods that are designed for exchange rather than for the direct support of working-class bodies, but through his dinner scheme, he is increasing Milton's capacity to use its existing resources to feed its working class more efficiently. In that sense, he is incorporating a theory of bioeconomic value into a system of exchange value production.

But even as Thornton institutes this bioeconomic project of which Malthus would approve, he suggests that the maximization of life is inextricable from the circulation of affect. In explaining his experiments to Mr. Colthurst, Thornton claims that personal intercourse between masters and workers is "the very breath of life," and that without it, his project "would lose its vitality, cease to be living" (421). The thing that makes this system "vital" (as opposed to the preceding pathoeconomic system) is the institution of "actual personal contact" between masters and men (32). Previously, we have seen how personal contact between masters and men was systematically eliminated in order to prevent the arousal of potentially disruptive sympathy. Thornton is reversing this pattern by deliberately building interclass personal contact into the institution of industrial capitalism. Gaskell thus drives home the point that capitalism's pathology is inextricably tied to its suppression of sympathy-producing embodied contact. Improving working-class access to higher-quality food is not sufficient to make capitalism "healthier," in Gaskell's depiction; it is only by altering the way affect circulates within industrial capitalism that Thornton can engender an alternative vital capitalism that supports life instead of producing death.

To bring this business model to fruition, however, Thornton ultimately needs the investment backing of Margaret Hale, who, as a recent heiress with a middle-class background, is uniquely positioned to fund Thornton's vital capitalism. As I have argued above, middle-class women's sympathy is not suppressed but rather produced and demanded in the bourgeois domestic space as emotional labor, filling the vacuum created by the systematic suppression of other channels of sympathy. Unlike traditional capitalist investors whose sympathy has been disciplined out of them, Margaret has been disciplined *into* heightened sympathy. And indeed, her investment in Thornton's mill is motivated by sympathy both for the workers of Milton and for Mr. Thornton himself, not by the desire for profit. She hopes to create jobs for unemployed workers in Milton and support the projects that Thornton has been forced to give up; she is not concerned with accruing more personal wealth. Notably, Margaret displays no desire to financially back Thornton's plans until she hears about his kitchen project and his newfound belief in close personal intercourse between masters and men. Only after Thornton transforms from a stakeholder of necroeconomics (in which bodies are raw materials that can be used and abused to produce money) into an advocate for vital capitalism (in which money is a raw material that can be used to produce healthy bodies) does Margaret offer her financial backing. The transfer of money at the conclusion of the novel is a model of the kind of investment that would support an alternative, health-based version of capitalism; it is capitalist investment as public health and community-building project. Moreover, Gaskell suggests that capitalism has created within itself the alternative investor who makes this new system possible—the middle-class woman, whose sympathy has not been suppressed but rather intensified.

Gaskell's solution, then, involves and requires sympathy, but it is not a simple call for readers to be more sympathetic toward the poor. She imagines, rather, an unfamiliar and almost uncategorizable alternative economic system to replace profit-driven industrial capitalism. In Gaskell's system, land-based wealth gets transferred to middle-class women, who then invest that wealth according to their sense of sympathy rather than their desire to accrue profit. It is not exactly philanthropy, because money is still distributed as wages for labor; it is not exactly socialism, because the means of production are still privately owned; and it is not exactly capitalism, because it is does not operate according to the logic of profits. It is a strange hybrid of the three, in which women like Margaret Hale privately own the means of production and, like an ideal socialist state, manage those means of production, with no private desire for profit, in order to generate a healthy social body. Gaskell's economic solution essentially imagines taking the means of production and putting them into the possession of her middle-class female readers. This solution brings us back around, oddly, to the novel's purported function as an instigator of imaginative readerly sympathy. In this fantasized alternative economy, Gaskell's novel serves an educational function, teaching her readers how to manage the means of production according to sympathy, like Margaret Hale. It is perhaps true, then, that Gaskell wants to inspire imaginative sympathy in her readers. She wants to do so, however, not to stimulate apolitical kindness or charity, but rather to facilitate the creation of a class of non-profit-driven female managers of capital who will make possible an alternative system of capitalism-as-public-health, which will in turn create healthy citizens and healthy communities and restore the natural flow of embodied sympathy through the social body.[18]

As a blueprint for actual political change, Gaskell's vision has some obvious shortcomings. It maintains a large degree of class hierarchy; it affords very limited agency to working-class characters except as collaborators with middle-class characters; it rejects working-class organizing in favor of a quasi-maternalistic system in which middle-class women own and operate the means of production.[19] Further, it structurally depends upon the production of women as sympathizers in a way that might appear to double down on gender difference. However, I argue that Gaskell does not participate in the reproduction of "fetishistic codes of sexual difference" when she draws attention to a sympathy differential between men and women under industrial capitalism (Hinton 3).[20] There is nothing intrinsic in women's heightened sympathy; it is produced, rather, by socioeconomic structures. Gaskell actually rejects any

18. In this sense, I both build upon and reframe Rachel Ablow's comparison in *The Marriage of Minds* between women and novels. Ablow suggests that, for Victorians, a novel was like a wife in that both were seen to "reproduce values associated with the home" (4), "encourage sympathy" (5), and "help us maintain and cultivate our best selves" (7). But in my reading, Gaskell's novels are more like unmarried women: they represent the potential for excessive sympathy, which, when routed in particular ways, can disrupt the affective structure of capitalism.

19. My argument converges here with that of Rosemarie Bodenheimer, who claims that in her imagination of Margaret as "female paternalist," Gaskell "transform[s] the idea of paternalism itself" (68).

20. Hinton suggests that "the propensity in feminist literary and often film criticism to emphasize sentiment's relation to women reproduces the very fetishistic codes of sexual difference these theories critique" (3).

inherent sex difference with regard to sympathy; outside of the artificial constraints produced by industrial capitalism, men and women sympathize in equal measure. Adam Smith makes a distinction between men's and women's intrinsic modes of sympathy; I argue that Gaskell does not. Instead, her novels reveal how necroeconomic capitalism structures sympathy, squashing it in some channels and directions and encouraging it in others. The perhaps utopian alternative that Gaskell imagines at the end of *North and South* has transformative potential not because of any direct political applicability but because it models the power of rerouting those channels of feeling to reshape economic systems.

CHAPTER 3

Letting Die Slowly

Necroeconomic Pleasure in Dickens's *Bleak House*

When it comes to violence, we have a bias toward the dramatic. Even as concerns about media consumers becoming desensitized to violence have become clichéd, our attention flows disproportionately toward the explosive, the visceral: the broken skin, the shock of blood, a scrum of emergency vehicles. But what about those forms of violence that we never became sensitized to in the first place—perhaps, never learned to recognize as violence at all? In his 2011 book, Rob Nixon uses the term "slow violence" to refer to "violence that occurs gradually and out of sight, a violence of delayed destruction that is dispersed across time and space, an attritional violence that is typically not viewed as violence at all . . . that is neither spectacular nor instantaneous, but rather incremental and accretive" (2). This is not the kind of violence that goes viral on Facebook or earns a video game its parental complaints. Slow violence is easy to ignore. And yet, it is perhaps the greatest threat to our continued existence on Planet Earth. It describes such "slowly unfolding environmental catastrophes" (2) as acidifying oceans, melting glaciers, deforestation, species loss, shrinking habitats, contaminated water supplies, and the (unequal) exposure to toxic waste, often outsourced to vulnerable populations on the other side of our slowly but catastrophically warming planet. "Slow violence" also describes the lethal working conditions we saw in the mills of Gaskell's Milton: the slow but fatal exposure of Milton's workers to the cotton "fluff" that kills Bessy Higgins (and the permanent semi-starvation wages that prompt

Milton's poor to accept such exposure). Gaskell would be disheartened to find that the Victorian period was only the beginning of the silent, unspectacular violence that makes breathing deadly. In the death of Bessy and other textile workers, we see a Victorian forerunner of what Nixon calls "the long dyings" of climate change (2).

I argue that in *Bleak House*, Dickens represents a different kind of slow violence—a slow *affective* violence that grounds the necroeconomic capitalism that continues to fuel the very climate catastrophe that Nixon describes. This affective violence, which takes place primarily in domestic spaces, produces the conditions of possibility for necroeconomics: oppositional relations between groups of people, felt divisions within the population, and most importantly, subjects who are willing to engage in necroeconomics. It produces, in other words, *necroeconomic feelings*. The slow violence that I describe in this chapter is different from the environmental violence that Nixon describes in two related ways. First, it is primarily affective—a particular form of unequal affective exchange that both justifies violence and is itself a form of violence. And second, it is meant to be witnessed. The necroeconomic system depicted in *Bleak House* does not displace its violence out of sight and out of mind, as Western countries do when we export toxic waste to developing nations in the Global South. It normalizes its violence not through displacement but through display. I speak deliberately of a vague, impersonal agency, because the necroeconomics I am describing is not a top-down, totalizing system imposed on a population by an agential, omnipotent state. It is an emergent form that creates effects by means of a dispersed agency. It bubbles up through interpersonal interactions both inside and outside of the official arms of the state through the actions and inactions of various partially disempowered actors: the rote rule-following of middle managers and the lower agents of the court, the private actions of the philanthropically minded housewife, the object-agency of paperwork and system-agency of bureaucracy, the thoughtless cruelty of the professional mooch, the futile pursuit of the lone police inspector, the aggressive preaching of the opportunistic evangelist, and so forth. It is in the affective interactions between these variably empowered actors that necroeconomic feelings emerge.

In describing necroeconomic feelings in this chapter, I follow on Achille Mbembe's claim that borders are not "merely a line of demarcation separating distinct sovereign entities" but "the name used to describe the organized violence that underpins both contemporary capitalism and our world order in general" (*Necropolitics* 99). Necroeconomic feelings manifest themselves as the creation, emergence, or calcification of affective borders between people. In order to understand the mechanics of necroeconomics, we need to recognize the connection between this grounding form of affective violence and the many forms of material violence that it enables. I argue that this connection is revealed in Dickens's *Bleak House*. In narrative form, we can see how borders are formed through repeated instances of performative affective violence and how those borders enable the violence of necroeconomics. And finally, we see an attempt—perhaps a stunted and a compromised one, but an attempt none-theless—to imagine ways of being in common that push back against those borders and the violence they enable.

BOUNDARY-PLEASURE AND BIOPOLITICAL RACISM

In this chapter, I explore a characteristically necroeconomic feeling that I call boundary-pleasure—that is, taking pleasure in the recognition and produc-tion of a boundary between the self and a suffering other. This feeling is first demonstrated by a character who tries to present himself as outside of eco-nomics entirely: Harold Skimpole, the manipulative hanger-on who neglects his own family while milking his "friend" Jarndyce for all he is worth. After Esther's illness, he claims that, because of her illness, he

> began to understand the mixture of good and evil in the world now; felt that
> he appreciated health the more, when somebody else was ill; didn't know
> but what it might be in the scheme of things that A should squint to make B
> happier in looking straight; or that C should carry a wooden leg to make D
> better satisfied with his flesh and bone in a silk stocking. (549)

Skimpole here is happy to let Esther suffer, but he is not exactly taking plea-sure in her suffering directly. Rather, he is taking pleasure in the contrast between her illness and his health—and that very contrast is making him feel more well. His pleasure centers not on her suffering itself, but on the differ-ence between their conditions. In the affective calculus that he sets up, his pleasure is located not in A's suffering as a quantity but in the mathematical relation by which it is both contrasted with and separated from B's health. This may seem like a trivial moment of schadenfreude, but I see it as absolutely crucial in that it sets up an affective relation that undergirds the technology of power that Foucault refers to as biopolitical racism, which is necessary to a necroeconomics that demands letting die.

Foucault situates biopolitical racism in response to what he sees as a cru-cial paradox of biopolitical power: how can a power structure that grounds its legitimacy in its ability to maximize the life of the population get away with letting and making people die on a massive scale? Biopower takes "life as both its object and its objective": it acts upon life, enacting discipline upon individual bodies and seeking to regulate population-wide biological trends, and it acts for life, aiming to maximize the vital force of the population as a whole (*"Society"* 254). If maximizing life is biopower's aim and function, then how can that power kill? The same biopolitical regimes that enforced mandatory vaccination, drained cesspools, and funded hospitals also built concentration camps, the modern prison-industrial complex, and the atomic bomb. The period during which biopower becomes the predominant mechanism of state control, according to Foucault, is simultaneously a time when states begin to expose citizens to death on an unprecedented scale. Foucault lingers on this apparent paradox:

> How can a power such as this kill, if it is true that its basic function is to improve life, to prolong its duration, to improve its chances, to avoid accidents, and to compensate for failings? How, under these conditions, is it possible for a political power to kill, to call for deaths, to demand deaths, to give the order to kill, and to expose not only its enemies but its own citizens to the risk of death? Given that this power's objective is essentially to make live, how can it let die? How can the power of death, the function of death, be exercised in a political system centered upon biopower? It is, I think, at this point that racism intervenes. (*"Society"* 254)

Racism is the technology that allows biopower to reconcile this apparent contradiction between claiming life as the desideratum of power and utilizing death as the instrument of power.

Foucault uses the term "biopolitical racism" to describe a very specific form of eighteenth- and nineteenth-century intra-European racialization, explicitly detached from what he calls "ethnic racism" and implicitly abstracted from Europe's constitutive history of imperial violence. When Foucault describes "biopolitical racism," he refers to a technology of state power that fragments a nation's internal population. This racism "establish[es] a biological-type caesura within a population," allowing the state to break up the presumed organic whole of the nation's citizenry into biologized subgroups that may or may not coincide with recognized ethnic divisions (*"Society"* 255). These subgroups are positioned vertically as a hierarchy by which human lives are ascribed differential value. Biopolitical racism's function is to "introduc[e] a break . . . between what must live and what must die" within the body of the nation (254). In excavating the relationships between race, colonialism, sexuality, and biopower in Foucault's archive, Ann Stoler explains that Foucault locates racism not in confrontations between phenotypically distinct groups, but rather in "the bifurcations within Europe's social fabric" (Stoler 60).

Racism creates these bifurcations by designating certain people as "unsuitable participants in the body politic" and then frames "such internal exclusions" as "necessary and noble pursuits to ensure the well-being and very survival of the social body" (Stoler 62). Instead of pointing outward toward the people of another nation, it points inward toward perceived threats or "others within" the state. Foucault's biopolitical racism is thus about the production of internal caesuras within the European nation-state through the exclusion of a range of racialized "others," many of whom are phenotypically white—like the pauper child Jo in *Bleak House.*

This setting aside of the history of colonialism and systemic anti-Blackness[1] has educed justified criticism from scholars such as Alexander Weheliye, particularly for the erroneous separation Foucault establishes between biopolitical racism and "ethnic racism." Weheliye highlights how Foucault's project of marking out modern European internal racism as a novel historical phenomenon leads him to "uncritically embrace[ ] an ontological differentiation between ethnic and biopolitical racism, leaving the door open for the naturalization of racial categories and the existence of a biological sphere that is not always already subject to ethnic racism" (59–60). In his characterization of biopolitical racism, in other words, Foucault imagines the possibility of a "pure" racialization abstracted from ethnic, cultural, or phenotypic difference. Weheliye identifies this with Agamben's similarly problematic claim in *The Remnants of Auschwitz* that "the biopolitics of racism so to speak transcends race" (85).[2] Both theorists seek to "authenticate the uniqueness and novelty of European biopolitical racism" by placing it in contrast to an imagined racism "always already situated in a primitive elsewhere" (60). As Weheliye argues, however, there is no setting aside so-called "ethnic racism" from biopolitical racism. We can see the inextricability of biopolitical racism and anti-Blackness, for example, in Ruth Wilson Gilmore's analysis of racism (in the context of California's prison system) as the "state-sanctioned and/or extralegal production and exploitation of group-differentiated vulnerability to premature death" (247). Gilmore's definition encompasses the production of caesuras within the population that justify the letting die of certain groups but also shows how the United States' systemic anti-Black racism disproportionately places Black Americans on the dangerous side of those divisions. In using Foucault's account of racism in this chapter, I do not wish to suggest that

---

1. This is, as Weheliye notes, a particularly egregious omission given the influence of radical Black thinkers such as Angela Davis and George Jackson on Foucault's thinking (62–63).

2. Weheliye traces this, in part, to "a strong 'anti-identity politics' strain in the Anglo-American academy" that "position[s] bare life and biopolitics as uncontaminated by or prior to reductive or essentialist political identities such as race and gender" and thus "proper objects of knowledge" (7).

it is adequate. Rather, I mean to suggest that it is uniquely appropriate for analyzing Dickens, whose critique of racialization is productive and inadequate
in much the same ways as Foucault's theorization of it is. I will argue that,
in *Bleak House,* Dickens criticizes the affective structure that undergirds the
biopolitical racism that Agamben and Foucault describe without interrogating
anti-Black racism or acknowledging the transimperial reality from which that
technology is born. In this sense, Dickens shares the same analytic gaps that
Weheliye points out in Foucault and Agamben—criticizing intra-European
racialization without interrogating (when not actively replicating) anti-Black
racism, while displacing "ethnic racism" to an unspecific "primitive elsewhere."

The racial politics of *Bleak House* are complex, ambivalent, and deeply
problematic. As Daniel Hack has shown, the novel puts forth an "ethics of
proximity" that seems to dismiss the need for and value of transatlantic abo-
litionism—or any ethical duty to physically distant others at all (26). And yet,
Frederick Douglass chose *Bleak House* as the only Victorian novel to serialize
in his periodical. The novel lived a variety of apparently contradictory after-
lives: it was simultaneously condemned by abolitionists[3] and transformed by
an escaped slave into a narrative of resistance and freedom.[4] In this chapter,
I certainly do not wish to "redeem" *Bleak House* of its localism or Dickens of
his racism. It is incontrovertible that the novel advocates for a localist ethics
that dismisses imagined others in Borrioboola-Gha as outside its purview and
that Dickens as author largely disregards people of color entirely except when
using racist caricatures as metonymic shorthand for "that which is uncivilized." Daniel Hack argues that Douglass's determination to persist in publishing the entirety of the massive novel stemmed from "a determination to enlist
'the universal favorite of the people' in the cause [of abolition], *if necessary*

---

3. The British abolitionist Lord Denman criticized the novel for its depiction of Mrs. Jellyby, suggesting that it ridicules those making an effort to combat slavery and asking, "Who
but the slave traders can gain by this course of argument?" (5). Crucially, Denman is interpret-
ing Mrs. Jellyby as an abolitionist, as many readers did. Both the text and the novelist resist
this interpretation, however. Dickens replied to Denman's criticism by stating that "No kind of
reference to Slavery is made or intended" (Dickens to Mrs. Cropper, 20 December 1852, qtd.
in Stone 195). Although Dickens's somewhat flippant rejoinder does not acknowledge that this
characterization did lend fuel to the proslavery fire, whether he intended so or not, I do think
it is important to note that Mrs. Jellyby's project actually sounds more like imperialism than
abolition. Her aim is to send the "superabundant" population of England to Africa "with a view
to the general cultivation of the coffee berry—*and* the natives" (44). The people of Africa are, at
best, an afterthought in Mrs. Jellyby's plan. She is essentially organizing colonialism under the
guise of philanthropy, sending British people to farm distant land already occupied by people
she scarcely considers. She is certainly not engaged in antislavery work; in fact, her project is
barely concerned with people of color at all.

4. Hannah Crafts's *Bondswoman's Narrative,* written in the mid-nineteenth century but
not published until 2002, draws heavily upon the plot, characters, and language of *Bleak House*
for inspiration. For more on this adaptation, see Hack, ch. 1.

despite himself" (29, emphasis added). Perhaps, in my analysis, I am motivated by a similar determination. In this chapter, I will argue that Dickens gives us crucial insight into the accretive power of repeated affective interactions to make racist ideologies real, to give them form and purchase. If we can see how those affective mechanics work, then we can intervene and alter them. Thus, I do wish to argue that we can extract (limited, compromised, but still productive) antiracist potential from the non-necroeconomic affective relations that Dickens imagines, even as the novel itself replicates racist stereotypes and seems to dismiss the value of transatlantic activism.

This potential comes in the dismantling of the boundary-pleasure that biopolitical racism enables and depends upon. Foucault's biopolitical racism establishes an inverse relation between the health and well-being of groups on either side of the boundary it creates, imagining a causal connection between the death of the other and the vitality of the self:

> The fact that the other dies does not mean simply that I live in the sense that his death guarantees my safety; the death of the other, the death of the bad race, of the inferior race (or the degenerate, or the abnormal) is something that will make life in general healthier: healthier and purer. (255)

Biopolitical racism thus creates an ideological foundation for the idea that my health is inversely proportional to the health of those on the other side of the caesura and enables the promise that the suffering of the other will translate into my health and the threat that the other's health or prosperity must result in my suffering or death. This inverse relation is simultaneously affective and material. The persistence of racism, of course, leads to adverse health outcomes for marginalized groups in myriad ways—systemic discrimination in the healthcare system, unequal access to nutritious food, unsafe working conditions, disproportionate exposure to environmental hazards, and so forth, not to mention racially motivated violence—and privileged groups certainly benefit materially from the outsourcing of risk to immigrants and communities of color. This imagined relation functions as an impetus to and a justification for public policies and business practices that do physiological harm to marginalized groups. But the direct inverse relation remains imaginary; the death of the other does not directly make the in-group physiologically healthier. Rather, it makes them *feel* healthier and better; that affective experience then motivates and justifies the discriminatory policies that make the imagined relation into a material reality.

It is by setting up this inverse relationship between the death of some people and the affective experience of health in others that racism functions as "the precondition for exercising the right to kill" in the name of life. This is what enables the "necro" function of biopower. In order for a system of power to position itself as being in service of life and simultaneously to kill or to expose its citizens to death, it needs this racist ideology. Racism both starts with and creates this affective relation in a mutually amplificatory cycle: affect travels across a felt racial boundary in an inverse manner, transforming from positive to negative as it crosses. This inverse relation is both a result of racism and its technology, as the exercise of this affective relation instantiates and shores up the boundary on which it operates. This inverse affective relation is thus vital to necroeconomics, because it supports the *feltness* of the boundary between what must live and what must die—the boundary that justifies killing in the name of life, the boundary that neutralizes and holds in check the potentially destabilizing paradox of (necro)biopower. This foundational role of affective relations is, ultimately, why it matters to read novels like *Bleak House* in an attempt to understand the mechanics of necroeconomics. The long form of the serialized novel enables Dickens to show the slow, accretive process by which interpersonal, seemingly apolitical affective relations work to crystallize and make real the boundaries that justify necroeconomic violence. Reading *Bleak House* in the context of necroeconomics illuminates the stakes of the interpersonal and the affective, shedding light in two directions. It makes visible the politics of *Bleak House,* helping us see the political stakes of repeated affective interactions over time, and it highlights the affective foundations of necroeconomics, revealing how interpersonal affective encounters over time create the conditions under which it is possible to let other people die. This connection, between the subtle violence of an inverse affective relation and the killing function of necroeconomics, is further illuminated in Harold Skimpole's treatment of Jo, the young street sweeper.

Jo, an orphaned pauper child, pops up repeatedly in the novel as a friend to the mysterious Nemo, a rejected witness at Nemo's inquest, a secret guide to Lady Dedlock in disguise, and a confused informant to Mr. Tulkinghorn. Esther encounters the "wretched boy" after he has fallen gravely ill and her young maid, Charley, an orphan herself, hears about his case from a common acquaintance named Jenny (450). Esther and Charley go to Jenny's cottage and, after seeing the state of the case, bring the ailing Jo back to Bleak House to care for him. Skimpole's relation to Jo, both materially and affectively, stands in sharp contrast to that of Esther and Jarndyce. Materially, Esther and Jarndyce bring him near to themselves, touch him, provide physical comforts, and take him into Bleak House. In contrast, when Mr. Jarndyce consults Skimpole (who, although he never actually practices medicine in the novel, was originally trained as a physician) on the question of what to do with Jo, Skimpole suggests that Jarndyce "had better turn him out" (454). Unfazed by Jarndyce's rare "almost stern" response, Skimpole goes on to explain, "I have a constitutional objection to this sort of thing" (454). Skimpole is making a claim of exclusion on behalf of a perceived opposition between his body and Jo's body. His "constitution" is threatened by Jo's inclusion in the domestic space, and in Skimpole's mind, this serves as sufficient justification for turning Jo out into the street. The act of exclusion that Skimpole calls for is, of course, an act of indirect killing. When Skimpole instructs Jarndyce to "put him out in the road," Jarndyce asks, "And what is he to do then?" (455). Skimpole responds, "Upon my life, I have not the least idea what he is to do then. But I have no doubt he'll do it" (455). But, of course, Jo is going to die if they put him out in the road. He is going to suffer, starve, freeze, and die. By calling on Jarndyce to turn Jo out of Bleak House, he is calling on Jarndyce to (passively) let Jo (slowly, painfully) die.

The contrast between these two material approaches to the suffering boy maps onto a similar contrast between affective responses. Both Jarndyce and Esther respond to Jo in what we might call a direct affective relationship: Jo's suffering causes them to feel negative emotions. Jarndyce is "uneasy," pacing "up and down and rumpling his hair" (455) as he considers what he calls a "sorrowful case" (454). Esther identifies with the boy so directly that she almost seems to exchange subject positions with him. When he is frightened by her resemblance to Lady Dedlock, she begins to feel "half frightened at [her]self," as if she has moved outside of her own body into Jo's and is viewing herself from Jo's perspective (454). Skimpole, in contrast, seems to derive pleasure from the boy's suffering. Throughout his encounter with Jo, he wears an "engaging smile" (455) and speaks "gaily" (454) and "cheerfully" (456). Later, he is "delighted" and "extremely gay all the rest of the evening," singing whimsical songs about the suffering of little orphan boys (457). Skimpole's reaction here is not mere callousness (although it certainly is that too); rather, it is an illustration of the inverse affective relation that grounds necroeconomics. In the span of just a few pages, Skimpole enacts the whole process by which the inverse affective relation supports a biopolitical form of racism that justifies the "letting die" of certain individuals in the name of health. He establishes an inverse affective relation with Jo, performing pleasure as he witnesses Jo's suffering; that inverse relation both stems from and shores up the rhetorical boundary between himself and Jo; that rhetorical boundary justifies the material exclusion of Jo from a domestic space of safety and care into a space of slow death.

As was the case in the pathoeconomic structures illuminated in Gaskell's novels, this relation operates not merely at the moment of death. Rather, the inverse affective relation extends over time, across the many weeks of suffering and struggle that expire before Jo finally follows suit. But unlike the mill owners of Gaskell's fictionalized Manchester, Skimpole's engagement in this relation is not instrumental; he is not trying to utilize Jo's vulnerability to gain the upper hand in a labor dispute. For Skimpole, this relation is primarily about *pleasure*. He is, of course, perfectly willing to profit off of Jo's suffering, as we see when he sells Jo out to Bucket for five pounds. But initially and fundamentally, Skimpole's relation to Jo is one of schadenfreude—finding enjoyment in witnessing Jo's suffering as he slowly coughs and rattles his way toward death. This brief instance of not-too-close contact with the suffering boy brings Skimpole pleasure. It is crucial that the boy is brought near enough to see but repulsed before he is near enough to touch. With the boundary between them reconstituted, Skimpole spends the rest of the evening singing songs and imagining stories about the past and future suffering of his "young friend," deriving continued gaiety and delight as he dwells upon Jo's pain (457). This behavior is almost sadistic—but Skimpole takes pleasure not in doing harm, but rather in *witnessing* it. Skimpole does not have a specific, targeted desire to do direct harm to Jo. Instead, he wants to passively stand by and *watch* as Jo lingers on, deriving pleasure from Jo's destitution and gradual destruction. His is not the active, acute sadism of a Mrs. Squeers or a Daniel Quilp; it is, instead, a slow, passive, voyeuristic boundary-pleasure that takes no ownership of violence, indeed pretends that it is not violence, and yet finds enjoyment in violence's effects.[5] It is, in other words, the schadenfreude of the

---

5. Skimpole also enacts other forms of racially affective violence in the text, for example, when he takes pleasure in an aestheticized imagining of plantation slavery in the American South: "Take the case of the Slaves on American plantations. I dare say they are worked hard, I dare say they don't altogether like it, I dare say theirs is an unpleasant experience on the whole; but, they people the landscape for me, they give it a poetry for me, and perhaps that is one of the pleasanter objects of their existence. I am very sensible of it, if it be, and I shouldn't wonder if it were!" (273). It is unclear in the text where Skimpole got this image of enslaved people in the Southern United States, but we can presume that it is based on his exposure to a visual representation in British media and not on actual travel to the US. (See Marcus Wood's *Blind Memory* for a wide-reaching analysis of the "utterly problematic nature of the visual representation of slavery in Europe and North America" [4]). Saidiya Hartman's *Scenes of Subjection* helps in understanding why (beyond the obvious) this is so unsettling. Analyzing an antislavery letter by John Rankin, Hartman details how his sympathy seems to require an imaginative projection by which he "phantasmically becom[es] the enslaved" and then "begins to feel for himself rather than those whom this exercise in imagination presumably is designed to reach" (Hartman 19). The fact that he can imagine "black sentience only by feeling for himself" implies that "black sentience is inconceivable and unimaginable" (19). It is the enslaved body's status as property that undergirds this relation: the "fungibility of the commodity makes the captive body an abstract and empty vessel vulnerable to the projection of others' feelings" (21). Skimpole enacts a similar kind of affective violence as Rankin's but without the abolitionist goals and without any attempt to sympathize with the enslaved person. He recognizes that the enslaved people suffer, but he makes no attempt whatsoever to imagine that suffering even through projection. Instead, he makes the absurd proposition that enslaved people might derive pleasure from providing him with the material for the pleasurable imaginative experience of their suffering. The enslaved people are thus rendered as utterly interchangeable vessels for white feeling that completely disregards black sentience.

complicit witness. Skimpole's pleasure is founded upon the disposability of its object; he takes as his unspoken premise that it is acceptable to let Jo die. But his pleasure comes not from *letting* someone die; it comes from *watching* them die.

BOUNDARY-PLEASURE AS PHILANTHROPY

Harold Skimpole is not the only character in *Bleak House* who makes a habit of watching people die. The so-called philanthropist Mrs. Pardiggle, who spends all of her time visiting and haranguing the local poor, does so as well. While slow sadism was for Skimpole a leisurely hobby, Mrs. Pardiggle makes a philanthropic career—indeed, an entire self-identity—of it. She is, to all appearances, the exact opposite of Skimpole—as committed to the concept of "work" as Skimpole is to leisure. Like Skimpole, she engages in performative self-mythologizing, but her mythology centers on her inexhaustible capacity for exertion. Upon meeting Esther and Ada, she says of herself:

> I love hard work; I enjoy hard work. The excitement does me good. I am so accustomed and inured to hard work that I don't know what fatigue is. . . . I do not understand what it is to be tired; you cannot tire me if you try! . . . The quantity of exertion (which is no exertion to me), the amount of business (which I regard as nothing) that I go through, sometimes astonishes myself. I have seen my young family, and Mr. Pardiggle, quite worn out with witnessing it, when I may truly say I have been as fresh as a lark! (116)

Besides just setting Mrs. Pardiggle up as a self-congratulatory try-hard, this passage also crucially reveals that her efforts align with the inverse affective model that we saw in the interaction between Skimpole and Jo. There is an inverse relationship between Mrs. Pardiggle's experience and that of her family—the excitement "does her good" while her family is "worn out" from witnessing it. The effect of her philanthropic efforts, on the level of her family, is to make her feel better and to make her husband and children feel worse.

The actual content of the "hard work" to which she is so devoted—the "excitement" that "does her good"—seems to be *witnessing the suffering of the cottagers*. Aside from the reading of a didactic sermon, which is unnarrated in the novel, Mrs. Pardiggle's visit mainly consists of an angry litany in which the man of the house preempts Mrs. Pardiggle's questions, asserting all the ways in which he and his family are dirty and unhealthy:

Is my daughter a washin? Yes, she *is* a washin. Look at the water. Smell it! That's wot we drinks. How do you like it, and what do you think of gin, instead! An't my place dirty? Yes, it is dirty—it's nat'rally dirty, and it's nat'rally onwholesome; and we've had five dirty and onwholesome children, as is all dead infants, and so much the better for them, and for us besides. (121)

Finally, as if to actualize this inverse relationship between Mrs. Pardiggle and the people she patronizes, the sick "gasping baby" dies just as Mrs. Pardiggle leaves the cottage, asserting again that she is "never fatigued" (122). Her energy increases in proportion with the suffering and ill health of others. Although she claims to be helping the poor, her philanthropy conforms to the same logic that Foucault refers to as racism under biopolitics: "the death of the other, the death of the bad race, of the inferior race (or the degenerate, or the abnormal) is something that will make life in general healthier" ("*Society*" 255). Mrs. Pardiggle seems to literalize this relationship, growing "fresh as a lark" through her exchange with the "onwholesome" poor and their dead and dying children.

Mrs. Pardiggle and her unwilling assistants do not provide any goods or services to the brickmaker's family; this is not a scene of material exchange or resource circulation at all. Rather, this scene centers on the circulation of affect—on the social and performative witnessing of pain, both physical and psychical. As many scholars have illuminated,[6] pain draws attention to surfaces, to boundaries. Pain intensifies our awareness of the boundaries of our bodies and selves at the same time as and *because* it threatens those boundaries. Paying attention to the social experience of feeling and witnessing pain helps us to see "the dynamic nature of surfacing itself" (Ahmed 26). That is, we can see how boundaries are constituted and upheld through various social acts, both instinctive and performative, that respond to pain, both felt in ourselves and witnessed in others. At the most instinctive level, think of the impulse to turn inward, curl up, in response to internal pain or the impulse to turn away, to shield oneself, at the sight of an open wound in an attempt to solidify the boundaries of one's own body. At the other end of the spectrum, imagine the performative and social act of the bully laughing at the pain of his victim in order to solidify the social boundary between them; imagine the similarly performative act of the friend moving toward, embracing the victim, solidifying a social bond of community between them. The performed

6. Drew Leder explains how the intensity of pain draws attention to the surfaces of the body and often causes it to turn in on itself (71–75); Judith Butler discusses the constitutive role of injury in the "materialization" of boundaries and surfaces (53). See also Scarry; Rey.

emotional response of the onlooker who witnesses pain, instinctual and visceral as it might feel, participates in the production of the social boundaries to which it seems to respond. Occasions of pain are opportunities for dynamic surfacing, for the negotiation of social boundaries through affective performance and response.

In this case, the ultimate purpose of Mrs. Pardiggle's visit seems to be to use the occasion of the brickmaker family's pain as an opportunity to shore up social boundaries through affective performance. Esther's narrative describes Mrs. Pardiggle's mode of responding to the brickmaker in distinctly performative terms: she notes Mrs. Pardiggle's "demonstrative cheerfulness" and twice describes Mrs. Pardiggle as making "a great show" of determination (118, 122–23). And crucially, the positive affect that Mrs. Pardiggle performs is the opposite of the deeply negative affect she is witnessing. She witnesses the physical pain of injury and hunger and the psychological pain of domestic violence and loss; she responds with "cheerfulness." This stands in contrast to Esther and to Ada, who weeps and is "full of grief" (124) after witnessing the family's suffering. Esther notes that Mrs. Pardiggle cannot get through to the objects of her philanthropy because "there was an iron barrier, which could not be removed" between herself and them (122). In fact, her inverse affective performance in the cottage works to constitute that iron barrier—between herself and the brickmaker's family specifically, and between a worthy middle class (who must live) and a disposable pauper class (who can be let to die) generally.

Mrs. Pardiggle thus engages in what we might call compulsive immunizing. Roberto Esposito has written extensively about immunity as a dialectical counterpart to community.[7] Immunity is a mode of protecting life from the risks of community, of being-in-common—but it does so through a controlled exposure to those risks. Immunity is about using what you seek to exclude as a tool to exclude it. It moves paradoxically, drawing the threat close in order to exclude it, just as vaccination prevents disease by introducing an inert form of that disease into the body (9). An immune response "discriminate[s] things

---

7. He places *immunitas* in a dialectical relationship with his other key term, *communitas*. Whereas *communitas* is the being-in-common and the obligation that we are compelled to have toward those with whom we share common life, *immunitas* is what places a barrier around what is proper, what is not common, and what exempts us from the obligation of the *munus*, the gift that we owe to the community. *Immunitas* is inherently anticommunal. Community is risky; to be in common is to be vulnerable, to be open to influence from others. Taken to the extreme, community becomes nondifferentiation, the dissolution of individuality. The *munus*, the gift, becomes the giving over of the entire self. *Immunitas* appears as a response to the threatening entropic potential of radical community; it acts as "an antidote needed to defend life from the dissolutive possibility of being 'put in common'" (15).

as not belonging" by reacting against them; in doing so, it reinstantiates the boundaries that being-in-common threatens to break down completely (49). Mrs. Pardiggle enacts this paradoxical movement in the novel as she compulsively visits the paupers who metonymically stand in for every threat to Victorian bourgeois society: violence, filth, disease, animality, sexual promiscuity, "savagery." These are the anxieties of a (rapidly) growing society, a (slowly) democratizing, urbanizing society, a society build on imperialism—and the threats that bourgeois morality sought to keep at bay. By bringing herself into proximity with these people, allowing into her life this controlled dose of that which threatens her, she seeks to inoculate herself against those threats and to reinstantiate that iron barrier between them and herself. Reading Mrs. Pardiggle in this way illuminates the affective structure of Esposito's immune function. There are, of course, ways of coming into contact with people that break down boundaries—ways of drawing near that do not create iron barriers. We see this in Esther and Ada's fundamentally different experience with the cottagers, as I discuss later in the chapter. It is, I argue, the particular inverse affective relation Mrs. Pardiggle establishes with these people, wherein their suffering produces her strength, that creates the immunitary effect.

Dickens's indictment of Mrs. Pardiggle thus expands the scope and escalates the stakes of his economic critique, moving beyond a more comfortable liberal critique of a lazy aristocratic parasitism to a potentially much more radical critique of bourgeois morality as a tool of necroeconomics. It is easy to read Skimpole as a figure for a kind of leisured parasitism without unsettling the premises of Victorian necroeconomics in any real way. Despite not actually having any wealth, Skimpole fashions himself a man of leisure and lives quite comfortably off the wealth and unpaid labor of others. Mr. Turveydrop (dancing master and father-in-law to Caddy Jellyby) does something similar, pretending to be a grand gentleman of great "deportment" while actually living off the pathoeconomic labor of his wife, who "works herself to death." Both men depend upon a kind of theft to maintain their lifestyle, with Turveydrop exploiting the unpaid labor of his wife and son while Skimpole just fails to pay for the goods and services he uses, either passing off the bill to Jarndyce or accumulating debt that he leaves Esther and Richard to pay with their life savings. Both men are also willing to produce suffering and death as a byproduct of their parasitic lifestyles, as Mr. Turveydrop's family sickens and dies due to overwork and Skimpole sends Jo off to near-certain death in exchange for five pounds.

But criticizing men who consume everything but refuse to produce anything does not particularly unsettle the narrative of mid-nineteenth-century necroeconomic capitalism. Indeed, it could be seen to support a liberal narrative that values people according to their economic productivity, grouping together aristocrats and paupers under a rubric of lazy parasitism. This is the narrative that transforms the (grievable) death of the poor into the (laudable) disposal of a parasitic group that is "living off the state." But what we get with Mrs. Pardiggle makes *Bleak House*'s economic critique much more expansive, and in my view, much more interesting, because bourgeois morality and the Protestant work ethic come in for indictment. Just as the cottagers are metonyms for Victorian anxieties, Mrs. Pardiggle is a sort of metonym for bourgeois morality. But crucially, Mrs. Pardiggle's bourgeois work ethic is not an actual engine for production or a genuinely superior code for living well. It is, rather, a quasi-sadistic compulsion. She does not seek to improve the well-being of the cottagers; nor does she wish to eradicate them. Instead, like a more systematic Skimpole, she is invested in keeping them around in their suffering state so that she can continue her compulsive practice of immunitary witnessing. Mrs. Pardiggle is constantly talking about her hard work, but the only thing that work is actually producing is an imagined and deeply felt boundary between herself, the valuable citizen, and the poor as a disposable subgroup. The depiction of Mrs. Pardiggle's "philanthropy" thus reveals that bourgeois morality is implicated in necroeconomics, because it both produces and justifies the barrier between the worthy and the unworthy, between who must live and who can die—and it does so in a more insidious way than Skimpole's flat refusal to countenance the ailing Jo. It makes the production of this iron barrier, this "biological-type caesura within [the] population," appear as a moral good ("*Society*" 255).

Reading Mrs. Pardiggle's "hard work" as an immunitary compulsion to produce racialized boundaries helps to reframe one of the more unsettling moments in the text—the description of her own children as racial others. After Mrs. Pardiggle introduces her children to Esther and Ada, listing the "voluntary" contribution she has forced each child to make, Esther describes their physical and emotional condition in terms of racial stereotypes:

> It was not merely that they were weazened and shriveled—though they were certainly that too—but they looked absolutely ferocious with discontent. At the mention of the Tockahoopo Indians, I could really have supposed Egbert to be one of the most baleful members of that tribe, he gave me such a savage frown. The face of each child, as the amount of his contribution was mentioned, darkened in a peculiarly vindictive manner, but his was by far the worst. (114)

It is a particularly uncomfortable moment because it is not spoken by the villainous Skimpole but the ethically trustworthy Esther. Esther implies that the Pardiggle children have become part of the racialized pauper class from which Mrs. Pardiggle seeks to distinguish herself. In their appearance, the health and maintenance of their bodies, their manners, their desires, their ways of interacting with the world, they are somehow not really English. In other words, they are on the other side of the iron barrier that Mrs. Pardiggle's affective othering works to establish.

Various critics have discussed Dickens's use of racial stereotypes to convey the karmic irony of Mrs. Pardiggle's situation: obsessed with establishing the boundary between herself, as representative of bourgeois morality, and everything that threatens it, Mrs. Pardiggle ends up reproducing all those threats within her own family. The fate of the Pardiggle (as well as the Jellyby) children is not just, as David Plotkin suggests, a result of maternal neglect—their mothers' failure to create the "neatly ordered homes . . . necessary for the cultivation and growth of English children" (17). For Plotkin, the problem with Mrs. Pardiggle is what she *does not do*. I argue that the problem is what she *does*. Mrs. Pardiggle is an immunizing machine, compulsively creating boundaries all around her. Her children are not racially othered because they are neglected but because the racial otherness that Mrs. Pardiggle actively and compulsively produces catches them in its crossfire. Her immunitary defense against otherness quickly becomes an autoimmune reaction—it turns on her own flesh and blood. The fact, moreover, that her own children end up on the other side tells us that the barrier is not based on any positive biological difference; rather, it is formed through affective relation. The Pardiggle children occupy the same inverse affective relation to their mother as the brickmaker's family, all growing "quite worn out with witnessing" her performance while their suffering "does her good." In other words, this immunitary reaction is not a reliable way of (to paraphrase Esposito) discriminating what does not belong. It is instead a compulsion, motivated by boundary-pleasure, that operates via the circulation of affects and works in service of necroeconomics.

While Mrs. Pardiggle is rhetorically producing racial otherness through inverse affective performance, her philanthropic counterpart Mrs. Jellyby is making that rhetorical barrier into a material one. Mrs. Jellyby's "philanthropy" involves resettling England's unemployed population in Africa to farm coffee beans on "the left bank of the Niger" (48)—a project she primarily manages via the writing of an enormous number of letters, sending "five thousand circulars from one post-office at one time" (51). From the outset, her project is one of systematically placing the barrier of distance between herself and a racialized subgroup of English people—the pauperized unemployed. The ultimate outcome of the scheme highlights Mrs. Jellyby's involvement in a project of racial othering even further, to the point of tragic absurdity. In the last chapter of the novel, in which Esther recounts the fate of several of the minor characters, readers learn that Mrs. Jellyby's "African project" (47, 114) ended up failing "in consequence of the king of Borrioboola wanting to sell everybody—who survived the climate—for rum" (912). In effect, what Mrs. Jellyby's philanthropic scheme ends up doing is sending England's surplus population out of the country to be sold as slaves in Africa. She ultimately actualizes the inverse relation that was, for Skimpole, only an imaginative one—founding her own sense of health and well-being on a process of racializing and excluding an English subgroup. Moreover, her seemingly endless energy quite literally derives from the labor of those she excludes—that is, from African coffee. Esther marvels at Mrs. Jellyby's capacity to work without rest, noting that when she went to bed at "nearly midnight," Mrs. Jellyby was still "among her papers drinking coffee" (52). In this way, Mrs. Jellyby represents this inverse affective economics taken to its logical extreme: she takes that rhetorical racial boundary, that "caesura" in the population between those who must live and those who can die, and she makes it material, sending the "other" away to the racially coded continent of Africa to die or be enslaved in the process of producing the very substance that fuels her. This is necroeconomics materialized, operating through the technology of biopolitical racialization. Yet even as Dickens criticizes that racialization, he leaves unexamined the "ethnic racism" that he simultaneously attributes to and exercises upon the imagined African king of Borrioboola. In constructing this ironic conclusion to Mrs. Jellyby's project, Dickens seems to characterize a geographically homogenized Africa as not only uncivilized and dangerous but also *responsible for slavery*. He thus, like Foucault, exiles so-called ethnic racism to a "primitive elsewhere" even as he criticizes domestic racialization.

Focusing on their role as producers of racialization gives us a new way of reading Dickens's representation of Mrs. Pardiggle and Mrs. Jellyby. There is, of course, misogyny in it. Ambitious women do not come out well in this novel. As many scholars have rightly pointed out, Dickens contrasts these two overbearing, overreaching, overly public women with the domestic, self-effacing "little woman" Esther in such a way that leaves no doubt about whom he considers to be doing womanhood correctly. Moreover, he seems to mock these women for their ambition while simultaneously criticizing Richard Carstone for his lack of ambition in a way that reifies traditional gender roles. And setting aside Dickens's intentions, Mrs. Jellyby and Mrs. Pardiggle have certainly been taken up, then and now, as argumentative fuel for opponents of women's involvement in public life and political activism.[8] But it is not *just* misogyny. I contend that observing the similarities between these women and Skimpole in the context of necroeconomics can help us see how Dickens's condemnation of these women exceeds a problematic critique of their transgressive gender positions—it is also a critique of their implication in the affective foundations of necroeconomics.

The three characters I have just described—Mr. Skimpole, Mrs. Pardiggle, and Mrs. Jellyby—are unlikely figureheads for necroeconomic capitalism in that they are functionally quite marginal to its operation. An unemployed man playing tunes on the piano in the country houses of his wealthier friends, claiming no interest in matters of money or business; two middle-class wives doing unpaid charity work. None of them actually owns capital, employs laborers, determines wages, or sells goods; they all operate off to the side of the cash nexus that Gaskell found so damaging to community health. And yet, I argue that they become figures or metonyms for the logic of necroeconomics, crystalizing the ideological premises and affective modes of relating to other people that ground necroeconomic capitalism and make it possible. They model ways of feeling, enacted as social practice, that make economic exploitation not only thinkable, not only defensible, but felt as natural and healthy. They illustrate what it means to *feel necroeconomically* and model how those feelings are produced and continually reproduced through the social practice of affective performance and response. In this sense, these characters make sense as metonyms for necroeconomic feelings not in spite of their separation from actual monetary exchange but because of it—they show how the feelings of capitalism are produced and ratified in domestic and social spaces. The long narrative durée of *Bleak House* thus reveals what theories of political economy, which focus on natural laws abstracted from time and place, must necessarily leave out: the repetitive, durational work of producing the affective relations that enable people to behave like the *homo economicus* whose existence political economists retroactively assume.[9]

---

8. Wisconsin politician Edward G. Ryan, for example, gave a series of lectures in 1854 arguing for the importance of separate spheres for men and women. He titled the lecture series "Mrs. Jellyby" (Cook 361). Even today, a Google search for "Mrs. Jellyby" and "feminist" reveals an alarming number of recent blog posts and other commentaries that continue to use Mrs. Jellyby as an example of the danger of female activism to the well-being of children. Blogger Laura Wood uses the example of Mrs. Jellyby as recently as 2018 to complain about women who "become obsessed with political causes" and subsequently "emasculat[e]" their husbands and "imperil the hygiene and health of their children," ultimately encouraging her readers to "learn from the mistakes of do-gooders of the past such [sic] Mrs. Jellyby of Mr. Dickens' masterpiece."

9. Claudia Klaver shows how Ricardo in particular was keen to remove all narrative elements from his writing in an attempt to disaggregate economics from noneconomic concerns and legitimize his work as "science" (14–25).

ANTI-IMMUNITY AS ALTERNATIVE

If the feelings of capitalism are produced in social and domestic spaces, then economic structures can also be challenged and reformed through domestic and social interventions. *Bleak House* has often been criticized for turning to the domestic as an escape from politics, ultimately offering no political solutions to the problems it highlights. Pamela Gilbert claims that "Dickens finally has nothing better to offer than the ever-more-perfect separation between domestic and public life, in which the public is hopelessly corrupt and the domestic offers a tenuous and limited salvation for those within a small 'circle of duty'" (*Citizen's Body* 151). Nancy Armstrong raises this issue more generally when she notes the limitations of Victorian novels that use the household as the "model for imagining social relations" (143). Even progressive or feminist novels often fall into the trap, she claims, of merely "replacing a household composed of the heterosexually monogamous couple and their biological offspring with another version of that household that can do little to change the way a nation distributes goods and services to its population" (144). But I argue that the domestic is more than a model for social and economic relations—it is actually the space wherein the premises that ground necroeconomic capitalism are iteratively (re)produced and come to be felt as real, as logical, and as healthy. An intervention within that space that changes how those feelings are produced, then, does have the potential to change economic systems and ultimately to change the distribution of resources and services on a material level.

Indeed, the novel begins with John Jarndyce deciding to make a domestic intervention into an economic problem—that is, to try to undermine Chancery by bringing Richard and Ada into his home. Chancery is itself a necroeconomic institution. Its entire raison d'être is to enforce a material version of the inverse relation I have described above. That is, Chancery mandates that one person can win only to the extent that another loses, even against the wishes of the "interested parties." Chancery is fundamentally opposed to the communal, to the possibility of being or holding in common. Indeed, its function is to eradicate the common and enforce the proper. Resources cannot be shared; the parties in a suit must be opponents; one party can only gain if the other party loses; if that inverse relation cannot be established, then no one can gain anything. This compulsory inverse relation unsurprisingly generates "iron barriers" between people; those who have inherited an interest in the suit have "inherited legendary hatreds" along with it (14). Ada expresses her frustration at this compulsory oppositionality: "I am grieved that I should be the enemy—as I suppose I am—of a great number of relations and others; and that they should be my enemies—as I suppose they are; and that we should all be ruining one another, without knowing how or why" (71). Even those who gain by the suit (the lawyers and clerks of court) are compelled into this inverse relation, like the receiver in the cause who has "acquired a goodly sum of money by it but has acquired too a distrust of his own mother and a contempt for his own kind" (15). Like Skimpole, Mrs. Pardiggle, and Mrs. Jellyby, Chancery does not produce anything of value; instead, it operates as a kind of necroeconomic machine, producing iron barriers by forcing inverse affective relations on the people compelled into its suits.

And also like Mrs. Pardiggle, it uses bourgeois respectability as a tool to recast predatory practices as morally justifiable business. Mr. Vholes, the vampiric lawyer who encourages Richard in his relentless and futile pursuit of a "judgment" in the case, is a walking personification of this sleight of hand. Mr. Vholes is, the narrator tells us, a "respectable man. He never misses a chance in his practice, which is a mark of respectability. He never takes any pleasure, which is another mark of respectability. He is reserved and serious, which is another mark of respectability. His digestion is impaired, which is highly respectable" (573). And this respectability is used as a weapon against anyone who sees the "coherent scheme" (573) of Chancery for what it is and ventures to complain about it: "This respectability of Mr. Vholes is brought into powerful play against them" (574). This same "respectability of Mr. Vholes has even been cited with crushing effect before Parliamentary committees" that have inquired into Chancery's practices (574). Even in the face of overwhelming evidence that Chancery does harm, the respectability of Vholes works like a talisman to protect the predatory institution from regulation:

> "Question: But you think that their abolition would damage a class of practitioners? Answer: I have no doubt of it. Question: Can you instance any type of that class? Answer: Yes. I would unhesitatingly mention Mr. Vholes. He would be ruined. Question: Mr. Vholes is considered, in the profession, a respectable man? Answer:"—which proved fatal to the inquiry for ten years—"Mr. Vholes is considered, in the profession, a MOST respectable man." (574)

Vholes's respectability places him firmly on the "good" side of the iron barrier; he is part of the population that matters, that must be preserved, that must live. Thus, the institution that provides his livelihood must be healthy and good and anything that would threaten it must be wrong: "As though, Mr. Vholes and his relations being minor cannibal chiefs and it being proposed to abolish cannibalism, indignant champions were to put the case thus: Make man-eating unlawful, and you starve the Vholeses!" (574–75). Any proposal to reform Chancery, to stop doing harm to the suitors, is recast as a proposal to harm Vholes—but Vholes is respectable; he is one of "us"; we cannot do him harm. This is the trick of necroeconomics. It places groups of people on either side of an iron barrier and establishes an inverse relation between them: when "they" get healthier, "we" get less healthy, and vice versa. Suddenly, when someone proposes to stop harming the people on the other side of the barrier—to stop harming *them*—I can interpret that as a threat to myself, to *us.* The defenders of Chancery are supported here by the same line of thinking that fuels groups like men's rights activists and white nationalists (and, I suppose, the "indignant champions" of cannibal rights): if *those* people become healthier and happier and more free, *I* must necessarily become less healthy and less free. Thus, if you stop doing harm to those people, you are threatening my well-being. Mr. Vholes's primary role in the machine of Chancery is to continually reaffirm this ideological logic by performing respectability and thus affirming his position on the right side of the iron barrier:

> In a word, Mr. Vholes, with his three daughters and his father in the Vale of Taunton, is continually doing duty, like a piece of timber, to shore up some decayed foundation that has become a pitfall and a nuisance. And with a great many people in a great many instances, the question is never one of a change from wrong to right (which is quite an extraneous consideration), but is always one of injury or advantage to that eminently respectable legion, Vholes. (575)

The "decayed foundation" that Mr. Vholes is tasked with shoring up is Chancery, of course, but it is also necroeconomics.

And indeed, Chancery is quite literally necroeconomic in that it is actually producing disease and death. The third-person narrator describes the suit's pathological influence in terms that sound like figurative language, stating that "Jarndyce and Jarndyce has stretched forth its unwholesome hand to spoil and corrupt," but this statement operates materially as well (15). The suit leads to Ms. Flite's mental illness, Gridley's premature death, and Tom Jarndyce's suicide. Most memorably, it leads to Richard's death. In the moments after the suit collapses, the entirety of the estate expended in legal costs, the lawyer Mr. Vholes takes "one gasp as if he had swallowed the last morsel of this client" (901); Richard's mouth suddenly fills with blood; he dies that very evening. There is no physiological cause for his death at the end of the novel; on the day of his death, Esther says that "his illness was still of the mind" (898).

He is, I suggest, infected by the extreme immunitary logic of Chancery; he loses all sense of *communitas* and the common; he becomes obsessed with establishing the boundaries of the proper; he begins to see members of his own community (particularly Jarndyce) as threats and tries to build defensive barriers against them. While Richard is unlike Mrs. Pardiggle is most ways, he is similarly engaged in a form of compulsive immunitary behavior, as he becomes obsessed with demarcating the boundaries between himself and the other parties in the case. Ultimately, he is destroyed from the inside out, as if by a morbidly overactive immune system that has lost its ability to distinguish friend from foe, self from pathogen.

Chancery is also responsible for producing the diseased space of Tom-All-Alone's. Dickens describes this space as a sort of unburied corpse, producing disease in the same manner as the half-buried decomposing bodies in the pauper graveyards that so concerned him:

> As on the ruined human wretch vermin parasites appear, so these ruined shelters have bred a crowd of foul existence that crawls in and out of gaps in walls and boards; and coils itself to sleep, in maggot numbers, where the rain drips in; and comes and goes, fetching and carrying fever and sowing more evil in its every footprint than Lord Coodle, and Sir Thomas Doodle, and the Duke of Foodle, and all the fine gentlemen in office, down to Zoodle, shall set right in five hundred years—though born expressly to do it. (236)

Dickens reminds readers that this property is "in Chancery, of course" (236). This is the material result of the rhetorical "iron barrier"—the production of a space that is materially neglected because its residents are part of a racialized subgroup whose deaths are ratified as being paradoxically healthy for the social body as a whole, from which they are excluded. And this, of course, is the space that produces the illness that infects Jo and then spreads to Charley and Esther. It is the epicenter of disease and death in the novel, and it is produced by Chancery. It is thus not just a figure of speech to say that the "legion of bills in the suit have been transformed into mere bills of mortality" (14). Chancery is figuratively and literally a necroeconomic machine, simultaneously producing the ideological premises that enable necroeconomics *and* producing disease and death in service of economic gain.

What we are seeing here is a society with an autoimmunity problem. We see characters like Richard and Mrs. Pardiggle compulsively engaging in immunitary behaviors, destroying themselves and their loved ones as they lose all sense of what is genuinely malignant and what is benign. I argue that necroeconomics is the root of this destructive autoimmunity. As I have described above, necro-economics works by creating subdivisions within the population—caesuras, iron barriers—and then establishing an inverse relation across those barriers. In other words, necroeconomics produces a social body that is confused about where its body ends and where the threats to its body begin. Mrs. Pardiggle thinks she is making herself healthier by inoculating herself against her neigh-bors; Mrs. Jellyby thinks she is solving the nation's problems by exporting its citizens to Africa; Richard thinks he is serving his own cause by defending himself against his most devoted benefactor. Like a physiological body with an autoimmune disease, the necroeconomic social body mobilizes its defenses against itself. Chancery both systematically generates this autoimmune confu-sion on an individual level, turning brother against brother and mother against son, and systematically profits off it. Many necroeconomic actors utilize the divisions between people to generate profit for themselves, but none do so more straightforwardly than Chancery. Chancery is telling people they need to build a wall with one hand and is selling bricks with the other. Simultaneously a met-onym for necroeconomics and a parody of it, Chancery compresses into one absurd institution the process by which necroeconomic systems produce and then profit off "iron barriers," getting people to buy into their own destruction.

But not everyone falls for Chancery's trick. John Jarndyce wants noth-ing more than to opt out of the oppositional relations that Chancery tries to impose on him. The action of the novel is set off by his attempt to undermine its power by bringing his ostensible opponents—Richard and Ada—into his domestic space and creating a particular affective relationship with them. Jarn-dyce tries to fast-track their intimacy, sending each young person a letter prior to their meeting asking them to "take the past for granted" and "meet as old friends" (74). He then tells them when they first arrive at his house, "You are at home" (76). In other words, he tries to remove from their interactions any sense of his private property ownership, instead suggesting that what is his is also theirs. He repeatedly insists upon (and indeed demonstrates) a direct affective relation between himself and the wards of court, suggesting that their happiness makes him happy and their suffering causes him suffering, even from the very first moment of their meeting. His intense aversion to displays of gratitude functions not just as a charming idiosyncrasy but also as a repeated affective performance that functions in the opposite way as that of Mrs. Par-diggle. By threatening to "run away" (74) or jump out the window when his wards express their sense of obligation to him, he performs (perhaps overact-ing a bit) his direct affective relation with them. There is no obligation; he has not sacrificed anything; by giving them happiness, he is also giving himself happiness. He seeks to counteract the Chancery machine, to break down the iron barrier it would place between him and his wards, by performing a direct affective relation with them with as much gusto as that with which Mrs. Pardiggle acts out the inverse relation in her philanthropic work.

Jarndyce performs a similar affective relation when he "gives" Esther (along with a miniature version of Bleak House) to Allan Woodcourt. While this moment has often been read as one of self-sacrifice—that is, Jarndyce sacrifices his own desire (to marry Esther) to satisfy what he realizes to be the desires of Esther and Woodcourt (to marry each other)—it seems to me that such a reading of Jarndyce's choice is only possible if we ignore or distrust both his own words and Esther's description of his affects and body language. Jarndyce is very clear that he does not view this choice as a sacrifice of his happiness. He calls the day a "day of joy" and tells Esther "exultingly" that he has "looked forward to it . . . for months and months" (890). Esther corroborates Jarndyce's claim of genuine happiness in her description of his appearance and behavior on the day that he reveals the new Bleak House to Esther. He is "so quaintly cheerful" as he shows Esther the house; Esther has seen the joy brewing "in [his] face for a long while" (888). As he leaves Esther and Woodcourt together, he notes that the wind is "due West"—his way of saying that all is right with the world and he is pleased (891). There are multiple ways of reading this. We could interpret this, perhaps, as Jarndyce just trying to be nice and prevent the happy couple from feeling bad for him. Alternately, we could read his response as a particularly managerial joy: the puppet master's pleasure in managing and executing a plan to perfection. Or, we could take his language seriously and conclude that he is genuinely made happy by the happiness of others. In this light, his "gift" of Esther to Woodcourt really is not a sacrifice, because it makes Esther and Woodcourt deeply happy, and their happiness spreads to and multiplies in Jarndyce. If we do not assume that affects are contained within the individual, if we allow that they might spread in direct relation between individuals and across social spaces, then Jarndyce's demeanor here reads differently—not as generous self-forgetfulness but as genuine happiness felt across the boundaries of selves. His performative expression of happiness in direct relation to the happiness of Esther and Woodcourt has real social effects, constituting them as part of a community of mutual feeling—directly responsive and responsible to each other.

Ultimately, Jarndyce's success in these affective machinations is limited. Richard still falls prey to the machine of Chancery and dies as a result. But Jarndyce's attempt here introduces an affective method for undoing the ideological work of necroeconomics that comes to be more fully realized in Esther.[10] While Jarndyce manifests community with his distant relations through living beside them in direct affective relation, Esther both embodies this relation and expands it outward, practicing an ethical being-beside that threatens the ideological foundations of necroeconomics much more deeply. Like Jarndyce (and unlike Skimpole and Mrs. Pardiggle), she displays a direct affective relation in her everyday interactions with the people around her: she feels happiness at Richard and Ada's romantic bliss; she feels grief in response to Jenny's loss; she feels concern and sadness as she witnesses Richard's decline (and indeed warns him against imagining an oppositional relation between himself and Jarndyce). But beyond this, she embodies this process in a way that Jarndyce does not. What Jarndyce did with his words and his property, Esther does with her body. We get description after description of Esther engaging in direct bodily contact with others. She takes up the body of Jenny's baby in her arms after it dies (123); she "take[s] [Peepy] up to nurse" after he has been injured and holds him until he falls "fast asleep in [her] arms" (49); she sits "by Charley, holding her head in [her] arms" while Charley is ill (460). Her first visit to the Jellyby household—the occasion upon which Ada describes her as a beneficent force of nature, stating that it "rained Esther"—comes to a head during an encounter of transformative contact with Caddy Jellyby, in which the disgruntled girl falls asleep with her head in Esther's lap and subsequently embarks upon a journey of self-improvement. The contact between the two young women is pivotal, both the impetus that sets off Caddy's development and the encapsulation of Esther's almost supernaturally good influence on those around her. Esther's embodied approach accounts for why she is more successful than Jarndyce in breaking down iron barriers. Her body seems to be transparently legible in a way that Jarndyce's words are not. Richard can mistrust and misinterpret Jarndyce's words, but no one can misinterpret Esther's body.[11]

It is crucial to note that close physical contact does not inevitably break down barriers and produce bonds of communal feeling. Proximity and con-

---

10. In making this claim, I diverge from Elizabeth Langland, who sees Mrs. Pardiggle and Esther as being essentially the same: both engaged in the work of disciplining the working classes, both preaching the "same values," both aligned with bourgeois interests. In Langland's reading, they are divided only in approach: Mrs. Pardiggle's "abstract humanitarianism" versus the "soft voice and gentle touch of Esther" (297). But I argue here that Mrs. Pardiggle and Esther are actually working toward opposite goals: the affective production of versus the erosion of the boundaries that enable necrocapitalism.

11. Indeed, the transparent legibility of Esther's body is a problem for her in the novel. Guppy reads Esther's body as evidence against Lady Dedlock, and although she mourns the supposed loss of her beauty, Esther is relieved when illness alters her facial features enough to make her less readable.

tact are occasions of affective intensity; different ways of responding to that intensity can produce a range of social effects. Sara Ahmed demonstrates this in *The Cultural Politics of Emotions*, showing how contact between bodies can solidify social boundaries, sticking hate to particular bodies and cohering others together as collectives. It comes across particularly poignantly in her reading of a short excerpt from Audre Lorde's *Sister Outsider*. In the essay, Lorde recalls sitting beside a white woman on a New York City subway train when she was a child. The woman recoils from the space between them in horror; Lorde assumes there is a roach crawling between them, only to discover that the woman's horror was provoked by contact with her own black body. In this case, bodily contact—and specifically, the white woman's affective performance of horror and physical response of recoiling away from the contact—reconstitutes racial boundaries. The moment of affective intensity occasioned by the chance contact between these two bodies on a subway train reproduces the social divisions to which it appears to respond:

> The white woman's refusal to touch the black child does not simply stand for the expulsion of blackness from white social space, but actually re-forms that social space through re-forming the apartness of the white body. The re-forming of bodily and social space involves a process of making the skin crawl; the threat posed by the bodies of others to bodily and social integrity is registered on the skin. (54)

We see Lady Dedlock respond to Jo in a similar way, "recoiling from him" in horror (240), "shrinking from him . . . and putting out her two hands, and passionately telling him to keep away from her, for he is loathsome to her," taking care not to touch him when she gives him his payment and "shuddering as their hands approach" (243). Lady Dedlock might be posing (rather unconvincingly) as a servant during their interaction, but her physical response to proximity with Jo's body re-forms the very real class boundary, the iron barrier, between them, in a way that is clear even to Jo. Although much less systematic than Mrs. Pardiggle and her compulsive slum-shaming, Lady Dedlock performs a similar rejection of poor bodies that also instantiates the boundaries of *immunitas*.

Esther's interaction with Caddy at the Jellyby household models a different kind of contact: a nonrepulsive contact that breaks down social boundaries rather than shoring them up. Far from repelling the girl, filthy from her work as her mother's unpaid amanuensis, Esther initiates contact with Caddy, "put[ting] [her] hand upon her head, and touch[ing] her forehead" (56). At this moment, Caddy's hostility cracks and falls away; she kneels at Esther's side, weeping, buries her face in Esther's skirts, and remains in that position of intimate proximity for the entirety of the night:

> I could not persuade her to sit by me or to do anything but move a ragged stool to where she was kneeling, and take that, and still hold my dress in the same manner. By degrees the poor tired girl fell asleep, and then I contrived to raise her head so that it should rest on my lap, and to cover us both with shawls. The fire went out, and all night long she slumbered thus before the ashy grate. At first I was painfully awake and vainly tried to lose myself, with my eyes closed, among the scenes of the day. At length, by slow degrees, they became indistinct and mingled. I began to lose the identity of the sleeper resting on me. Now it was Ada, now one of my old Reading friends from whom I could not believe I had so recently parted. Now it was the little mad woman worn out with curtsying and smiling, now some one in authority at Bleak House. Lastly, it was no one, and I was no one.

The protraction of this contact seems almost unreasonable; surely Esther could have made her excuses and taken to her bed. And yet, it is the very protraction of the contact that highlights it as a performative action that intervenes in the organization of social space. This is not the angelic, apolitical union of two women in an idealized domestic space that is separate from a wider social sphere. Rather, it is an *intervention in* the social sphere. Esther is performing the converse of the white woman's repulsion of Audre Lorde, or Lady Dedlock's horror in response to Jo. She is using her body to re-form social boundaries by communicating that Caddy's touch, the impression of Caddy's body on her own, does not register as a threat. It is a refusal to recoil, a commitment to maintaining contact for a particular social purpose. There is risk here: the boundaries of individuality seem to threaten to dissolve altogether as Esther loses track of Caddy's identity as well as her own. But in the context of necroeconomics, we can see the political potential of this dissolution of boundaries. Through this exaggerated refusal to recoil, Esther is producing an embodied affective relation between herself and Caddy that breaks down the iron barrier between them.

This contact is antinecroeconomic in that it breaks down the barriers on which necroeconomics depends. It also seems, at times, to be antinecroeconomic in that it appears to literally promote or generate good health. When Caddy falls ill later in the novel after giving birth to a baby girl, Esther goes to nurse her during her illness. In her narrative, Esther relates,

> Caddy had a superstition about me, which had been strengthening in her mind ever since that night long ago, when she had lain asleep with her head

in my lap. She almost—I think I must say quite—believed that I did her good whenever I was near her. Now, although this was such a fancy of the affectionate girl's, that I'm almost ashamed to mention it, still it might have all the force of a fact when she was really ill. (711)

Esther's close physical presence acts upon Caddy like medicine, making her healthier with "the force of a fact" regardless of any actual physiological explanation. And while Caddy draws on Esther's strength, Esther is adamant that this withdrawal does not lessen her own stock of health in proportion. After Esther travels to London to visit Caddy several days in a row, Jarndyce suggests that they take possession of lodgings in London so that Esther will not become worn out by constant traveling. To this offer, Esther replies, "Not for me, dear guardian . . . for I never feel tired," and she goes on to note in her private narration that this is "strictly true" (711). In these moments of ethical contact between Esther and Caddy, vitality is not obeying the inverse relation of necroeconomics, wherein one can gain only to the extent that the other loses. Instead, Dickens depicts wellness growing in direct relation between the two, proliferating as it is shared. This is what it means when Ada says that it "rained Esther" (77). Esther's commitment to antinecroeconomic contact seems to have a salutary effect on everyone around her, short-circuiting the inverse economy of affect, introducing an alternative direct model of health and happiness, and improving communal well-being to an extent that Jarndyce's sugarplums cannot.

CONTAGIOUS COMMUNITY

If the problematic system that Dickens critiques in this novel looks like a destructive immune system, then the alternative he offers looks like a healthy epidemic. Of course, *Bleak House* does not offer any specific suggestions for political reform, no fully realized alternative economic or political model to replace the pathological system that it critiques; rather, *Bleak House* gives us Esther. But in her quietly presented personal philosophy of ethical responsibility to those around her, we can see the seeds of a potentially radical alternative to necroeconomics. She tells Mrs. Pardiggle, "I thought it best to be as useful as I could, and to render what kind services I could to those immediately about me, and to try to let that circle of duty gradually and naturally expand itself" (117). Esther describes here a sort of contagion model of ethical responsibility, wherein responsibility spreads through contact. The multiple overlapping plots of the serial novel serve particularly well to illuminate this contagious spread of responsibility. Esther and Richard become linked to

Skimpole through their contact with him at Bleak House and feel compelled
to pay his debt when the collector comes to arrest him; as a result of this
episode, Esther, Ada, and Jarndyce feel compelled to check on and care for
the debt collector's young children after he dies; the eldest of these children,
Charley, becomes Esther's maid; Charley knows Jenny, the brickmaker's wife,
who knows Jo, the sick child, and tells Esther of his plight; Esther visits and
feels compelled to care for Jo; through connection with Esther, both Woodcourt and George Rouncewell later feel compelled to care for Jo. Duty to one
another spreads like a contagion—it happens through contact, it occurs "naturally" without effort or forethought, and is indiscriminate with respect to class
and social group. Like an epidemiological map of an airborne illness, it builds
outward as moments of contact multiply, exponentially growing the web of
ethical responsibility.

There is a problem here, of course: this ethical epidemic starts with and
hinges on the vulnerable body of a largely disempowered woman. Esther is
radically dependent on others throughout the novel. Although she views Jarndyce's patronage as a great kindness, he is essentially the puppet master of her
life. She is subject to his whims before she even knows who he is and does not
seem to feel empowered to push back against his decisions, as we see when
she accepts his marriage proposal out of gratitude rather than desire. Her
childhood self is broken down emotionally by her aunt's abuse and her adult
self is broken down physically by her illness. In her reading of Esther, Helena
Michie focuses on the "making and unmaking through pain" of the female
self, claiming that female selfhood in *Bleak House* is constructed through pain
and disfigurement (200). The model for political change that I see in this
novel, which takes the form of the "making and unmaking" of iron barriers,
similarly depends on a female character making herself vulnerable to pain and
disfigurement—to being herself unmade in the process of unmaking iron barriers. And although Robert Newsom characterizes Esther as a model that all
readers are meant to emulate,[12] I would venture to say that most readers are
left wishing to *know* an Esther rather than aspiring to *be* an Esther. The risky,
embodied work of breaking down iron barriers is placed on the shoulders of a
young woman, raised in trauma and shaped by suffering, who acts with unfail-
ing selflessness throughout the novel and never seems to resent the often more
privileged others who draw on her affective labor while she is trying to process

---

12. Newsom pushes back against the idea that *Bleak House* singles out women in its turn
to domesticity, claiming that male characters are criticized for their domestic failures as well.
He claims that this novel utilizes female characters as its models for all readers, both male and
female. In Newsom's reading, goodness is equivalent to self-sacrifice in this and other novels,
so "to the extent that they accept the association of women with self-sacrifice they are urging
their readers all to act like women" (78).

her own trauma. As readers, we would be forgiven for feeling that we cannot live up to this model—further, that we might not want to.

And yet, there is something potentially radical in the indiscriminate inclusiveness of this epidemiological model of ethical responsibility. It is crucial that this contagious duty applies not just to meritorious characters but to everyone—including Jo, the street-sweeping urchin that Lady Dedlock found so profoundly repulsive. Indeed, Dickens dwells on Jo's mundane repulsiveness in every description of him. He is like the "blinded oxen" (237) in the marketplace; he is like a stray, "degenerate" dog (238); he is a "horrible creature" (240); he is "dirty, ugly, disagreeable to all the senses" (669); his clothes are like "like a bundle of rank leaves of swampy growth, that rotted long ago" (659); and he himself is like a "growth of fungus . . . produced in neglect and impurity" (660). He disgusts Lady Dedlock when he is excited to see a rat crawling into the ground in the graveyard (243); he offends Mrs. Snagsby by yawning at the Reverend Chadband's proselytizing (290); he frightens Charley with his fear of Esther when she cares for him in the brickmaker's cottage (454). He is a beggar—one of that category of people who Adam Smith claims are most likely to be "objects rather of contempt than of fellow-feeling" (*Theory* 144). Nor does Jo "moderate" his expression of his own suffering or show stoic "self-command" so that observers will be more likely to sympathize with him, as Adam Smith suggests (146). Rather, he whimpers, complains of being "a chivied and a chivied, fust by one on you and nixt by another on you, till I'm worrited to skins and bones," and threatens to "go and make a hole in the water"—that is, to commit suicide (660). Jo is no Oliver Twist or Little Nell, no misplaced paragon of bourgeois values who, given a bath and a modest income, would resemble the most traditional middle-class protagonist. There is nothing about Jo that makes him merit special attention or "deserve" Esther's care. He is, in his own words, just a "reg'lar one" (239).

This is key because it means that Esther is not just moving misplaced characters from one side of the iron barrier to the other; rather, she is troubling it altogether. A skeptic could say that Caddy is a middle-class girl who has been pushed to the wrong side of the iron barrier by her mother's domestic failures; Esther restores her to her rightful class position. Even the working-class Charley is so unfailingly virtuous—hardworking, resourceful, prematurely maternal, wholeheartedly grateful to her benefactors—that she could be said to "deserve" Esther's care (as well as her own subsequent rise in class status). But Jo does not fit this pattern; he is just a regular one. He is

> a common creature of the common streets, only in soul a heathen. Homely filth begrimes him, homely parasites devour him, homely sores are in him, homely rags are on him; native ignorance, the growth of English soil and

climate, sinks his immortal nature lower than the beasts that perish. Stand
forth, Jo, in uncompromising colours! From the sole of thy foot to the crown
of thy head, there is nothing interesting about thee. (669)

Jo is little more than a prototype for the unsuitable participant in the body
politic, the "other within" that biopolitical racism places on the other side
of a barrier—the one who can be allowed to die, whose death is rewritten as
medicine, the one who can be killed in the name of life. If Esther's ethically
contagious community includes Jo, then it must not exclude anyone. Esther
gives us a model of community that seems to have no iron barriers, no subdivisions within it—and thus, no conditions under which the citizen is excused
from caring for his or her neighbor.

Although this radically inclusive social body remains fictional, the act of
imagining it is still a powerful political challenge. In his influential essay "Necropolitics," Achille Mbembe writes, "Sovereignty means the capacity to define
who matters and who does not, who is disposable and who is not" (27). That is
to say that the boundary-making function that undergirds necroeconomics—
the establishment of iron barriers between those who must live and those who
can die—is the very basis of political power. Dickens shows us in *Bleak House*
that this boundary between the valued and the disposable is actually negoti-
ated in the home, in the sitting room, in the cottage, through experiences and
performances of affect. That boundary is produced and made real through the
action of feelings, felt and expressed in social and domestic spaces. So even if
the only blueprint for change that *Bleak House* has to offer is an alteration in
the circulation and performance of affects primarily contained within domestic space, that alternative affective economy has the potential to shift or even
eliminate those crucial boundaries and thus the potential to effect political
change. This is not a retreat from politics but an attempt to unsettle the foundation upon which the political status quo is based.

CHAPTER 4

Unfeeling Capitalism, Future and Past

Middlemarch, Felix Holt, and *News from Nowhere*

In considering the problem of capitalist feelings, the authors I have examined so far in this book have all approached the problem with an oscillating sense of scale. They zoom in and out between the macro of capitalism and the micro of feelings, highlighting the interplay between the two. Writing in the final third of the nineteenth century, the two authors who form the focus of this final chapter—George Eliot and William Morris—share the premise that capitalist feelings are a problem, but they approach that problem from opposite directions. Morris zooms all the way out, subsuming all affective conflicts under the umbrella of anticapitalist struggle. For Morris, capitalism is always necroeconomic. Letting die is not just one emotionally problematic technology of a capitalist market, as it was for Martineau or Gaskell; it is the purpose and effect of what Morris views as a fundamentally pathological system. Eliot, meanwhile, zooms all the way in, collapsing capitalism's necroeconomic function into the dynamics of interpersonal feeling. "Letting die" now looks like Nicholas Bulstrode deciding not to interfere with a nurse's incorrect treatment of Raffles, the only man who knows the dubious origins of Bulstrode's wealth. Eliot still presents us with the scene of a capitalist crime, but the action of "letting die" has been abstracted from economic modes of production, wage labor, strikes, employment, and so forth.[1] We are left with the image of

---

1. This is not to say, of course, that Eliot was not personally aware of contemporary debates in political economy. For a detailed account of her knowledge and engagement with political economy, see Coleman.

Bulstrode watching at the sickbed as Raffles dies, thinking of plausible deniability and the silence of the dead.

To first appearances, the novels paired together in this chapter seem quite disparate. Morris's account of an agrarian communist utopia, set 150 years in Britain's future, is simultaneously dreamlike and polemical, staking no claim to realism. *News from Nowhere* (1890) is an unapologetic escape to a dream of what might be, making no concessions to what is. Inhabited by characters who function as mouthpieces for Morris as a political visionary, it has remained in the criticism more as an exhibition of late-Victorian socialist thought than as a literary achievement. Eliot's *Felix Holt* (1866) and, to a much greater extent, *Middlemarch* (1872) have been celebrated as triumphs of nineteenth-century realism. A scientist of human nature, Eliot "plung[es] the dissecting-knife"[2] into her characters in order to produce the fullest and most accurate "picture of human life," illuminating the "unhistoric acts" that subtly shape our world ("Natural History" 54; *Middlemarch* 515). Referring to the depictions of Lydgate and Rosamond in *Middlemarch,* Henry James said that there was "nothing more powerfully *real* than these scenes in all English fiction" (580). I argue, though, that all three texts are united by a shared character-type—embodied by the title character in *Felix Holt,* by Caleb Garth and Dorothea Brooke in *Middlemarch,* and by Richard Hammond (and many others) in *News from Nowhere*—defined by their total lack of affective investment in capital or social mobility. Moreover, although Eliot's novels may not include time travel like Morris's does, these characters are all examples of speculative thinking: How would people operate in the absence of capitalist feelings? Morris projects forward into the future, creating a utopian setting and imagining the individuals it would produce; Eliot creates very similar characters and projects them backward into retrospective realism. *Felix Holt* may be realism, but Felix is utopian. For Morris, these characters show us how people might feel in a capitalism-free future. For Eliot, they show us how people would have needed to feel in the past in order to solve the contradictions of capitalism in the present.

MIDDLEMARCH:
STICKY MONEY

Although George Eliot's *Middlemarch* does not dwell upon the processes of industrial production in the way that Gaskell's novels do, I argue that the

---

2. R. H. Hutton, unsigned review from the *Spectator,* 1872, qtd. in Carroll 305. For more on the connection between Eliot's novelistic method and dissection and an analysis of these reviews in particular, see Menke 636.

novel is haunted by the specter of necroeconomics—specifically, that there undergirds the narrative a profound concern about the sticky feelings that circulate around the capitalist act of letting die. I begin with the only character whom Eliot repeatedly describes in terms of his role as an owner and circulator of "capital": Nicholas Bulstrode. In fact, the novel seems to figure Bulstrode as the *only* source of capital in Middlemarch. Nearly every time the word "capital" is used in its economic sense, it refers either directly or indirectly to Bulstrode's money.[3] Readers learn of the substantial "capital" Bulstrode has infused into Middlemarch, much of which he plans to quietly withdraw in order to run away from the impending scandal that Raffles's appearance portends (383), and some of which he offers to Will Ladislaw, the son of the lost stepdaughter whose whereabouts Bulstrode paid Raffles to conceal (386). Meanwhile, the merchant Mr. Vincy is described as having capital only to the extent that Bulstrode has given it to him. He "can't spare" any capital for Fred (318); he tells his daughter Rosamond that he is already trading on "borrowed capital" (419). Bulstrode is confirmed to be the source of that borrowed capital when he privately tells his wife (Mr. Vincy's sister), "I have supplied your brother with a great deal of capital" (427). Lydgate can turn only to Bulstrode when he "finds that his furniture and other initial expenses come to between four and five hundred pounds more than he has capital to pay for" (363). Even Joshua Rigg, the illegitimate son whose unexpected inheritance of Featherstone's estate disappoints Vincys and Featherstones alike, only acquires the "capital" he wants to fund his money-changing business by selling his newly inherited estate of Stone Court to Bulstrode.

If *Middlemarch* is an economy, Bulstrode is both its primary and most problematic source of capital. Eliot, of course, is no Marxist—and yet, it is notable that nearly all the capital that circulates in this novel can be traced back to an originary capitalist theft. That is, Middlemarch's capital traces back to Bulstrode, and Bulstrode's capital traces back to theft. When explaining why so many townspeople object to Bulstrode, Lydgate tells Dorothea, "He is concerned with trade, which has complaints of its own that I know nothing about" (272). Lydgate will soon come to understand those complaints all too well when the origins of Bulstrode's wealth come to light (and destroy his own reputation by proxy). Up to this point, Bulstrode has successfully concealed from the people of Middlemarch that his wealth originates from his employment at and eventually ownership (via marriage) of a London pawnbroker,

---

3. The word is used only twelve times to refer to money. Seven of those refer to Bulstrode's money. Four of the remaining five refer not to capital but to its absence: Fred Vincy lacks capital; Lydgate lacks capital to pay his debts; Will Ladislaw's "only capital" is his "brain" (183); Mr. Brooke has not invested capital in his estate. The fifth, which I discuss later in this chapter, refers to Caleb Garth's desire to avoid "handling capital" despite a career in business.

the source of whose "magnificent profit was the easy reception of any goods offered, without strict inquiry as to where they came from" (381). He is, in other words, making money by trafficking stolen goods. While he admits to initially "shrinking" from a business whose "profits [are] made out of lost souls," he manages to train himself into feeling comfortable with it: "His religious activity could not be incompatible with his business as soon as he had argued himself into not feeling it incompatible" (381–82). With the "vista of a fortune" before him, he abstains from making any inquiries into the origins of the goods (381).

After the shop's owner dies and Bulstrode prepares to marry his widow, Bulstrode's desire to hold onto the capital thus obtained leads him to strategically fail to find the long-lost daughter of his betrothed. One way of putting this would be to say that Bulstrode keeps his stolen capital by stealing the intended inheritance of his absent stepdaughter Sarah and her young son Will. Eliot, however, does not put it this way. Instead, the crime is figured passively, in terms of what Bulstrode does *not* do rather than what he does. Eliot writes,

> The daughter had been found; but only one man besides Bulstrode knew
> it, and he was paid for keeping silence and carrying himself away. . . . Bul-
> strode had never said to himself beforehand, "The daughter shall not be
> found"—nevertheless when the moment came he kept her existence hidden;
> and when other moments followed, he soothed the mother with consolation
> in the probability that the unhappy young woman might be no more. (382)

The crimes that lead to Bulstrode's wealth—the trafficking of presumably stolen goods and the concealment of Sarah Ladislaw—are both acts of strategic nonintervention. He opts not to investigate the source of the shop's wares; he opts not to inform the widowed Mrs. Dunkirk of her daughter's whereabouts. His criminality is not characterized by decisive action but rather by a morally suspect tendency to "let well enough alone." Thus, the only character who accumulates substantial capital in *Middlemarch* does so via a morally suspect process of "laissez-faire."

Bulstrode's abandonment of his stepdaughter in itself shows his willingness to let die in service of the accumulation of capital. It leaves the Ladislaws critically poor, to the point that Will remembers being "very hungry" as a child and having "only a little bit of bread" until Casaubon steps in to provide for them (228). It also occasions Bulstrode's extended bribery of the troublesome Raffles, who will eventually be allowed to die under Bulstrode's roof. His debauched former associate's appearance in Middlemarch sends Bulstrode reeling; he cannot help hoping for the death of the only man who could enlighten the townsfolk about the origins of Bulstrode's esteemed capital. In paying Raffles to buy his silence, Bulstrode is aware that he is also giving an alcoholic the means to hasten his own death. When Bulstrode provides Raffles with one hundred pounds in cash, Eliot's narrator notes that "various motives urged Bulstrode to this open-handedness, but he did not himself inquire closely into all of them. As he had stood watching Raffles in his uneasy sleep, it had certainly entered his mind that the man had been much shattered since the first gift of two hundred pounds" (425). Yet even as he feels an "intense desire . . . that the will of God might be the death of that hated man" (431) and sees in that death "his own deliverance" (435), he strives to avoid taking any positive action to bring that death to fruition. He reflects that "there was no sin in contemplating death as the desirable issue—if he kept his hands from hastening it—if he scrupulously did what was prescribed" (435). But as he watches through Raffles's illness, he becomes frustrated that his desires do not have material force in the world: "Bulstrode felt himself getting irritated at the persistent life in this man, whom he would fain have seen sinking into the silence of death: imperious will stirred murderous impulses towards this brute life, over which will, by itself, had no power" (437). Indeed, Raffles in his raving seems to be aware of Bulstrode's unspoken desire; he "imagine[s] a doctor present, addressing him and declaring that Bulstrode wanted to starve him to death out of revenge for telling" (435). Raffles's erroneous word choice— suggesting that Bulstrode is going to "starve" him—raises the specter of the industrial "clemming" we saw in Gaskell's novels in this very different act of letting die. Bulstrode finally abdicates his post to the housekeeper Mrs. Abel, giving her a vial of opium but conveniently failing to pass on Lydgate's instructions about how much to give the patient. When she appeals to Bulstrode for alcohol, which Lydgate has strictly forbidden, to relieve Raffles's pain, he gives her the key to the wine cellar and allows her to administer it at her discretion. Raffles dies the following morning, and Bulstrode feels "more at rest than he had done for many months" (439).

Dr. Lydgate, however, is more troubled and unfortunately will find that Bulstrode's scandal sticks to him and adheres with some stubbornness. I am drawing here on Sara Ahmed's *The Cultural Politics of Emotion*, in which she describes how feelings circulate via "sticky" signs and objects. Some objects are especially sticky, like globs of slime; things stick to them, and they stick to you. Affects and meanings get stuck to the sign as an effect of the history of its circulation; the more "saturated with affect" the sign is (as in the case of, say, a racial slur), the harder those associations are to unstick. Those meanings then threaten to "stick" to the individuals, groups, or ideas to which the sticky sign is applied. Affects thus travel by a kind of slimy metonymy, via the vector of the sticky object. In this sense, Ahmed claims that "emotions work as a form of capital: affect does not reside positively in the sign or commodity, but is produced as an effect of its circulation" (45). In this case, however, the sticky object is *capital itself*. Bulstrode's money in *Middlemarch* is sticky; it picks up grime as it circulates, and it threatens to leave a slimy film on anyone who touches it. As Ahmed notes, the "quality of sliminess is that it 'clings'" (90). She quotes Sartre, who describes slime as "a fluidity which holds me and which compromises me; I can not slide on this slime, all its suction cups hold me back; it can not slide over me, it clings to me like a leech" (qtd. in 90). In her depiction of the circulation of Bulstrode's money, Eliot suggests that this is also the nature of capital's fluidity.

To enter into the exchange of capital is to enter into this chain of metonymic signification—unfortunately for Lydgate, to whom Bulstrode's shame clings like a leech. When Lydgate first settles in Middlemarch, he is confident that he can benefit from Bulstrode's patronage without compromising his own independence. He "proudly" claims that he will ignore religious sectarianism and local politics, asserting that he is only concerned with how Bulstrode "spends large sums on useful public objects" and thus "might help [Lydgate] a good deal in carrying out [his] ideas" (112). Lydgate's friend Farebrother is rather more wary, however, and takes time to warn the overconfident Lydgate about the risks of becoming tied to others and being driven by their inclinations and goals—of "wear[ing] the harness and draw[ing] a good deal where your yoke-fellows pull you" (111). Lydgate believes that settling in provincial Middlemarch is precaution enough, because it will remove him from the "empty bigwiggism, and obstructive trickery" of London (112), but Farebrother warns that Middlemarchers "have our intrigues and our parties" as well and argues that Lydgate needs to be careful to "keep [him]self independent" (111). Lydgate thinks that Farebrother is referring to avoiding the ties of marriage, but Farebrother resists this interpretation. He claims that marrying "a good unworldly woman . . . may really help a man, and keep him more independent," citing Caleb Garth's wife as an example (112). Instead, Farebrother turns the conversation back to Bulstrode, who is in the process of campaigning against Farebrother for the chaplaincy of the new hospital. Although Farebrother acknowledges that he "should be glad of the forty pounds" given as salary for the chaplaincy, he abdicates any claim on Lydgate's loyalty, giving Lydgate leave to vote against him to avoid offending Bulstrode and assuring Lydgate that their friendship will not be damaged as a result (113). Farebrother shows an awareness here that the exchange of money can get sticky and chooses to act against his own financial interest in order to preserve his friendship with Lydgate, whom he claims he "can't spare" (113).

Lydgate, however, is not quite so careful, nor quite so willing to give up material wealth. Despite his cutting-edge scientific training and progressive plans for medical reform, Lydgate retains traditional ideas about wealth and consumption:

> That distinction of mind which belonged to his intellectual ardour, did not penetrate his feeling and judgment about furniture, or women, or the desirability of its being known (without his telling) that he was better born than other country surgeons. He did not mean to think about furniture at present; but whenever he did so, it was to be feared that neither biology nor schemes of reform would lift him above the vulgarity of feeling that there would be an incompatibility in his furniture not being of the best. (97)

Indeed, when he marries, he does not choose the type of "unworldly" woman that Farebrother admires, but rather the refined, materialistic, social-climbing Rosamond, who Mrs. Bulstrode claims was brought up "in too worldly a way" (216). And when Lydgate prepares for marriage, he rents an expensive home and purchases all the household goods that he considers, based on his upper-class upbringing, to be "ordinary" without any particular "notion of being extravagant" (217). Rosamond continues this precedent in her housekeeping once they are married, "simply . . . ordering the best of everything" (364). Soon afterward, having "bought and used a great many things which might have been done without, and which he is unable to pay for," Lydgate finds himself deep in debt (364).

It is this complacent desire for material goods that leads Lydgate to appeal to Bulstrode for a personal loan and results in him losing the independence that Farebrother cautioned him to protect. Distracted by his troubles, Bulstrode initially responds to Lydgate's request with a terse refusal. Shortly afterward, however, an ill and raving Raffles returns to Middlemarch, and Bulstrode calls Lydgate in to oversee his care. As he worries about what Raffles might say in the presence of the doctor, Bulstrode regrets missing the opportunity to create in Lydgate "a strong sense of personal obligation" to him that might serve as some "defense" against any accusations made by Raffles (435). He changes course and offers Lydgate an interest-free loan of one thousand pounds to clear his debts. Lydgate is temporarily "overjoyed" when Bulstrode extends to him the loan, but there soon "crossed his mind, with an unpleasant impression, as from a dark-winged flight of evil augury across his vision, the thought of that contrast in himself which a few months had brought" (237). His misgiving is well placed: Raffles dies the next day, but his secrets do not die with him. The news of Bulstrode's past spreads like wildfire through Middlemarch just as Lydgate is paying off his very public debts with Bulstrode's money, and before Lydgate is even aware of Bulstrode's backstory, "the world believes that [Bulstrode] somehow or other poisoned the man and that [Lydgate] winked at the crime, if [he] didn't help in it" (456). Bulstrode's money is doubly sticky: it sticks Lydgate and Bulstrode together, and it sticks Bulstrode's "diseased motive" to Lydgate. Indeed, Lydgate quickly realizes that establishing this adherence was Bulstrode's goal in giving him the loan: "He was afraid of some betrayal in my hearing: all he wanted was to *bind me to him* by a strong obligation" (456, emphasis added). And in this, Bulstrode is successful; Lydgate tells Dorothea that "Bulstrode's character has enveloped me, because I took his money" (471). Lydgate's contact with Bulstrode's money has made him sticky too; suspicions "cling" to him (471). The suspicion that sticks "most obstinately" is that Lydgate is a person who is willing to let die (471). In light of the scandal, the townsfolks' fear that Lydgate "meant to let the people die in the Hospital, if not to poison them, for the sake of cutting them up" (274) hardens into a certainty that he is a medical murderer on the scale of Burke and Hare (447). Bulstrode's sticky capital bears the history of letting die; the feelings that such a history provokes get stuck to Lydgate by metonymic association when he takes that capital.

Given that "the sticky and the disgusting" are often "linked, if not reduced to each other," it is no surprise that the characters who handle sticky capital are frequently characterized as objects of disgust (Ahmed 89). Bulstrode imagines Raffles as disgusting precisely because he is sticky: even after Bulstrode is out of Raffles's "repulsive presence," he cannot "shake off its images with their hateful kindred of sensations—as if on all the pleasant surroundings of his life a dangerous reptile had left his slimy traces" (425). But of course, Raffles's presence is only repulsive to Bulstrode because it recalls a previous exchange of money for the concealment of Sarah Ladislaw's whereabouts. Raffles becomes slimy through his history of contact with Bulstrode's money—as does Lydgate, who already felt "disgust with himself" following a passing attempt to gamble his way out of debt (364, 419). After he accepts Bulstrode's slimy loan, the people of Middlemarch treat him "as if [he] were a leper" whose infection was liable to stick to them at the slightest contact (457). Even his wife Rosamond begins to feel "disgust" (411) and "repulsion" (434) toward him. Only once in the novel is the word "disgusting" used to describe physical filth, and this occurs in the context of an unscrupulous attempt to acquire capital: when Fred enters an "unsanitary" alleyway in hopes of "disposing advantageously of his horse" (151) for quick money in order to pay off his debts and get out of a "disgusting dilemma" (71).

Ahmed characterizes disgust as a culturally dependent response to prox-imity with an object that threatens to breach or otherwise undermine the boundaries of the individual.[4] Disgust does important cultural work, per-formatively (re)instantiating the boundaries that were threatened by the dis-gusting object by "registering [its] proximity as an offense" (85). Given this definition, we might expect the characters to feel disgust in response to some-thing like cholera—one of the key diseases that Lydgate hopes to control with his Bulstrode-funded fever hospital. Cholera literally threatens to breach the body's boundaries, entering and overtaking the body and undermining its continence. In the violence of its symptoms, cholera seems to mock our pre-sumption of individual human boundedness, coming inside the body and turning the body inside out. In this retrospective novel set during the first outbreak of cholera in England, however, Eliot almost never presents char-acters becoming disgusted by diseased bodies—by the breaching of physical boundaries or any literal undermining of the body's continence. She draws attention, instead, to the desire for and exchange of capital as the primary threat to individual boundedness and the integrity of the self. Fittingly, the binding together of Lydgate and Bulstrode is actualized in the Middlemarch public mind at a meeting held to address the first occurrence of cholera in the town. Bulstrode and Lydgate attend the meeting in hopes of controlling the physical spread of a disease that compromises individual boundaries; instead, they demonstrate the power of sticky money to undermine those very bound-aries. Lydgate's choice to "[give] his arm to Bulstrode" (450) confirms the sus-picions of the onlookers that Lydgate accepted Bulstrode's money as a bribe and eliminates any doubt that Lydgate will be "enveloped" by Bulstrode's char-acter. It is capital, not cholera, that threatens the integrity of the individual in *Middlemarch*.

Crucially, though, not everyone in Middlemarch feels the same disgust in response to people who have become "sticky" through the exchange of capital. It is, in fact, those who most desire capital themselves who most strongly feel "disgusted" or "repulsed" in response to others who compromise themselves for monetary gain. Ahmed highlights how disgust is always "deeply ambiva-lent, involving desire for, or an attraction towards, the very objects that are felt to be repellent" (84). Think, for example, of the desire to look at a grue-some injury, followed by the pulling away in disgust; only because we are

---

4. Zachary Samalin explains how Darwin's theory of disgust in *Expressions* diverges from Ahmed in that Darwin's disgust "has no objects" (128). See chapter 2 of *The Masses Are Revolt-ing* for Samalin's fascinating account of Darwin's idiosyncratic understanding of the physical disgust reaction as an evolutionary holdover from early forms of human communication.

first compelled to look are we subsequently compelled to distance ourselves. All the characters mentioned above—Bulstrode, Lydgate, Rosamond, Fred Vincy—feel the desire to accumulate material wealth in one way or another. It is this desire that puts their individual boundaries at risk and thus compels the distancing action of the disgust reaction in order to reinstantiate those boundaries. This differential disgust reaction is on display during the controversial reading of Featherstone's will, in which he bequeaths his estate to his illegitimate son, Joshua Rigg. Featherstone's many would-be legatees eye the "frog-faced" Rigg with near-universal disgust. But this response is notably absent in Caleb Garth, a man whom Eliot describes as almost compulsively uninterested in the accumulation of wealth: "Caleb's were the only eyes, except the lawyer's, which examined the stranger with more of inquiry than of disgust" (207). While Caleb is an enthusiastic businessman, "it must be remembered that by 'business' Caleb never meant money transactions, but the skillful application of labor" (341). He has "no keenness of imagination for monetary results in the shape of profit and loss" and only participates in "the many kinds of work which he could do *without handling capital*," often "declin[ing] to charge at all" for his labor (159, emphasis added). Caleb's indifference toward capital corresponds with a freedom from the disgust reaction that his neighbors feel in response to people rendered figuratively sticky and socially incontinent through their engagement in the circulation of money. His boundaries are not vulnerable in the way that those of other characters are, and thus, he does not need the corollary performative distancing of disgust to shore them up. In other words: Caleb is not drawn to capital, so he does not have to draw away from it.

I posit that Caleb serves as a model for how to engage in a slimy world without getting sticky—through an almost compulsive abnegation of personal financial gain. Both Caleb and his like-minded daughter, Mary, undergo separate trials in which they are offered money in exchange for acting on behalf of another person. For Mary, this occurs when Featherstone attempts to bribe her into privately burning his latest will just before his death. The tactless Featherstone explains his proposition in bald-faced terms, saying, "Missy . . . look here! take the money—the notes and gold—look here—take it—you shall have it all—do as I tell you" (199). Meanwhile, after Caleb Garth hears about Bulstrode's past indiscretions from Raffles and decides to give up working for him as a result, Caleb receives a somewhat similar proposition, though Bulstrode phrases it in much more guarded terms: "You would not wish to injure me by being too ready to believe a slander. . . . That is a poor reason for giving up a connection which I think I may say will be mutually beneficial" (429). Bulstrode and Featherstone both are attempting to use money to buy the Garths' agency, both offering "gold" (199) or "benefits" (430) in hopes of getting the Garths to act as their "agent" (429). Both Garths show themselves to be immune to financial temptation, rejecting the money and refusing to be recruited into the metonymic chain of sticky social contagion. They respond to the respective offers with repetitive actions of both verbal and physical rebuff. To the imploring, increasingly desperate Featherstone, Mary repeats the same basic repulsing phrase several times: "I cannot touch your iron chest or your will. . . . I will not touch your iron chest or your will. . . . I will not touch your key or your money, sir. . . . I will not touch your money. I will do anything else I can to comfort you; but I will not touch your keys or your money" (199–200). In his parallel interaction with Bulstrode, Caleb repeatedly makes a physical gesture of rebuff, putting up his hand against Bulstrode's offers and pleas; over the course of the short interaction, he is described as "making a slight gesture with his right hand" (429), "waving his hand" (430), "lifting up his hand" (430), and "lifting his hand deprecatingly" (430). In response to these resolute refusals, both Bulstrode and Featherstone are beaten into submission, with Featherstone breaking down and "cry[ing] childishly" (199) and Bulstrode "cower[ing]" before Caleb (429). Through this renunciation of monetary desire, Caleb and Mary seem to become cling-proof. They continue to do business with the individuals involved in the scandal: Caleb later arranges for Mary and her husband, Fred Vincy, to live at and manage Stone Court, the former estate of Featherstone, inherited by the illegitimate Rigg and purchased by the disgraced Bulstrode, and yet none of the scandal attached to Featherstone, Rigg, or Bulstrode gets transferred to the Garths. Nothing sticks; the Garths maintain the independence that Lydgate lost, and while Garth is able to successfully pursue his land management goals and turn Fred Vincy into a "rather distinguished" farmer at Stone Court (511), Lydgate is forced to quit Middlemarch and give up his medical reform goals, for which he "always regard[s] himself as a failure" (512).

GETTING UNSTUCK: CALEB GARTH, DOROTHEA BROOKE, AND FELIX HOLT

In her analysis of the feelings that circulate around the act of letting die, Eliot ultimately seems more concerned with the capacity of those feelings to move than with the acts that occasion them. The tragedy is not the death of Raffles; the tragedy is that the death of Raffles *sticks to Lydgate*. Eliot takes issue not with capital itself but with its capacity to act as an affective vector whose circulation puts independence of action at risk. Eliot is thus left with the problem

of how to sustain the exchange of capital without producing the affective satu-
ration that makes capital so sticky. Her solution comes in the form of characters like Caleb Garth and Dorothea Brooke, whose idealized prosocial desires
obviate the need for the mediating mechanism of capitalism's invisible hand.
Caleb and Dorothea (both of whom bear a notable emotional resemblance to
the inhabitants of Morris's postrevolutionary utopia in *News from Nowhere*)
feel a direct and passionate desire to do labor that sustains the social body,
unmediated by a self-interested desire for profit. Caleb is affectively invested
not in capital but in labor itself, speaking of it with "fervid veneration," with
"religious regard" (158). The sights and sounds of productive labor—the
"echoes of the great hammer where roof or keel were a-making, the signal-
shouts of the workmen, the roar of the furnace, the thunder and plash of the
engine"—are to him "a sublime music" and impact him like "poetry without
the aid of the poets" (158–59). He feels a passionate, almost religious desire to
"have as effective a share as possible in this sublime labor," looking at "good
practical schemes, accurate work, and the faithful completion of undertak-
ings" as his "divinities" (159). He is interested in "business" only as a generator
of material improvements for the social body—in the "indispensable might
of that myriad-headed, myriad-handed labour *by which the social body is fed,
clothed, and housed*"—and not as means of generating personal wealth (159,
emphasis added).

Dorothea shows a similar fervency of desire to help feed, clothe, and house
the social body, though her efforts are more often dismissed or frustrated than
Caleb's. He is reminded of his own ambitions when she describes hers thus:
"I should like to feel, if I lived to be old, that I had improved a great piece of
land and built a great many good cottages, because the work is of a healthy
kind while it is being done, and after it is done, men are the better for it" (341).
Dorothea and Caleb feel the same strong desire to care for the social body—to
protect it, to shelter it, to make it stronger and healthier. And as with Caleb,
Dorothea feels this not as a social obligation or a means to some other end;
she feels it as a positive desire, a personal longing. She does not feel this desire
to help in response to a suffering other in the way that John Barton or Margaret Hale does; instead, it is a constant and character-defining desire that she
feels even in the absence of any need. Upon moving to her married home of
Lowick, for example, she feels "some disappointment, of which she was yet
ashamed, that there was nothing for her to do in Lowick; and in the next few
minutes her mind had glanced over the possibility, which she would have preferred, of finding that her home would be in a parish which had a larger share
of the world's misery, so that she might have had more active duties in it" (50).
When Casaubon wonders why she "seem[s] a little sad," Dorothea admits that

she is "feeling something which is perhaps foolish and wrong . . . almost wishing that the people wanted more to be done for them here" (50). Dorothea's desire to be of use to the social body cannot be satisfied by the knowledge that her help is not presently needed, because she is not motivated by a theoretical sense of duty but rather by a deep personal longing. Neither Dorothea nor Caleb needs to be led by an "invisible hand" to "advance the interest of the society" (Smith, *Theory* 184–85); they do so of their own accord, directly led by a prosocial desire to engage in labor that supports the well-being of their communities. In a society populated by Calebs and Dorotheas, Smith's assertion that "it is not from the benevolence of the butcher, the brewer, or the baker that we expect our dinner, but from their regard to their own interest" would be null and void (*Wealth* 17). Furthermore (and crucially for Eliot), capital would no longer be sticky. In the absence of financial self-interest, capital would become a pure cipher of exchange, invested with no affect whatsoever and thus impossibly smooth. Eliminating the mediating mechanism of the invisible hand, whose input is financial self-interest and whose output is social improvement, thus also eliminates the threat of affective contagion posed by the circulation of sticky capital.

We see what this alternative model of feeling might look like in the middle-class man (in Caleb Garth) and in the formerly wealthy woman who elects to become middle-class (in Dorothea). Notably, however, we do not see what it might look like for those most likely to be allowed to die in the name of capitalism—that is, the poor. Indeed, the feelings of working-class characters barely appear in *Middlemarch*. There might be some indirect benefits for the working class in the proliferation of subjects who feel like Caleb and Dorothea: Caleb Garth will presumably be a better boss than Featherstone, and Dorothea's cottage management will certainly be superior to that of her useless uncle. But Eliot's intervention focuses, both as means and as object, on bourgeois feelings. How must bourgeois feelings change, she asks, in order to protect people like Lydgate from getting mired in capitalism's slime? Eliot's critique of necroeconomic feelings, then, follows a pattern that Carolyn Betensky identifies in the Victorian social-problem novel: it is oriented toward "bourgeois selving" rather than working-class health or well-being (4). Betensky argues that the social-problem novel produces bourgeois feeling as an end unto itself—specifically, it produces "feeling for the poor" that redeems the class and marks the sympathizing bourgeois self as deserving of sympathy without changing any of the material conditions of capitalism. I argue that, in *Middlemarch,* sympathy for the poor is in fact secondary to the renunciation of financial desire. What matters most, for the production and protection of the bourgeois self, is the elimination of the bourgeois individual's personal desire for financial gain. The elimination of that financial desire protects the bourgeois individual—not from the threat of external cross-class enmity or internal bourgeois guilt, but rather from *intra*-class metonymic slippage that threatens to compromise the autonomy upon which the fiction of the bourgeois individual rests.

But even more crucially, Eliot's intervention into capitalist feelings serves to protect the system to which the fiction of the bourgeois individual belongs: liberalism. Specifically, she attempts to resolve an inherent conflict between liberalism and capitalism or, more precisely, an internal tension within liberal capitalism. I build here upon Elaine Hadley's characterization of mid-century liberalism as a tradition that "is deeply committed to disinterest, the capacity to detach from one's own local and personal interests and think in various registers of abstraction beyond the self and that self's body: nationally, altruistically, globally" (*Living* 237). For Hadley, Victorian liberalism was not a politics of content (a particular set of opinions that liberals shared), but rather a politics of form (particular modes of coming to an opinion, expressing that opinion, and engaging with other opinions, whatever the content of those opinions might be). The liberal individual is independent of any allegiance to a collective (party, corporation, class consciousness, or otherwise) that would predetermine his stance on an issue; he practices a "principled disinterest" which is "manifested through internal devil's advocacy" (81). He is defined more by his freedom *not* to believe, not to fall into the party line, than by the positive content of his opinions.

In *Middlemarch,* Eliot shows that monetary interest threatens an individual's capacity to practice this principled disinterest. Lydgate first feels this threat when he must cast the deciding vote between Farebrother and Tyke for the chaplaincy of the infirmary. As Lydgate stews over the decision, he feels that his freedom to decide is hampered by the inevitable involvement of his own interest. Like a junior MP, his party loyalty is being tested: "He could not help hearing within him the distinct declaration that Bulstrode was prime minister, and that the Tyke affair was a question of office or no office; and he could not help an equally pronounced dislike to giving up the prospect of office" (114). Lydgate responds "defiantly" when Wrench sees his vote as a forgone conclusion (119), but he votes with Bulstrode anyway—the first step in the process of becoming Bulstrode's "party man," unfree to practice the habits of disinterest and detachment necessary to liberal individualism (112). The only way to protect an individual's access to liberalism is to become like Caleb Garth—that is, to replace individuated self-interest with a passionate desire to labor on behalf of the social body as a whole. While Lydgate is ahead of his time as a medical man—more like the professionalized, scientific doctors of the novel's composition than those of its setting—his enactment of liberal individualism is outdated. His failure sounds the alarm on rational self-interest, revealing the need for a new kind of liberal individual: one who, like Caleb, shorts the circuit of the invisible hand by "[feeling] intensely the moral and rational imperatives of the nation, the state, and the empire" (Hadley, *Living* 15). He is the model of the mid-Victorian liberal individual, whose "objectivity was presumed to be passionately embraced, [his] disinterested ideas sincerely articulated, and [his] abstracting techniques suffused with altruistic sentiment" (14). Caleb preserves the ideal of the liberal individual whose pursuit of his own authentic personal desires[5] produces the social good, but he eliminates the financial content of those desires that was so fundamental to eighteenth- and early nineteenth-century political economists. In other words, Caleb redeems the *form* of bourgeois individualism by emptying it of its capitalist content. As the model of what Hadley calls "passionate disinterest" (282), Caleb becomes a means of resolving the tension between the interest fundamental to capitalism and the *dis*interest fundamental to liberalism.

We have to look backward in Eliot's oeuvre to *Felix Holt* (1866) to see a working-class version of this character—the titular Felix, who *feels* much like Caleb and Dorothea. It is useful to examine this earlier work in the context of the affective shift that *Middlemarch* proposes because it allows us to see the implications of that shift for working-class politics. Like *Middlemarch*, *Felix Holt* is strategically retrospective, set just before the passage of the First Reform Act (1832)—a moment when England is making crucial decisions about the relationship between economic class and electoral politics. As many scholars have noted, this novel about a "radical" leans surprisingly conservative,[6] registering a profound discomfort with the expansion of the franchise to include

---

5. Eliot does suggest that abstract beliefs or theoretical intentions are insufficient motives for action; it must be authentic personal desire. Eliot illustrates this particularly in the character of Bulstrode, who struggles between his religious theories and his personal desire for money. When Eliot relates Bulstrode's personal history—his decision to become involved in a morally questionable business, his choice to cover up his knowledge of his stepdaughter in order to keep the money that would have been hers—she describes him as "a man whose desires had been stronger than his theoretic beliefs" (383). Later, when Bulstrode longs for Raffles's death but resolves not to do anything to hasten it, Eliot writes that "Bulstrode set himself to keep his intention separate from his desire" (435). Discipline and self-control do not, in *Middlemarch*, seem to offer much promise; characters like Bulstrode need to *have different desires*. Diverging from the political economists of the late eighteenth century, Eliot suggests that Bulstrode does not simply need to do a better job of placing quantitative ethical limits upon his normal desire to acquire personal wealth; rather, Bulstrode needs to replace his desire for personal wealth with a qualitatively different desire to care for the social body.

6. Raymond Williams, Catherine Gallagher, Ruth Yeazell, Rosemarie Bodenheimer, Sally Shuttleworth, and Carolyn Betensky all point up the novel's striking conservatism. There are a few critics, however, who do make an argument either for its intended but unrealized radicalism (Bruce Robbins, Stefanie Markovits) or its genuine alignment with working-class radical goals (Christopher Z. Hobson).

middle-income men. This discomfort centers around the fear that middle-income voters would be as readily "buyable" as Raffles and thus that electoral politics would be reduced to competitive bribery. This threat is actualized in the Sproxton pub owner Chubb, a man so straightforwardly driven by rational self-interest that he functions as a sort of *homo economicus*-made-flesh. Chubb "had thoroughly considered what calling would yield him the best livelihood with the least possible exertion, and . . . had prospered according to the merits of such judicious calculation," becoming "a forty-shilling freeholder" (128). He looks forward to his vote, not being "one of those mean-spirited men who found the franchise embarrassing, and would rather have been without it: he regarded his vote as part of his investment, and meant to make the best of it" (128). "Making the best" of his vote does not, of course, mean using it to bring about healthy political change or to achieve the enactment of his values. He approaches the vote with the same calculating self-interest with which he chose his profession: "There's no man more independent than me, I'll plump or I'll split for them as treat me the handsomest and are the most of what I call gentlemen; that's my idee. And in the way of hacting for any man, them are fools that don't employ me" (132). Chubb embodies a certain definition of independent citizenship in that he is self-employed, financially independent, and free from the amalgamating ties of class consciousness or political party affiliation. In practice, however, this means that Chubb is happy to become an agent for whichever politician will pay him best; his vote is a commodity for sale to the highest bidder. Financial self-interest not only informs but entirely subsumes political decision-making.

Felix Holt is the opposite of Chubb; to the same extent that Chubb is motivated by his own financial self-interest, Felix rejects financial gain as a motive. Indeed, his most defining characteristic is his propensity to act against his own financial self-interest, choosing to work as an artisan despite the access that his higher level of education could give him to the middle class. He begins the novel as a son who stops his mother from profiting from the sale of harmless but ineffective quack medicines (61), and he ends as a husband who proclaims that "he will always be poor" (476). Like an evangelical Caleb Garth, Felix not only personally rejects but also encourages others to reject both wealth and the commodities it can buy: "Let a man once throttle himself with a satin stock, and he'll get new wants and new motives. Metamorphosis will have begun at his neck-joint, and it will go on till it has changed his likings first and then his reasoning, which will follow his likings as the feet of a hungry dog follow his nose" (64–65). Felix figures wealth as not only sticky but also morbidly transformative. Luxury goods, according to Felix, work like alien slime in a science fiction movie—the slightest contact sets off a metamorphosis that reprograms desire and thought and turns a previously autonomous individual into a sort of consumerist zombie—and as such, he refuses to touch them as decisively as Mary Garth refused to touch Featherstone's money. Because of this, Felix is as difficult to buy as Chubb is easy. Harold Transome's unscrupulous election manager Jermyn is frustrated by the inconvenience posed by Felix, "whom he knew very well by Trebian report to be a young man with so little of the ordinary Christian motives as to making an appearance and getting on in the world, that *he presented no handle to any judicious and respectable person who might be willing to make use of him*" (185, emphasis added). His abdication of financial self-interest makes him impossible to instrumentalize and enables genuinely independent action, thus making him worthy of the franchise in a way that Eliot suggests someone like Chubb is not.

Indeed, Felix presages the feelings of Morris's utopians when he argues in favor of every man working "in the way he's best fit for" (435). Richard Hammond (Morris's mouthpiece in *News from Nowhere*) similarly argues for the value of allowing "the freedom for every man to do what he can do best" (123); he marks the beginning of utopia as the point at which "people found out what they were fit for, and gave up attempting to push themselves into occupations in which they must needs fail" (104). Unlike Morris's futurians, however, Felix develops these utopian feelings absent any actual political or economic change. In fact, Felix seems to want to bring about the same change in others *instead of* (or at least before) working toward political change. He tells Esther:

> I don't mean to be illustrious, you know, and make a new era, else it would be kind of you to get a raven and teach it to croak "failure" in my ears. Where great things can't happen, I care for very small things, such as will never be known beyond a few garrets and workshops. And then, as to one thing I believe in, I don't think I can altogether fail. If there's anything our people want convincing of, it is, that *there's some dignity and happiness for a man other than changing his station.* That's one of the beliefs I choose to consecrate my life to. (435; emphasis added)

Morris would certainly agree with Felix's proposition that there should be dignity and happiness in a laboring life. But Morris makes this argument in the context of a postrevolution utopia in which both capitalism and class have been eliminated; everyone can do what they are best fit for and live in the same state of plenitude. The same is not true of Felix's world. If someone is best fit for manual labor, that person is going to live in materially inferior conditions compared to someone who happens to be "fit for" law or finance. While Morris will argue for everyone engaging in whatever form of labor they are most fit for *on the condition of the elimination of class hierarchy,* Felix essentially ends up arguing for working-class acceptance of class hierarchy.

The conservative impulse of Felix's thinking becomes more explicit in the "Address to Working Men" that Eliot writes in his voice in 1868. As Carolyn Betensky and others point out, the purported audience of the address could not be much further from its actual readership; published in the Tory-leaning, decidedly bourgeois *Blackwood's Edinburgh Magazine,* the address was highly unlikely to reach more than the odd handful of actual working-class readers (Betensky 139–40). Nor would, I speculate, working-class readers have found much to enjoy in the essay, as Felix essentially blames the working classes for "the general state of the country,"[7] calls their wisdom and virtue into question, and describes the poor who are led into vice by a "too craving body" as "the hideous margin of society" (492). He goes on to urge working men to use their newfound franchise for "general good" and not for "Class Interests" (489, 491). Indeed, the essay largely becomes an argument for the necessity of class hierarchy. He attempts to persuade his imaginary working-class reader that

> the only safe way by which society can be steadily improved and our worst evils reduced, is not by any attempt to do away directly with the actually existing class distinctions and advantages, as if everybody could have the same sort of work, or lead the same sort of life (which none of my hearers would be stupid enough to suppose), but by the turning of Class Interests into Class Functions or duties. What I mean is, that each class should be urged by the surrounding conditions to perform its particular work under strong pressure of responsibility to the nation at large; that our public affairs

---

7. He says that working men must not be "very wise nor very virtuous" because

> any nation that had within it a majority of men—and we are the majority— possessed of much wisdom and virtue would not tolerate the bad practices, the commercial lying and swindling, the poisonous adulteration of goods, the retail cheating, and the political bribery which are carried on boldly in the midst of us. A majority has the power of creating a public opinion. We could groan and hiss before we had the franchise: if we had groaned and hissed in the right place, if we had discerned better between good and evil, if the multitude of us artisans, and factory hands, and miners, and labourers of all sorts, had been skillful, faithful, well-judging, industrious, sober—and I don't see how there can be wisdom and virtue anywhere without those qualities—we should have made an audience that would have shamed the other classes out of their share in the national vices. We should have had better members of Parliament, better religious teachers, honester tradesmen, fewer foolish demagogues, less impudence in infamous and brutal men . . . I say, it is not possible for any society in which there is a very large body of wise and virtuous men to be as vicious as our society is. (485–86)

should be got into a state in which there should be no impunity for foolish or faithless conduct. (491)

His argument seems to be for the preservation of an existing class hierarchy, altered only in the feelings of its constituents, who are now motivated to work by their responsibility toward the general good rather than by financial self-interest.

Perhaps surprisingly, this includes the preservation of privilege for the upper classes. Felix claims that they hold the "treasure of knowledge, science, poetry, refinement of thought, feeling, and manners" (494) and thus must not be "robbed of the chances by which they may be influential and pre-eminent" (495), nor should working-class voters (whose power he greatly overestimates) "stop too suddenly any of the sources by which their leisure and ease are furnished" (495). He argues in favor of "the great law of inheritance," claiming that working-class people who question the premise of intergenerational wealth are "just as bigoted, just as narrow, just as wanting in that religion which keeps an open ear and an obedient mind to the teachings of fact" as upper-class people who argue against the expansion of the franchise (499). While some have seen Felix of the novel and Felix of the address as different speakers with different politics, I would argue that the novel displays a similar commitment to preserving an existing class hierarchy. The only revolution we get in this novel is Esther Lyons's transformation from aspiring member of a leisure class to "dignified and happy" member of the lower-middle class, which Eliot describes as a "revolutionary struggle" (464). Not only does she reject Harold Transome's offer of marriage, but she also gives up her rightful claim to the Transome estate, allowing the Transomes to maintain their upper-class position and privilege. The "revolutionary" goal here is not improving the lives of the working classes; it is not even establishing sympathy for the working class. The goal is renunciation itself: the establishment of Esther as an individual who is free from financial desire and thus as a match for Felix, "the person of means who has chosen not to be a person of means" (Betensky 142). The risk of class upheaval is neutralized by Esther's newfound rejection of capitalist desire; order is restored through the enlightenment of the middle-class subject, and the Transomes return, emotionally chastened but materially unchanged, to their upper-class home.

We are left with Felix and Esther, members of an elective working class who have proven themselves deserving of the franchise by renouncing any desire for social mobility or, I would argue, radical social change. Committed to a working-class identity but devoid of capitalist self-interest, they represent the promise of a stable, continuous, nondisruptive transition to a post–Reform Act era of increasingly inclusive political representation. Social commentators in the earlier Victorian period deliberately sought to instill financial self-interest in Britain's working classes; they criticized and feared an unmanageable pauper class that was not motivated by a normativized desire for social mobility.[8] But as the franchise expands to include voters with less and less wealth, that financial self-interest becomes dangerous: explicitly, because voters will be buyable, like Chubb; implicitly, because of the threat that a working-class majority might vote as a bloc, claim real political power, and use that power to radically upend the political and economic status quo. Whether she means to do so or not (I am not making a claim about authorial intention), Eliot's depiction of Felix envisions a way to avert this problem: premise working-class political inclusion on their abdication of the financial self-interest that would make their inclusion threatening. While the depiction of Chubb seems to pit liberalism and capitalism against each other (in that his rational self-interest voids his disinterested, autonomous political decision-making), this solution ends up shoring up both. It protects the autonomous decision-making of liberalism by making null the threat of bribery at the ballot box. It simultaneously protects the economic status quo by making desire for social mobility and fitness for the franchise mutually exclusive. It offers access to middle-class rights on the condition of the renunciation of middle-class pleasures. It puts working-class citizens in a double bind: If you want to ascend to a middle-class lifestyle, then you do not deserve the voting rights that would enable you to gain the political power to do so. If you do not want middle-class pleasures, then you can have the voting rights that would enable you to gain them on the condition that you do not use them. I agree with Christopher Z. Hobson's contention that this novel differs from other social-problem novels "not because it melts the worker into a general 'culture,' but because it recognizes, as social development imperatively demanded, the end of the paternalist conception of social power and the emergence of the workers as an independent force in society"—that "Felix's aim is the improvement of the class so that it can meaningfully act in politics" (21, 27).[9] The primary substance of that "improvement," however, is an abdication of financial self-interest that functions to guard against any genuinely radical political action that would fundamentally alter existing economic hierarchies, modes of production, or systems of resource distribution. In *News from Nowhere*, William Morris will call for precisely such radical action.

---

8. See Gilbert, *Citizen's Body*.

9. Similarly, while I agree with Dermot Coleman's assessment that "Eliot is emphatic that education of the working classes must precede electoral enfranchisement," (26) I emphasize that the content of such education seems to be the eradication of any desire to upset existing class hierarchy.

NEWS FROM NOWHERE:
FEELINGS WITHOUT CAPITALISM

I began this book with its most overtly procapitalist author in Harriet Martineau; at the end, I turn to its only avowed anticapitalist in William Morris. Morris and Martineau are the most similar and, simultaneously, the most diametrically opposed of the authors I consider. Both wrote overtly political fiction intended to persuade their audiences of the correctness of a particular economic ideology; both have largely fallen out of the canon compared with the other authors represented in this study. But of course, while Martineau regarded free-market capitalism as a quasi-divine providential system, immutable and natural as life itself, Morris was a revolutionary socialist who actively worked toward the global overthrow of capitalism. Born in 1834 to a wealthy middle-class family, Morris first became known as a poet and textile artist associated with medieval revivalism and linked with the pre-Raphaelite brotherhood (particularly through Dante Gabriel Rosetti). He experienced his political epiphany a bit later in life than Martineau but took to his cause with just as much evangelical enthusiasm. He very publicly declared himself a socialist in a controversial lecture at Oxford's University College on November 14, 1883, in which he rallied undergraduates to look beneath "outside appearance of order in our plutocratic society" to see the "mangled bodies" that "competitive commerce" produces—all while the Oxford Masters, who expected an academic lecture on the role of art in democracy, looked on aghast (MacCarthy 478). By the time he wrote *News from Nowhere* in 1890, he had become a central figure in the British Socialist movement: first as an influential member of the Social Democratic Federation and subsequently as the reluctant leader of the Socialist League and editor of the League's newspaper, *Commonweal*, after a schism within the former group. Frustrated by the political infighting that plagued the movement he had previously invested with such hope, Morris escaped to *News from Nowhere,* a postrevolutionary dreamworld in which the contagious sympathy and radical inclusivity that Gaskell and Dickens just began to imagine is fully and effortlessly realized.

Compared to the authors studied in previous chapters, Morris raises the stakes on capitalist feelings. He shares, for example, Gaskell's concern about how necroeconomic capitalism works to reshape, reroute, or pervert human beings' natural feelings. But Gaskell was specifically concerned with sympathy, illuminating how capitalism interferes with a natural, embodied impulse to care that threatens its operative mode of exploitation. Morris is concerned with feelings writ large—all our pleasures, desires, intimacies, and fears. For Morris, capitalism intervenes at the level of human nature itself. When Guest claims that "political strife [is] a necessary result of human nature," Hammond replies, "What human nature? The human nature of paupers, of slaves, or slave-holders, or the human nature of wealthy freemen? Which?" (118). Morris here rejects outright the concept of a fixed, ahistorical, apolitical human nature. In his view, there is no universal human nature that can be abstracted from historical and material conditions and taken as the premise upon which political claims are founded. Human nature, rather, is a product of political, historical, and material conditions. Human feelings and desires are fundamentally malleable, shaped by the political and (most importantly to Morris) economic systems in which they circulate and function as operative parts. Human nature as abstract universal given, then, is a fiction used to entrench a particular political order and make other political formations unthinkable.

Yet even as Morris suggests that all human desires are contingent, he insists that capitalism and communism have fundamentally different relationships to that contingency. He insists that global capitalism—which his fictional mouthpiece Hammond, following Marx, refers to as "the World-Market"—is defined by its foundational need to produce new and insatiable desires. Essentially, Morris characterizes nineteenth-century industrial capitalism as an apparatus for producing an ever-increasing stock of wares that no one necessarily wants—"wares made to sell and not to use" (126)—and then producing consumers who want them. The goods come first; the desires are produced retroactively, in response to the need to sell the goods. He argues that capitalism is, at its core, a "vicious circle" (121) of boundless, indiscriminate production that produces "a never-ending series [of] sham or artificial necessaries" (124). Rich and poor alike are "cast into the jaws of this ravening monster," forced to toil endlessly and live in or among squalor to support the "dire necessity of 'cheap production' of things, a great part of which were not worth producing at all" (124). This last clause is crucial to Morris's understanding of desire under capitalism. A system that produces an enormous amount of worthless goods must also produce consumers who are willing to buy those goods, or else it will fail. The production of historically contingent, "artificial" desires is thus at the very heart of the operation of capitalism.

Indeed, Hammond describes the morbidly transformative effects of capitalism on human society in much the same way that Felix Holt described those of luxury goods on an individual. Hammond zooms way out, characterizing capitalism as a virus or parasite that infects human civilization as a whole, hijacking our desires and making us destroy our own lives in order to reproduce itself ad infinitum. Morris seems to agree with Eliot's depiction of capital as a sticky, disgusting object—but he implies that in a capitalist society, it has already touched everything. Everything is already covered with goo. The individual does not have the capacity to, like Felix, simply opt out through emotional self-management. Hammond describes capitalism as a systemic "infestation"—and not just a domestic infestation but an invasive species that spreads itself across the globe (126).[10] In a scathing critique of British imperialism, Morris characterizes nineteenth-century imperial conquest as the natural outgrowth of this domestic infestation:

> The appetite of the World-Market grew with what it fed on: the countries within the ring of "civilization" (that is, organised misery) were glutted with the abortions of the market, and force and fraud were used unsparingly to "open up" countries outside that pale. This process of "opening up" is a strange one to those who have read the professions of the men of that period and do not understand their practice; and perhaps shows us at its worst the great vice of the nineteenth century, the use of hypocrisy and cant to evade the responsibility of vicarious ferocity. When the civilised World-Market coveted a country not yet in its clutches, some transparent pretext was found—the suppression of a slavery different from and not so cruel as that of commerce; the pushing of a religion no longer believed in by its promoters; the "rescue" of some desperado or homicidal madman whose misdeeds had got him into trouble amongst the natives of the "barbarous" country—any stick, in short, which would beat the dog at all. Then some bold, unprincipled, ignorant adventurer was found (no difficult task in the days of competition), and he was bribed to "create a market" by breaking up whatever traditional society there might be in the doomed country, and by destroying whatever leisure or pleasure he found there. He forced wares on the natives which they did not want, and took their natural products in "exchange," as this form of robbery was called, and thereby he "created new wants," to supply which (that is, to be allowed to live by their new masters) the hapless, helpless people had to sell themselves into the slavery of hopeless toil so that they might have something wherewith to purchase the nullities of "civilisation." (125)

The purpose of colonialism is, in Morris's view, the expansion of the market; any nationalistic, cultural, or religious justification for British intervention in other nations is just "transparent pretext" to forcibly induct new consumers into the compulsively productive machine of capitalism. Both domestically and imperially, capitalism is a virus that works by "creating new wants" in

---

10. Zachary Samalin cites Morris as an example of a paradoxical trend in Victorian discourse to characterize the expression of disgust toward the conditions of modern civilization as evidence of one's civilized nature. Being "civilized," in other words, means being disgusted by civilization. See Samalin 12–16.

the people it infects. Thus, while Morris expresses the contingency of human desires, he is not suggesting that the desires produced by capitalism and communism (or other systems) are equally contingent. He posits, rather, that capitalism is founded upon that very contingency; it is only through the endless, pathological production of artificial desires that capitalism can sustain and reproduce itself.

Morris thus highlights the premise of this project: that a purportedly laissez-faire system of capitalism cannot actually just let things alone. It may present itself as passive on the surface, but like the proverbial duck, it is paddling like hell underneath. Morris shows that capitalism not only demands excessive labor to produce (in his view, too many) goods; it also requires an enormous investment of energy to maintain itself as a system. Getting people to labor under unpleasant conditions takes work; producing the "sham" desire to buy the goods produced by those workers takes work; preventing workers from rising up against their masters takes work. Communism still requires some quantity of the first category of work: farms must be sown and goods produced, although the people of Morris's utopia have done without anything that was "too disagreeable or troublesome" to produce (127). But Morris suggests that communism requires a lot less of the second category of work. Producing the kinds of subjects that can sustain Morris's agrarian anarcho-communism, which is not invested in the compulsive production of new wants, requires substantially less deployment of power than producing the subjects invested with the "sham" feelings necessary for the sustainment of capitalism. In making this comparison, Morris implicitly rejects a fundamental claim of nineteenth-century advocates of laissez-faire ideology: that the free market is a self-regulating, low-maintenance system that works best when left alone. While followers of Adam Smith disagree about his position on regulation— significantly enough that Alan Greenspan can cite Smith as the legitimating source for the claim that state regulation of the market can never work at the same time sociologist Giovanni Arrighi claims that Smith forecasts the necessity of state control of the market to protect against financial crisis[11]—it remains true today that most people associate communism with "big government," assuming that any communist system will necessarily require a higher level of state intervention to motivate, discipline, and subdue its people than its capitalist counterpart. Morris (following Marx) unequivocally disputes this. For him, capitalism is compulsively high maintenance, requiring the continual deployment of state power to discipline workers, produce consumers, and open up new markets. He echoes this sentiment in his political writing; in the

11. See Hill and Montag 1–5; see also Arrighi.

"Statement of Principles" he penned for the Hammersmith Socialist Society, he claims that a capitalist society "cannot be stable; it holds within itself the elements of its own dissolution; and it can only go on existing by the repression by force and fraud of all serious and truthful thought and all aspirations for betterment" (*Collected Letters* 490). His communism, on the other hand, is so self-sustaining that it quickly makes the state obsolete and allows state power to die out. In the anarcho-communist society that Morris imagines will arise after global revolution, there are no nation-states and no state as such.

In referring to Morris's version of communism as "anarchic," I am affiliating him with a term that he would not have claimed in his own lifetime. Although Morris had many anarchist friends and even bailed some out of jail,[12] he was skeptical of their methods and did not refer to himself as an anarchist. Biographers and critics disagree somewhat about Morris's feelings about anarchism; E. P. Thompson characterizes him as a textbook Marxist, while Fiona MacCarthy highlights both his intellectual sympathy and "warm personal friendship" with the "leading London Anarchists" of the late 1880s and 1890s (MacCarthy 543). My position is that Morris sought to distance himself from his anarchist friends because he disagreed with their means; his desired end, however, is a fundamentally anarchic form of communism. When Morris wrote *News from Nowhere* in 1890, his life had been consumed for over a decade by debate and infighting among British Socialists about the best means to bring about a socialist revolution. As the treasurer and de facto leader of the Socialist League, Morris was at the center of an ongoing, heated debate between the parliamentarians, who wanted to work on more incremental reform (and who ultimately won out and were influential in the formation of the Labour Party), and the anarchists, who wanted to use more violent and disruptive tactics. The League split in 1884 with the parliamentarian-led Social-Democratic Federation (SDF) in dramatic fashion over this same debate (MacCarthy 493–505). Morris was not particularly comfortable with either branch of the movement. He was "vehemently anti-Parliament"; he viewed the legislature as irredeemably corrupt and thought that genuine change from "within the institution" was impossible (MacCarthy 493). But he was also very uncomfortable, on both moral and strategic grounds, with the disruptive and sometimes violent tactics to which his anarchist friends tried

---

12. After the harsh sentencing of the Walsall Anarchists on dubious evidence that they had manufactured a bomb, Morris's former collaborators Charles Mowbray and David Nicoll were arrested for publishing an article that appeared to encourage violence against the judge in the case. Morris bailed out Mowbray and later wrote a letter in support of the Walsall Anarchists, several of whom he also knew personally. He also later gave evidence on behalf of Tom Cantwell when he was arrested on suspicion of "soliciting the murder of members of the royal family" (MacCarthy 641–42).

to urge him;[13] he disliked violence and believed that it would alienate potential socialist converts and turn public opinion against the cause.[14] Morris preferred activism via persuasion; he devoted his almost superhuman energy (and much of his own money) to giving public lectures, writing articles, and editing and producing *Commonweal,* the newspaper of the Socialist League. Ultimately, he was pushed out of one of those activities—editing *Commonweal*—by his anarchist comrades in the League, who saw him as too conciliatory (Mac-Carthy 581).

But *News from Nowhere* is not really about the means. The novel is quite literally constructed as an imaginative escape from the sordid debates about strategy that dogged Morris's real life during this period. Just as Morris himself would frequently have done, the narrator who comes to be known as William Guest muses "discontentedly and unhappily" over a frustrating day of contentious debate at a meeting of the Hammersmith Socialist Society, at which "there were six persons present, and consequently six sections of the party were represented, four of which had strong but divergent Anarchist opinions" (43). He wishes, as Morris certainly wished, that he could just "see a day of" the future society that they were laboring to produce (44). *News from Nowhere* is the fulfillment of that wish—to leapfrog the messy question of means and jump straight to the fulfillment of the ends. While Morris briefly addresses the means when Old Hammond recollects the painful past to an eager Guest, this novel is about what the world will look like after the dust settles. And Morris makes it clear that the state does not have a role in that new world. While he expressed skepticism about (violent) anarchism as a strategy to be utilized en route to the revolution, he makes clear in *News from Nowhere* that the post-revolutionary communist society he (like Marx) envisions as an end goal of that revolution is fundamentally stateless.

Nation-states no longer exist, in name or in fact, in the world that Morris imagines in *News from Nowhere*. While different regions still vary in architectural styles, cuisine, and "amusements," the people of Morris's utopia have done away with "the whole system of rival and contending nations" (117).

---

13. By the late 1880s, the Anarchist contingent in the Socialist League was pushing Morris to shift the goals of the group toward violent revolution. He says: "The Anarchist element in us seems determined to drive things to extremity and break us up if we do not declare for anarchy; which I for one will not do" (qtd. in MacCarthy 578).

14. He wrote in *Justice* in 1894 that acts of violence are "criminal because inexpedient and stupid, and criminal in as much as they are attacks on people who are personally innocent, and are as destructive and harmful out of all proportion to any possible good they might produce" (qtd. in MacCarthy 642); "I cannot for the life of me see how such principles, which propose the abolition of compulsion, can admit of promiscuous slaughter as a means of converting people" (545).

Morris insists, though, that nineteenth-century capitalism had *already* made nations meaningless. Capitalist exploitation of workers nullifies the protections of nationhood and makes citizenship into another "sham." Hammond illustrates this to Guest by imagining the effects of a French conquest of England. The English masters, he claims, already "took from their workmen as much of their livelihood as they dared" (110). If the French took over, they could "not have taken more still from the English workmen" because "in that case the English workmen would have died of starvation; and then the French conquest would have ruined the French, just as if the English horses and cattle had died of under-feeding. So that after all, the English workmen would have been no worse off for the conquest: their French masters could have got no more from them than their English masters did" (110). Hammond's thought experiment here suggests that national identity is meaningless to working-class people under the conditions of free-market capitalism. The exact same amount of surplus value will be extracted from them—that is, the maximum amount that can be extracted without killing them and thus losing their utility as workers—regardless of the national identity of the ruling class. Interestingly, in making this argument, Morris comes the closest he ever does to agreeing with his capitalist opponents. That is, he accepts the truth of their claim that people (at least people in power) *will* act according to their own rational self-interest—because of course, these imaginary French conquerors could just murder everyone. If they were motivated by pure jingoistic enmity, they could simply ravage England, perhaps grab a few valuables, and return to France. But Morris assumes they will not, because they will follow their own financial self-interest to keep the workers alive and extract surplus value from them. In this sense, Morris engages in the same methodology that Marx does in volume 1 of *Capital*; in David Harvey's words, Marx takes the "theories of the classical political economists seriously and ask[s] what kind of world would emerge if they got to implement their utopian liberal vision of perfectly functioning markets, personal liberty, private property, and free trade" (285). In practice, of course, this is not the case. Hammond's illustration assumes that all capitalists will exploit their workers in precisely the same way and to precisely the same extent, as established by the laws of a free market. It ignores any difference between economic regulation or workers' protections across nations; more crucially, it disregards entirely the unique exploitation of workers under conditions of imperial violence and slavery. Much as the novel itself is set in a communist utopia, Hammond's anecdote is set in a capitalist utopia. In essence, Morris shows that the logical end of the most perfect implementation of free-market capitalism, in which markets are fully unregulated and individuals act according to rational financial self-interest, is the destruction of any meaningful form of nationhood. Nationhood is nullified by free-market capitalism to precisely the same extent that the market is what classical political economists aim for it to be.

Capitalism also makes nationhood meaningless for the rich—but that does not stop them from capitalizing on the appearance of national conflict for profit. While their countries are at war, rich men on different sides "gamble with each other pretty much as usual, and even [sell] each other weapons wherewith to kill their own countrymen" (110). These men are driven solely by rational financial self-interest; any proclaimed investment in nationalism is a strategic sham, used to create the conditions for opportunistic stock trading and profiteering. State power is exercised in an international arena, but it is exercised transnationally on behalf of the interests of capital. Following Marx, Morris claims that the state exists for no "other purpose than the protection of the rich from the poor, the strong from the weak" (109). In other words, state power functions in service of class interests (the protection of the rich from the poor) rather than in service of national interests or sovereignty (e.g., the protection of the English from the French). In nineteenth-century England, state power *is* capitalist power. It follows, then, that Morris envisions a global workers' revolution that will eliminate not only capitalism, but also the state itself. For Morris, these are two parts of the same goal. To him, state power's essential purpose is to maintain inequality. There is thus no place for the state in the society he imagines in *News from Nowhere,* which is founded on the "complete equality" of all its members—a condition which is, according to Morris's future dwellers, the "the bond of all happy human society" (200). The futurians have methods for making collective decisions—through informal debate and consensus-building in a "Mote," based on the ancient Norse traditions that so fascinated Morris—but they have no nation, no state, and according to Morris, no politics. Hammond tells Guest, "We are very well off as to politics,—because we have none" (116). In his explanation, he defines "politics" in two ways. First, he rejects tribalistic party politics, claiming that "differences of opinion about real solid things need not, and with us do not, crystallize people into parties permanently hostile to one another, with different theories as to the build of the universe and the progress of time" (117). He goes on, however, to claim that these apparent "serious difference[s] of opinion" were always a smoke-and-mirrors game to distract the public from the exploitation of capitalism. He claims that "the masters of politics" strategically used the "*pretence* of serious difference of opinion" in order to "cajole or force the public to pay the expense of a luxurious life . . . for a few cliques of ambitious persons" (118). Morris suggests here that if you don't have capitalist exploitation, you won't have politics. The spurious debate of party politics is merely a smoke screen—a means of distracting from and enabling exploitation. A society founded on the perfect equality of its members does not have any systemic exploitation to maintain; thus, it does not have anything Morris is willing to call "politics."

This is the world with absolutely no condition for exclusion that Dickens only just hinted at in *Bleak House*. The problem with Dickens's venture into this imagined world of radical inclusivity is, of course, that it seems to depend upon a young woman being shaped into a perfect feeling machine through the experience of childhood abuse. For both Dickens and Gaskell, more inclusive, more ethical worlds seem to be producible only by means of women's feelings: women as overworked feeling machines, called on to supplement a capitalism that blocks up other pathways of sympathy; women as products of childhood trauma who produce themselves as affective necessities because they have been told they do not deserve to live and so had better earn their place by being unfailingly loving and lovable. Margaret Hale and Esther Summerson are women created by necrocapitalism: the half-intended byproducts of a capitalism that interferes with sympathy and denies a universal human right to life and to the resources needed to sustain it. I have argued that both authors show the radical potential of these feelings to unsettle the very foundations of the system that created them. It wouldn't be the first time the unconsidered byproducts of a system were its downfall. But Morris takes a different approach. Where Dickens's solution was Esther, Morris's solution is the global overthrow of capitalism. In Morris's postrevolutionary future, there are no Margarets or Esthers. The utopian anarcho-communism that Morris imagines does not produce them as supplemental, unidirectional, unremunerated feeling machines.

Instead, it produces subjects whose emotions resemble those of Eliot's Caleb Garth, Dorothea Brooke, and Felix Holt. Like Eliot's idealized characters, the inhabitants feel a direct desire to work in ways that contribute to social well-being without any mediating mechanism. (In this case, of course, the invisible hand of capitalism is not made superfluous; it no longer exists.) When the nineteenth-century Guest hesitantly claims that "there is . . . a natural desire not to work," the twenty-first-century Hammond proclaims the "ancient platitude . . . wholly untrue; indeed, to us quite meaningless" (122). For Morris, the desire to avoid work is not natural. The feelings surrounding labor have been produced through the conditions of capitalism, which alienates workers both from their labor and from their own human essence—their "Gattungswesen," as Marx terms it. Absent these conditions in Morris's utopia, "all work is now pleasurable" (122). But this change seems to have taken place largely through a withdrawal of power rather than a deployment of it.

Hammond explains that the Britons of the future achieved this state through "the absence of artificial coercion, and the freedom for every man to do what he can do best, joined to the knowledge of what productions of labour we really want" (123). Communism shapes desires through the removal of artifice: artificial coercion to perform labor that is not truly necessary to meet artificial demand for products that do not really give pleasure or meet human needs. And while Morris, skeptical of any ahistorical claims about human nature, will not quite describe these new modes of feeling as universally "natural," he certainly claims them as both healthier and "less artificial" than their capitalist predecessors.[15]

The removal of "artifice" in Morris's utopia also makes possible the unimpeded transindividual flow of affect. While Dickens is no communist, his portrayal of Mrs. Pardiggle suggests that he would agree with Morris on at least one point: producing affective boundaries between people—boundaries that convert the suffering of others into pleasure for the self—is a lot of work. The world that Morris envisions seems to be entirely free of not only the "hard work" that Mrs. Pardiggle took such pride in performing but also the products of that compulsive labor: the felt affective borders that enable the "letting suffer" and "letting die" functions of necropolitics. In Morris's "society of equals," pain and pleasure alike travel freely between individuals and throughout communities. As Guest spends more time in this world, he begins to share in this experience. When he visits Hampton Court (still standing in Morris's future and used freely as a boarding house by travelers), he writes that the place is largely unchanged "except that the people whom we met there had an indefinable kind of look of being at home and at ease, which communicated itself to me, so that I felt that the beautiful old place was mine in the best sense of the word" (171). Guest takes note here of an affective change from his native past to this utopian future: pleasure has become communicable. The pleasure of the people around him spreads and amplifies his own pleasure. This communicable sympathy seems to extend even beyond the limits of the human.

---

15. The one exception is sexual desire. This he is willing to term "natural," for both men and women (91). Both sexual desire and sexual jealousy are, in fact, natural for Morris. But he discards other things as unnatural—for example, the obsession with women's virginity, the legal bond of marriage, and the connection between property and sex. He wholeheartedly rejects the idea that a woman's access to goods, resources, housing, and so forth would be connected to her sexual or romantic status. People do get married in Morris's utopia, but those marriages hold no legal status. "Marriage" simply refers to any long-term romantic partnership, which lasts until one or both of the parties want to leave. Insomuch as a government exists in this society, it is not involved in the administration of sexual or romantic couplings, and in the absence of private property, there are no negative financial or social consequences for ending a romantic relationship (90–93).

During the hay harvest, Dick describes how he "sympathize[s] with the year and its gains and losses" (224). He explains to a mildly confused Guest that he "can't look upon [the world] as if I were sitting in a theatre seeing the play going on before me"; rather, he feels that he is "part of it all, and feel[s] the pain as well as the pleasure in [his] own person" (225). Morris, like Gaskell, imagines here a form of sympathy that is fundamentally different from the spectatorial sympathy of Adam Smith. For Gaskell, such genuinely transindividual sympathy was a threat that capitalism had to reroute in order to neutralize. In the absence of capitalism, it flows freely through Morris's utopia. It is not simply that individuals can sympathize more readily with other individuals in this society. Much more fundamentally, affect has become radically deindividualized, ceasing to operate as a property of any individual. Much like goods and resources in this postcapitalist utopia, affect circulates freely as a shared property of the community.

Perhaps most importantly, Morris makes it clear that this radical communicability also characterizes their experience of pain. Pain, too, is shared across individuals—not through the occasional movement of sympathy but as a fundamental, constant condition of coexistence. When Guest asks if his new acquaintances have prisons in their society, Dick "flush[es] red" and responds with surprise and anger:

> Man alive! how can you ask such a question? Have I not told you that we know what a prison means by the undoubted evidence of really trustworthy books, helped out by our own imaginations? And haven't you specially called me to notice that the people about the roads and streets look happy? and how could they look happy if they knew that their neighbours were shut up in prison, while they bore such things quietly? (80)

These people could not be happy, Dick claims, if they knew that others were suffering—even if those others were out of sight. The existence of suffering others would not just tinge his experience; it would actually preclude happiness. To some extent, this empathic discomfort makes Morris's futurians similar to Felix Holt and Dorothea Brooke, neither of whom can enjoy luxuries while others are suffering. While looking at art on her honeymoon in Rome, Dorothea tells Will, "It spoils my enjoyment of anything when I am made to think that most people are shut out from it" (140). Felix echoes that sentiment when he says that "fine things . . . are not to my taste—and if they were, the conditions of holding them while the world is what it is, are such as would jar on me like grating metal" (435). But Morris leaves behind the bounded liberal individual for whose sake Eliot wanted to eliminate capitalist feelings. We saw how feelings moved in Middlemarch; they move in Morris's utopia too. But instead of being transferred metonymically between individuals, affect in utopia spreads environmentally, saturating the community as whole.

Morris suggests that this radical affective sharing acts as a powerful and sufficient guard against interpersonal cruelty and violence. In a world where suffering is unstoppably shared between people—where no boundaries exist to prevent its spread—doing harm to another must inevitably do harm to the self. The same radical sharing that Hammond says makes prisons unbearable thus also makes them unnecessary. In Dickens's depiction of Mrs. Pardiggle, we saw the cyclical, amplificatory relationship between affective boundaries and sadism: felt divisions between people enable sadism; the performance of sadism reinforces divisions between people and makes those boundaries even more strongly felt as real; the reinforcement of those boundaries then further enables sadism, and so on. This cycle is doubly impossible in Morris's utopia. His society of equals admits no fundamental difference or boundary between people, so there are no felt divisions around which to begin this process. But further, the radical affective permeability of its citizens means that the suffering of one person directly spreads to that person's neighbors and causes those neighbors suffering as well. In this imagined world of communally shared goods and communally shared feelings, the quasi-sadistic pleasures of necro-economics have become unthinkable: "In a society of equals you will not find anyone to play the part of torturer" (115). This is not to say that the citizens of Morris's utopia are incapable of antisocial feelings or interpersonal conflict. They still experience occasional violence; the novel includes an unpremeditated murder—a crime of passion, a fight caused by a rivalry over a woman—but the murderer takes no pleasure in his victim's suffering. To the contrary, he feels immediate, crushing remorse. Aside from such occasional disruptions, this society also contains a low-level hum of various negative affects and "ugly feelings"—grumpy old men who preferred the old ways and complain to their grandchildren, jealous young men who are disappointed in love, awkwardness between ex-lovers forced to meet in society, and so forth. Morris does not suggest that the success of a global anarcho-communist revolution will eradicate all antisocial inclinations and painful human emotions, nor are those feelings suppressed or discounted by the future-dwellers. But there is none of the pure cruelty that Dickens describes—no one who takes pleasure in making die. Neither is there any of the iron hardness, the affective impermeability, of Gaskell's mill owners, nor even the calculated reluctance of Martineau's Dr. Burke, who suppresses his own sympathy in favor of his economic principles. There is, in other words, no one who can stomach the feeling of letting die. Morris thus indicates that the affective capacity for letting die is not an inherent part of human nature; it has to be created, and it is created through capitalism.

This is, in my view, Morris's most foundational belief: that all human cruelty, all truly pathological human behavior, is produced by capitalism. This is the belief upon which his utopia is built. Morris rides the line between materialism and essentialism here. He doesn't quite suggest that human beings are essentially good or naturally ethical. For him, people are fundamentally responsive to the conditions under which they live; they can certainly be produced as cruel, as mercenary, as sadistic, and there doesn't seem to be anything in the human that inherently resists such production. Morris accepts that human beings are susceptible to being produced as cruel under conditions that favor it. But he does suggest that under the right material conditions, everyone can quite easily be produced as good. Once the material conditions that favor cruelty are eradicated, people will no longer be cruel. There is no fundamental or essential human impulse to cruelty. Cruelty only exists to the extent that it is produced by external systems. In this belief, Morris's view of human nature again approaches the neat simplicity of the political economists' view. For the political economists, all interest is self-interest and all selves are basically the same. Classical political economy struggles to account for desires that fall outside of the realm of rational self-interest, i.e., that do not *serve capitalism*: for queer, other-directed interest, for the death drive, for desires that seek to divest the self of possessions, for religious fervor, and so forth. Morris, meanwhile, is incapable of imagining perversions that are not *produced by capitalism*. All perversion, all murderous desire, all sadism, all enmity is produced by capitalism. Despite disagreeing categorically with them about how to organize labor and distribute resources, Morris shares with political economists an analytic gap regarding human desires and drives that exceed economic explanation. For him, this takes the form of almost completely disregarding the possibility of human pathologies that are not explained and produced by the conditions of living under capitalism.

This commitment to the belief that all human cruelty is the product of the forces of capitalism makes strategic sense for the point that Morris is trying to make—get rid of capitalism and literally every problem will be fixed—but it does result in an oversimplified and somewhat inadequate theorization of racism. Morris is, without question, the most (perhaps the only) explicitly anti-imperialist writer of those I have addressed. He is expressly opposed to the European conquest of countries outside of what he calls "the ring of 'civilisation,'" the quotation marks conveying his scorn for the specious term (125). He describes imperialism as "the great vice of the nineteenth century" and characterizes the so-called civilizing mission as a "transparent pretext" for callous exploitation (125). He flatly rejects the whole idea of European cultural or racial superiority, calling out "the White Man's Burden" as a racist lie. He even directly calls out the British government for genocidal biowarfare, condemning the deliberate sending of "blankets infected with small-pox" to American Indian tribal peoples (126). He characterizes racism and white supremacy as "shams" that people have used strategically to justify their financial greed. In characterizing white supremacy as a set of ideas dreamed up to justify economic exploitation, Morris anticipates the argument of theorists such as Ibram X. Kendi, who illuminates the economic logic that fueled the beginnings of anti-Black racism in the United States.[16] And yet, his critique of racial violence is curiously devoid of any actual theorization of race. His description of imperialism reduces racism to a mere feature of exploitative capitalism, ignoring the deep imbrication of racism and capitalism that theorists like Cedric Robinson reveal as well as the extent to which racism becomes embedded in identity and structures of feeling.[17] While Angela Davis says that "there is no capitalism without racism," she certainly does not imagine that it works the other way: that is, that eliminating capitalism, without addressing the specific structures and affective staying power of white supremacy, would eliminate racism. Racism, for Morris, is always cleanly mercenary—an excuse for the exploitation of workers. He does not consider the possibility of deeply felt, irrational racial hatred outside or even in spite of financial self-interest; in other words, he cannot imagine necropolitical pleasures that exceed necroeconomics. Resembling again his political economist opponents, he imagines racism as an expression of coldly rational financial self-interest. Thus, for Morris, the socialist revolution encompasses and subsumes antiracism: get rid of capitalism, and you will inevitably also get rid of racism.

This is, perhaps, the most utopian element of Morris's work: capitalism produces every pathology, every undesirable trait, every antisocial drive. In Morris's postcapitalist world, you might get a few people who make occasional bad decisions, a few eccentrics, a few grumps, but you will not get any deeply repulsive people or genuinely pathological behaviors. In this society founded upon universal inclusion, you don't get anyone who is genuinely hard to include. Nearly everyone is healthy, productive, well-nourished, happy, and beautiful. The men are "well-knit . . . manly and refined" (47); the women are "thoroughly healthy-looking and strong . . . all at least comely" (53) and generally "so well-looking or even so handsome" that the narrator has to hold himself back from commenting on their robust beauty to his companion and guide (61). There is no dirty street urchin covered in infested rags—no one whose body or behavior would offend the sensibilities of even the most sensitive observer—no one from whom Lady Dedlock would shrink in horror.

16. See, for example, Kendi's *Stamped from the Beginning*.
17. See Robinson's *Black Marxism* and Ioanide's *Emotional Politics of Racism*.

There is no "unfit other." This is, of course, illustrative of Morris's key point: that necrocapitalist states produce their own others, not just discursively but *materially,* prior to exploiting and excluding them. He does not simply want to *include* people like Jo but to eradicate the performative, affective, and discursive practices of "othering" upon which Jo's exclusion is founded. He wants to create a world in which the dirty, unhealthy street urchin like Jo literally does not exist, is never produced in the first place. This tracks with both Morris's larger focus on systemic exploitation and this work's place in the genre of utopian fiction, but it also provides a loophole through which Morris avoids the messiness of radical inclusivity in the present—a problem that challenged Morris in his activist career. He was, at times, frustrated and depressed by his interactions with the working classes. He does not *blame* these people for their faults; he blames capitalism (lack of good nutrition, shelter, education, the degrading effects of repetitive labor and overwork, etc.). But he still finds it challenging and uncomfortable to interact with them and bring them into his community in the present.[18] Setting this novel in a postcapitalist world, Morris can be much more enthusiastic about including their beautiful, healthy, industrious, generous, nature-loving descendants. He does not need to explain what this future society would do with "unfit" people because that society does not *produce* any unfit people. Radical inclusivity *is* the goal, but it is premised on the accomplishment of a revolution that will eradicate most of the attributes that make people hard to include.

In other words, Morris's blueprint for inclusivity is not sacrificial in the way that Esther's is—or at least it will not be once it is complete. Utopian as Morris might be about the behavior and feelings of human beings under postrevolution communism, he is bluntly realistic about the rocky process of revolution itself. Old Hammond describes years of "strikes and lock-outs and starvation," public protests met with police violence, a general strike that brings society to a standstill, and an unprovoked military massacre of peaceful protestors that sparks a civil war (133). Morris frames those who took part in this revolution in terms of sacrifice; Hammond interrupts his tale to stand and proclaim, "Drink this glass to the memory of those who died there, for

18. In the detailed diary he kept at the beginning of 1887, for example, he frequently describes his frustration and disappointment after speaking engagements with working-class audiences. Some audiences, he complains, are outright "dull" (557), and he questions whether even the most attentive audiences understand him. Years into his activist career, he still seems to feel some culture shock during his interactions with working-class people, stating that the "frightful ignorance and want of impressibility of the average English workman floors me at times" (25 Jan., qtd. in MacCarthy 555). In Fiona MacCarthy's accounting, this feeling of intransigent class difference contributes to Morris's difficulty in "establishing a genuine rapport with the working class as individuals" (559).

indeed it would be a long tale to tell how much we owe them" (145). That is to say, Morris's plan for radical inclusion involves sacrifice, but with a different temporality and orientation than the radical inclusion for which Esther metonymically stands. Morris's preferred sacrifice is not inclusive contact in spite of the risk of interpersonal contagion; it is protest and revolution in spite of the risk of state violence. For Dickens, inclusion seems to inherently demand sacrifice; to include is to put oneself at risk. Morris imagines a world in which inclusion need not require sacrifice. He explicitly blames economic systems (and the political systems that are, for him, merely capitalism's henchmen) for producing the pathologies that make inclusion both difficult and dangerous. His solution, then, starts with the eradication of that system. From that starting point, he goes on to imagine how human bodies, feelings, and communities would be reshaped in capitalism's absence. Morris's blueprint might be summarized as follows: in order to change feelings in the future, you have to change systems in the present.

The characters that Morris and Eliot imagine in the works discussed in this chapter are all anachronistic. William Guest travels forward to a communist utopia; Caleb, Felix, and Dorothea resemble residents of that utopia, travelling backward to a capitalist past to confuse the Middlemarchers and Trebians with their lack of financial self-interest in the same way that Morris's future-dwellers confuse Guest. The similarity of these characters from these two very different authors makes sense in that Eliot and Morris yearn for the same thing: the achievement of a mutualistic community populated by individuals who are motivated to work by direct, deeply felt desire, unmediated by the corrupting exchange of capital. They are both highly attuned to the threat posed by the feelings that circulate around and through capital; they both want to eliminate those feelings—but they differ with regard to whether they view those feelings as the cause or the effect, the horse or the cart. For Morris, feelings are an effect of material conditions; in *News from Nowhere,* he envisions how eliminating capitalism might change social modes of feeling within a community. For Eliot, feelings come first. She imagines characters who have undergone the same emotional transformation that, for Morris's characters, takes place over several generations and only after a global workers' revolution—but for Eliot's characters, that transformation takes place independent of and as a precondition for political change. The emotional transformation *is* Eliot's revolution. Discussing *Middlemarch,* John Kucich states that "Eliot makes general melioration a wishful by-product of the self-reflexive transformation of the private individual" (135). I would go even further: in *Felix Holt,* Eliot makes political inclusion and subsequent change *contingent* upon a prior self-reflexive transformation of the private individual.

Considered together, these authors add a crucial perspective to the story of necroeconomic feelings that I have been tracing in this project, reminding us why it is so important to examine how feelings interact with the material conditions in which they emerge. The authors I read in this book all consider, in different ways, feeling's relationship to systems of material inequality. Both Martineau and Gaskell focus on the disruptive power of transindividual feeling: for Martineau, this is a problem to suppress, while for Gaskell, it holds the potential to be marshaled toward the reshaping of capitalism. They share the assumption, though, that there is no pleasure in necroeconomics. This changes in Dickens. While he, too, shows disruptive potential in transindividual affect, he also highlights how necroeconomic pleasure can calcify boundaries and facilitate inequality; feelings can support capitalism just as readily they disrupt it. We see this even more starkly in Eliot's novels, in which apparently anticapitalist feelings get folded back into capitalism in a way that neutralizes their threatening potential. In *Middlemarch* and *Felix Holt,* capitalism digests its own resistance. My aim in pointing this out (as I hope is clear) is not to condemn perhaps the greatest novelist of all time for being insufficiently progressive or for failing to solve the impossible problem of how to live under capitalism. Rather, my goal is to highlight the Victorian origins of the "convergence" Brian Massumi identifies between "the dynamic of capitalist power and the dynamic of resistance" (21). The line is blurred between the feelings that support capitalism and those that resist it, as the renunciation of the affective attachments that capitalism demands ends up neutralizing the possibility of meaningful working-class political action. Capitalism is affectively opportunistic; it can co-opt the very feelings that seem to be its antithesis. Reading Eliot simultaneously illuminates capitalism's flexibility and affirms the Victorian novel's place in the project of "render[ing] cognitively visible the discursive movements of the invisible hand" (Reber 46). Morris, conversely, affirms the Victorian novel's place in rendering narratively visible the world that might exist outside the grasp of the invisible hand of capitalism. He uses the utopian novel as a methodology for thinking through how we could restructure economies to better meet the material as well as the affective needs of human beings. Whereas Martineau took the principles of the free market as first premises and then worked to engineer feelings accordingly, Morris asks what social structures might look like if we started by imagining what kinds of feelings we wanted them to make possible. Following this methodology, Morris ends up with a society that has freed itself of the problem of letting die.

AFTERWORD

Our Necroeconomic Present

On January 12, 2017, a young-adult novelist named Lauren Morrill tweeted, "My biggest problem in these ACA [Affordable Care Act] debates? I don't know how to explain to you why you should care about other people." Her message received nearly forty thousand "likes" and was retweeted by over twenty thousand Twitter users, prompting the relatively unknown writer to temporarily shut down her account while she dealt with tens of thousands of unexpected notifications and emails. Since then, Morrill's pithy quotation has taken on a life of its own. Six months after the original tweet, Kayla Chadwick used Morrill's (uncredited) tweet as a title for a *Huffington Post* op-ed, further popularizing the quotation and detaching it from its source. Thousands of Twitter users have retweeted it, often in response to right-wing politicians and pundits who oppose robust social safety nets or, more recently, mask mandates, vaccines, or lockdowns amid the COVID-19 pandemic. In an unusually innocuous manifestation of the disinformation machine that is social media, hundreds of Instagram users began attributing the quotation to Dr. Anthony Fauci, chief medical advisor to the president and face of the medical response to the COVID-19 pandemic, in June 2020, although he has never said it publicly (Spencer). This tweet even has its own merch. A quick search of Etsy or TeePublic will turn up dozens of T-shirts, buttons, mugs, face masks, and handmade cross-stitches depicting the quotation, often listing Dr. Fauci as the source. Searching in December 2022, I could not find any items for sale that correctly attributed the quotation to Morrill.

The viral afterlife of the tweet can be attributed to a lot of things: the satisfying simplicity of the quotation, the brevity with which it recasts political policy as fundamental ethical breach, and, of course, its affirming power to mark the person who shares it as ethically "correct" in opposition to its target. But I would argue that the quotation has taken root in part because it points to a real strategic problem for left-leaning politics, from mainstream liberal policies (such as mask mandates) to more radical leftist projects (such as prison abolition). Armed only with the tools of rational debate, it is hard to argue that someone should feel empathy for someone they do not already empathize with or that someone should put themselves at risk for the sake of someone to whom they do not already feel a sense of ethical responsibility. It is very difficult to *explain why* we believe what we believe about ethical responsibility in a community. Such convictions about our responsibility to others—about what community I am a part of, about who is included in that community, about who I have to care about and who I need to be scared of, about whose health matters and who is a threat to my health—these convictions are held close to the body, in a place that "argument" or "explanation" often cannot access. Opposing arguments register as visceral affronts, and conversation fails. Morrill is right: it is really hard to persuade someone into empathy. While her tweet does not offer much to arm us in that challenge (and its afterlife as ready-made Twitter comeback and merchandising slogan offers even less), I believe that Victorian novels offer more.

Written as laissez-faire capitalism became embedded in British culture as a secular providentialism, Victorian novels highlight how these feelings have been part of the mechanics of necrocapitalism from its very beginning. How people feel about other people's suffering matters, and has always mattered, for capitalism; these novels provide insight into why. Martineau and Gaskell show how the feelings produced when the market demands death present a sticking point that puts stress on capitalism's internal logic, threatening its claim to naturalness and moral goodness. Dickens offers a crucial reminder that witnessing the suffering of another under capitalism does not necessarily produce empathetic investment; it can, just as readily, produce pleasure. And perhaps most crucially, reading Eliot and Morris together reminds us that caring about another person's suffering does not necessarily produce anticapitalist action—and indeed, that compassion can be rerouted to buoy capitalism itself. These novels provide a literary laboratory in which we can observe how the feelings that circulate around scenes of letting die work for or against necroeconomics. What kinds of interactions with and orientations toward the other produce sympathy, and which produce apathy? Which produce hatred and sadistic pleasure? And just as crucially, how do those feelings translate (or not) into political action? How can "good feelings" get neutralized—be made to stymie action or excuse inaction? Or more insidiously, how do they get co-opted, rerouted to serve the oppressive systems whose effects provoked them? I refer here not just to "desensitization" or compassion fatigue—that is, to feeling *less* in response to suffering due to overexposure—but also to processes by which intense feelings in response to the suffering of another might be mobilized to produce political effects that actually heighten that suffering. In examining Victorian novels, we can see the history of this mobilization. Reading these novels gives us tools with which to evaluate emotion's role in both the operation of and resistance against necrocapitalism. It also gives us a healthy skepticism of simplistic explanations of feeling (especially sympathetic feeling) as naturally and necessarily anticapitalist. This literature helps us examine in a more nuanced way the multidirectional circuit between feelings and politics: between what I feel when I see someone suffer or die; what those feelings make me open to, skeptical of, or vulnerable to; and how that changes me as a political subject and actor.

Nearly 150 years after Morris dreamed of utopia in *News from Nowhere*— and more than 75 years after he imagined it coming to fruition—our world feels no closer to his egalitarian vision. The COVID-19 pandemic brought capitalism's death function to the surface as some politicians, such as Texas lieutenant governor Dan Patrick, explicitly claimed that elders should be willing to sacrifice their lives for the economy—and many more implicitly demanded the same of low-wage workers in industries such as food processing, transit, and retail. Diabetics die because they cannot afford insulin; uninsured Americans face bankruptcy as a side effect of cancer; pharmaceutical company executives bring home multimillion-dollar salaries. Meanwhile, Black Americans are beaten in the streets as they protest a judicial system that disproportionately kills them with impunity, while incarcerated men in California are paid slave wages to put their bodies on the line fighting deadly wildfires. Gun manufacturers make billions while school shootings barely register as news. History repeats itself, with better weapons; we witness death (now streaming) from our phones. Social media is now the conduit of an unprecedented torrent of other people's suffering; we watch other people die before we go to sleep and after we wake. The question I began with—When does "letting die" become murder?—is perhaps even more urgent today than it was in the 1830s, and like Victorians, we work through that question with reference to what we feel as witnesses of death. We ask ourselves the same questions that the

Victorians were asking: How do I feel when I witness another person suffering or dying? How *should* I feel? And most unsettling: Does it even matter how I feel? Is it enough to care? Under what conditions can care produce systemic change, and under what conditions does it merely become our own suffering, detached from and useless to the other whose suffering initially provoked it?

I want to push beyond an assertion of mere relevance to make a hopeful claim for these novels' enduring value as tools for understanding our world. I was compelled to write this book by my belief in the radical potential of feeling—the power of interpersonal affective and emotional exchange to reshape macro-level systems. This project has only further persuaded me. Feeling does have, I believe, immense potential to shape political and economic systems—to make them work or to make them not work. But that potential can be captured, routed, and mobilized in all kinds of ways. Victorian novels show us that the feelings that arise in response to necroeconomics are multidirectional, dangerous, and unpredictable. Feeling can flow through a hegemonic system as its lifeblood, animating its power, or like kerosene, working its way into every gear and just waiting on a match. Reading these novels in the context of the problem of letting die, we are left not with a facile account of sympathy's inherent power to overcome hierarchy and division. Rather, we are challenged to attend to the complex dynamics of feeling that shaped necroeconomics in the Victorian period and still shape these forces today. Methodologically, this means looking at these authors not as the "unacknowledged legislators of the world," nor as well-meaning but hopelessly indoctrinated old fools who perpetuated the very cultural hegemony against which they positioned themselves, but rather as our predecessors in a continued struggle to figure out feeling under capitalism. I do not want to suggest that these novels contain "the answers," nor, on the other hand, that they express out-of-date ideologies that I, from the other side, can reveal as flawed. There is no other side; we are still in it. Taken "beside" us, these novels offer insight not only into how we got here but also, as Eve Sedgwick puts it, into "what *might have happened but didn't*" (8, 155, n. 5). In a world that increasingly resembles dystopian fiction, we need all the tools we can get for imagining the world that we might still create.

WORKS CITED

Ablow, Rachel. *The Marriage of Minds: Reading Sympathy in the Victorian Marriage Plot.* Stanford UP, 2007.

———. "Victorian Feelings." *The Cambridge Companion to the Victorian Novel,* 2nd ed., edited by Deirdre David, Cambridge UP, 2012, pp. 193–210.

Agamben, Giorgio. *Homo Sacer: Sovereign Power and Bare Life.* Translated by Daniel Heller-Roazen, Stanford UP, 1998.

———. *Remnants of Auschwitz: The Witness and the Archive.* Translated by Daniel Heller-Roazen, Zone, 1999.

Ahmed, Sara. *The Cultural Politics of Emotion.* Routledge, 2004.

Anderson, Benedict. *Imagined Communities: Reflections on the Origin and Spread of Nationalism.* Verso, 1983.

Arendt, Hannah. *The Origins of Totalitarianism.* Saint Lucia, Harcourt Brace Jovanovich, 1973.

Armstrong, Nancy. *How Novels Think: The Limits of Individualism from 1719–1900.* Columbia UP, 2006.

Arrighi, Giovanni. *Adam Smith in Beijing: Lineages of the Twenty-First Century.* Verso, 2007.

Augustine. *Concerning the City of God of God against the Pagans.* Translated by Henry Bettenson, Penguin, 1984.

Beckert, Sven. *Empire of Cotton: A Global History.* Penguin, 2014.

Berlant, Lauren. "Cruel Optimism." *The Affect Theory Reader,* edited by Melissa Gregg and Gregory J. Seigworth, Duke UP, 2010, pp. 93–118.

Betensky, Carolyn. *Feeling for the Poor: Bourgeois Compassion, Social Action, and the Victorian Novel.* U of Virginia P, 2010.

Bickers, Robert, and Jonathan J. Howlett, editors. *Britain and China, 1840–1970: Empire, Finance and War.* Routledge, 2016.

Biddick, Kathleen. *Make and Let Die: Untimely Sovereignties.* Punctum Books, 2016.

Bigelow, Gordon. *Fiction, Famine, and the Rise of Economics in Victorian Britain and Ireland.* Cambridge UP, 2003.

Blaug, Mark. *Ricardian Economics: A Historical Study.* Yale UP, 1958.

Bodenheimer, Rosemarie. *The Politics of Story in Victorian Fiction.* Cornell UP, 1988.

Brantlinger, Patrick. "The Case against Trade Unions in Early Victorian Fiction." *Victorian Studies,* vol. 13, 1969, pp. 37–52.

Burrell, Sean, and Geoffrey Gill. "The Liverpool Cholera Epidemic of 1832 and Anatomical Dissection—Medical Mistrust and Civil Unrest." *Journal of the History of Medicine and Allied Sciences,* vol. 60, 2005, pp. 478–98.

Butler, Judith. *Bodies That Matter: On the Discursive Limits of Sex.* Routledge, 1993.

Carnall, Geoffrey. "Dickens, Mrs. Gaskell, and the Preston Strike." *Victorian Studies,* vol. 8, 1964, pp. 31–48.

Carroll, David, editor. *George Eliot: The Critical Heritage.* Barnes and Noble, 1971.

Cazamian, Louis. *The Social Novel in English, 1830–1850: Dickens, Disraeli, Mrs. Gaskell, Kingsley.* Translated by Martin Fido, Routledge and Kegan Paul, 1973.

Chadwick, Edwin. *Report from the Poor Law Commissioners on an Inquiry into the Sanitary Conditions of the Laboring Population of Great Britain.* 1842. Clowes and Sons, 1843.

Clark, Anna. *The Struggle for the Breeches: Gender and the Making of the British Working Class.* U of California P, 1995.

Coleman, Dermot. *George Eliot and Money: Economics, Ethics and Literature.* Cambridge UP, 2014.

Connell, Philip. *Romanticism, Economics and the Question of "Culture."* Oxford UP, 2001.

Cook, Beverly. "Lecturing on Woman's Place: 'Mrs. Jellyby' in Wisconsin, 1854–1874." *Signs,* vol. 9, 1983, pp. 361–76.

Coté, Amy. "Parables and Unitarianism in Elizabeth Gaskell's *Mary Barton.*" *Victorian Review,* vol. 40, 2014, pp. 59–76.

Courtemanche, Eleanor. *The 'Invisible Hand' and British Fiction, 1818–1860: Adam Smith, Political Economy, and the Genre of Realism.* Palgrave Macmillan, 2011.

———. "'Naked Truth Is the Best Eloquence': Martineau, Dickens, and the Moral Science of Realism." *English Literary History,* vol. 73, no. 2, 2006, pp. 383–407.

Davidoff, Leonore. *Worlds Between: Historical Perspectives on Gender and Class.* Routledge, 1995.

Davis, Angela. "An Extraordinary Moment: Angela Davis Says Protests Recognize Long Overdue Anti-Racist Work." Interview by Peter O'Dowd, adapted for web by Allison Hagan. *WBUR,* 19 June 2020, https://www.wbur.org/hereandnow/2020/06/19/angela-davis-protests-anti-racism.

Dean, Britten. "British Informal Empire: The Case of China." *The Journal of Commonwealth and Comparative Politics,* vol. 14, 1976, pp. 64–81.

Deleuze, Gilles. *Expressionism in Philosophy: Spinoza.* Translated by Martin Joughin, Zone Books, 1990.

Lord Denman. Uncle Tom's Cabin, Bleak House, *Slavery and the Slave Trade.* Longman, Brown, Green and Longmans, 1853.

Dickens, Charles. *Bleak House.* 1852–53. Edited by Stephen Gill, Oxford UP, 1998.

———. *Oliver Twist.* 1846. Edited by Kathleen Tillotson, Oxford UP, 1999.

———. *Our Mutual Friend.* 1864–65. Edited by Michael Cotsell, Oxford UP, 1989.

Eliot, George. "Address to Working Men, by Felix Holt." 1867. Reprinted in *Felix Holt: The Radical*, edited by Lynda Mugglestone, Penguin, 1995.

———. *Felix Holt: The Radical*. 1866. Edited by Lynda Mugglestone, Penguin, 1995.

———. *Middlemarch*. 1871–72. Edited by Bert G. Hornback, Norton Critical Edition, 2nd ed., W. W. Norton, 2000.

———. "The Natural History of German Life." *Westminster Review*, vol. 66, July 1856, pp. 51–79.

Engels, Friedrich. *The Condition of the Working-Class in England in 1844*. Translated by Florence Kelley Wischnewetzky, Swan Sonnenschein, 1892.

Esposito, Roberto. *Immunitas: The Protection and Negation of Life*. Translated by Zakiya Hanafi, Polity, 2011.

Faulkner, Harold Underwood. *Chartism and the Churches: A Study in Democracy*. New York, 1916.

Foucault, Michel. *Security, Territory, Population: Lectures at the Collège de France, 1977–78*. Edited by Arnold I. Davidson, translated by Graham Burchell, Picador, 2009.

———. *"Society Must Be Defended": Lectures at the Collège de France, 1975–76*. Edited by Arnold I. Davidson, translated by David Macey, Picador, 2003.

Frankel, Oz. *States of Inquiry: Social Investigations and Print Culture in Nineteenth-Century Britain and the United States*. Johns Hopkins UP, 2006.

Freedgood, Elaine. "Banishing Panic: Harriet Martineau and the Popularization of Political Economy." *Victorian Studies*, vol. 38, 1995, pp. 33–53.

Fryckstedt, Monica Correa. "The Early Industrial Novel: *Mary Barton* and Its Predecessors." *The John Rylands University Library Bulletin*, vol. 63, 1980, pp. 11–30.

Gagnier, Regenia. *The Insatiability of Human Wants: Economics and Aesthetics in Market Society*. U of Chicago P, 2000.

Gallagher, Catherine. *The Body Economic: Life, Death, and Sensation in Political Economy and the Victorian Novel*. Princeton UP, 2005.

———. "The Body versus the Social Body in the Works of Thomas Malthus and Henry Mayhew." *The Making of the Modern Body: Sexuality and Society in the Nineteenth Century*, edited by Catherine Gallagher and Thomas Laqueur, U of California P, 1987, pp. 83–106.

———. *The Industrial Reformation of English Fiction: Social Discourse and Narrative Form, 1832–1867*. U of Chicago P, 1985.

———. *Nobody's Story: The Vanishing Acts of Women Writers in the Marketplace, 1670–1820*. U of California P, 1994.

Gallagher, John, and Ronald Robinson. "The Imperialism of Free Trade." *The Economic History Review*, vol. 6, 1953, pp. 1–15.

Gammage, R. G. *History of the Chartist Movement, 1837–1854*. Newcastle, 1894.

Gaskell, Elizabeth. *Mary Barton*. 1848. Edited by Shirley Foster, Oxford UP, 2006.

———. *North and South*. 1854. Edited by Patricia Ingham, Penguin, 1995.

Gilbert, Pamela. *Cholera and Nation: Doctoring the Social Body in Victorian England*. SUNY P, 2008.

———. *The Citizen's Body: Desire, Health, and the Social in Victorian England*. The Ohio State UP, 2007.

Gilmore, Ruth Wilson. *Golden Gulag: Prisons, Surplus, Crisis, and Opposition in Globalizing California*. E-book. U of California P, 2007.

Goodlad, Lauren. *Victorian Literature and the Victorian State: Character and Governance in a Liberal Society*. Johns Hopkins UP, 2004.

Gould, Deborah B. *Moving Politics: Emotion and ACT UP's Fight against AIDS*. U of Chicago P, 2009.

Gregg, Melissa, and Gregory J. Seigworth. "An Inventory of Shimmers." *The Affect Theory Reader*, edited by Melissa Gregg and Gregory J. Seigworth, Duke UP, 2010, pp. 1–27.

Greiner, Rae. *Sympathetic Realism in Nineteenth-Century British Fiction*. Johns Hopkins UP, 2012.

Gržinić, Marina, and Šefik Tatlić. *Necropolitics, Racialization, and Global Capitalism: Historicization of Biopolitics and Forensics of Politics, Art, and Life*. Lexington Books, 2014.

Hack, Daniel. *Reaping Something New: African American Transformations of Victorian Literature*. Princeton UP, 2019.

Hadley, Elaine. *Living Liberalism: Practical Citizenship in Mid-Victorian Britain*. U of Chicago P, 2010.

———. *Melodramatic Tactics: Theatrical Dissent in the English Marketplace, 1800–1885*. Stanford UP, 1995.

Hall, Catherine. "The Early Formation of Victorian Domestic Ideology." *Fit Work for Women*, edited by Sandra Burman, 1979, Routledge, 2013, pp. 15–32.

Hardt, Michael, and Antonio Negri. *Multitude: War and Democracy in the Age of Empire*. Penguin, 2004.

Hardy, Anne. *The Epidemic Streets: Infectious Diseases and the Rise of Preventive Medicine, 1856–1900*. Clarendon Press, 1993.

Haritaworn, Jin, Adi Kuntsman, and Silvia Posocco, editors. *Queer Necropolitics*. Routledge, 2014.

Hartman, Saidiya. *Scenes of Subjection: Terror, Slavery, and Self-Making in Nineteenth-Century America*. Oxford UP, 1997.

Harvey, David. *A Companion to Marx's Capital*. Verso, 2010.

Haywood, Ian. *The Revolution in Popular Literature: Print, Politics and the People, 1790–1860*. Cambridge UP, 2004.

Hazlitt, William. "A Reply to the Essay on Population by the Reverend T. R. Malthus." *The Complete Works of William Hazlitt*, edited by A. R. Waller and Arnold Glover, J. M. Dent and Co., 1902, pp. 1–184.

Higgins, T. "Stephens and Liberty: Address to the Agricultural Labourers of England and Wales." *The Champion*, 12 May 1839.

Hill, Mike, and Warren Montag. *The Other Adam Smith*. Stanford UP, 2014.

Himes, Norman E. "John Stuart Mill's Attitude toward Neo-Malthusianism." *The Economic Journal*, vol. 39, issue supplement no. 1, 1929, pp. 457–84.

Himmelfarb, Gertrude. *The Idea of Poverty: England in the Early Industrial Age*. Vintage, 1983.

Hinton, Laura. *The Perverse Gaze of Sympathy: Sadomasochistic Sentiments from Clarissa to Rescue 911*. SUNY P, 1999.

Hirschman, Albert O. *The Passions and the Interests: Political Arguments for Capitalism before Its Triumph*. Princeton UP, 1977.

Hobson, Christopher Z. "The Radicalism of *Felix Holt*: George Eliot and the Pioneers of Labor." *Victorian Literature and Culture*, vol. 26, no. 1, 1998, pp. 19–39.

Hochschild, Arlie. *The Managed Heart: Commercialization of Human Feeling*. U of California P, 1983.

Hodgart, Alan. *The Economics of European Imperialism*. W. W. Norton, 1977.

Holland, Sharon, Marcia Ochoa, and Kyla Wazana Tompkins. "Introduction: On the Visceral." *GLQ: A Journal of Lesbian and Gay Studies*, vol. 20, no. 4, 2014, pp. 391–406.

Hutcheson, Frances. *An Inquiry Concerning Moral Good and Evil.* (1725). *British Moralists: Being Selections from Writers Principally of the Eighteenth Century,* vol. 1, edited by L. A. Selby-Bigge, Dover, 1965, pp. 68–187.

Huzel, James P. *The Popularization of Malthus in Early Nineteenth-Century England: Martineau, Cobbett, and the Pauper Press.* Ashgate, 2006.

Ioanide, Paula. *The Emotional Politics of Racism: How Feelings Trump Facts in an Era of Color-blindness.* Stanford UP, 2015.

Jaffe, Audrey. "Affect and the Victorian Novel." *The Palgrave Handbook of Affect Studies and Textual Criticism,* edited by Donald R. Wehrs and Thomas Blake, Palgrave, 2017, pp. 713–33.

——. *Scenes of Sympathy: Identity and Representation in Victorian Fiction.* Cornell UP, 2000.

James, Henry. "George Eliot's *Middlemarch*." *Galaxy,* 1873, pp. 424–28. Reprinted in *Middlemarch,* edited by Bert Hornback, W. W. Norton, 2000, pp. 578–81.

Johnson, Paul. *Making the Market: Victorian Origins of Corporate Capitalism.* Cambridge UP, 2010.

Kantorowicz, Ernst. *The King's Two Bodies: A Study in Mediaeval Political Theology.* 1957. Princeton UP, 1997.

Kay-Shuttleworth, James. *The Moral and Physical Condition of the Working Class Employed in the Cotton Manufacture in Manchester.* Ridgway, 1832.

Keay, John. *The Honourable Company: A History of the English East India Company.* Scribner Press, 1994.

Kendi, Ibram X. *Stamped from the Beginning: The Definitive History of Racist Ideas in America.* Bold Type Books, 2016.

Klaver, Claudia. *A/Moral Economics: Classical Political Economy and Cultural Authority in Nineteenth-Century England.* The Ohio State UP, 2003.

Kornbluh, Anna. *Realizing Capital: Financial and Psychic Economies in Victorian Form.* Fordham UP, 2004.

Kowaleski-Wallace, Elizabeth. *Consuming Subjects: Women, Shopping, and Business in the Eighteenth Century.* Columbia UP, 1996.

Kreager, Phillip. "Smith or Malthus? A Sea-Change in the Concept of a Population." *Population and Development Review,* vol. 48, no. 3, 2022, pp. 645–88.

Kucich, John. *Repression in Victorian Fiction: Charlotte Brontë, George Eliot, and Charles Dickens.* U of California P, 1987.

Langer, William. "The Origins of the Birth Control Movement in England in the Early Nineteenth Century." *The Journal of Interdisciplinary History,* vol. 5, no. 4, 1975, pp. 669–86.

Langland, Elizabeth. "Nobody's Angels: Domestic Ideology and Middle-Class Women in the Victorian Novel." *PMLA,* vol. 107, 1992, pp. 290–304.

Leder, Drew. *The Absent Body.* U of Chicago P, 1990.

Logan, Deborah Anna. Introduction. *Illustrations of Political Economy: Selected Tales,* by Harriet Martineau, Broadview, 2004, pp. 9–50.

Lorde, Audre. *Sister Outsider: Essays and Speeches.* The Crossing Press, 1984.

Lucas, John. *The Literature of Change: Studies in the Nineteenth-Century Provincial Novel.* Barnes and Noble, 1977.

Lysack, Krista. *Come Buy, Come Buy: Shopping and the Culture of Consumption in Victorian Women's Writing.* Ohio UP, 2008.

MacCarthy, Fiona. *William Morris.* Faber and Faber Limited, 1994.

Malabou, Catherine. "The King's Two (Biopolitical) Bodies." *Representations,* vol. 127, 2014, pp. 98–106.

Malthus, Thomas. *An Essay on the Principle of Population.* Johnson, 1798.

———. "Observations on the Effects of the Corn Laws." 1814. *The Pamphlets of Thomas Robert Malthus,* edited by Arthur Monroe, Augustus Kelly Publications, 1970, pp. 95–131.

Marcus [pseudonym]. *The Book of Murder! A Vade-Mecum for the Commissioners and Guardians of the New Poor Law throughout Great Britain and Ireland.* John Hill, 1838. Reprinted by William Dugdale, 1839.

Markovits, Stefanie. *The Crisis of Action in Nineteenth-Century English Literature.* The Ohio State UP, 2006.

Marshall, David. *The Surprising Effects of Sympathy: Marivaux, Diderot, Rousseau and Mary Shelley.* U of Chicago P, 1988.

Martineau, Harriet. *Deerbrook.* 1838. Edited by Valerie Sanders, Penguin, 2004.

———. *Harriet Martineau's Autobiography.* Edited by Maria Weston Chapman, James R. Osgood and Co., 1877.

———. *Harriet Martineau: Writings on Slavery and the American Civil War.* Edited by Deborah Anna Logan, Northern Illinois UP, 2002.

———. *Illustrations of Political Economy: Selected Tales.* 1832–34. Edited by Deborah Anna Logan, Broadview, 2004.

———. Preface. *Illustrations of Political Economy, Volume 1.* Charles Fox, 1832.

Marx, Karl. *Capital, Volume 1.* Translated by Ben Fowkes, Penguin, 1990.

Massumi, Brian. *The Politics of Affect.* Polity, 2015.

Mbembe, Achille. *Necropolitics.* Translated by Steve Corcoran, Duke UP, 2019.

———. "Necropolitics." Translated by Libby Meintjes, *Public Culture,* vol. 15, 2003, pp. 11–40.

McDonagh, Josephine. *Child Murder and British Culture, 1720–1900.* Cambridge UP, 2003.

Menke, Richard. "Fiction as Vivisection: G. H. Lewes and George Eliot." *English Literary History,* vol. 67, 2000, pp. 617–53.

Michie, Helena. "'Who Is This in Pain?': Scarring, Disfigurement, and Female Identity in *Bleak House* and *Our Mutual Friend.*" *NOVEL: A Forum on Fiction,* vol. 22, 1989, pp. 199–212.

Midgley, Claire. *Women against Slavery: The British Campaigns, 1780–1870.* Routledge, 1992.

Miller, D. A. *The Novel and the Police.* U of California P, 1988.

Minogue, Sally. "Gender and Class in *Villette* and *North and South.*" *Problems for Feminist Criticism,* Routledge, 1990, pp. 70–108.

Morris, William. *News from Nowhere and Other Writings.* Edited by Clive Wilmer, Penguin, 1993.

———. "Statement of Principles of the Hammersmith Socialist Society." *The Collected Letters of William Morris, Volume 3,* Princeton UP, 2014, pp. 489–92.

Morrow, Glenn. *The Ethical and the Economic Theories of Adam Smith: A Study in the Social Philosophy of the Eighteenth Century.* Longmans, Green, and Co., 1923.

Neocleous, Mark. "The Political Economy of the Dead: Marx's Vampires." *History of Political Thought,* vol. 24, 2003, pp. 668–84.

Newsom, Robert. "*Villette* and *Bleak House*: Authorizing Women." *Nineteenth-Century Literature,* vol. 46, 1991, pp. 54–81.

Ngai, Sianne. *Ugly Feelings.* Harvard UP, 2005.

Nixon, Rob. *Slow Violence and the Environmentalism of the Poor.* Harvard UP, 2011.

Oncken, August. "The Consistency of Adam Smith." *Economic Journal,* vol. 7, no. 27, 1897, pp. 443–50.

Patterson, Orlando. *Slavery and Social Death: A Comparative Study.* Harvard UP, 1982.

Peterson, Linda. "From French Revolution to English Reform: Hannah More, Harriet Martineau, and the 'Little Book.'" *Nineteenth-Century Literature,* vol. 60, no. 4, 2006, pp. 409–45.

Pichanick, Valerie. *Harriet Martineau: The Woman and Her Work.* U of Michigan P, 1980.

Pinch, Adela. *Strange Fits of Passion: Epistemologies of Emotion, Hume to Austen.* Stanford UP, 1996.

Plotkin, David. "Home-Made Savages: Cultivating English Children in *Bleak House.*" *Pacific Coast Philology,* vol. 32, 1997, pp. 17–31.

Polanyi, Karl. *The Great Transformation: The Political and Economic Origins of Our Time.* 1944. 2nd ed., Beacon, 2001.

Poovey, Mary. *The Financial System in Nineteenth-Century Britain.* Oxford UP, 2002.

———. *Genres of the Credit Economy: Mediating Value in Eighteenth- and Nineteenth-Century Britain.* U of Chicago P, 2008.

———. *Making a Social Body: British Cultural Formation, 1830–1864.* U of Chicago P, 1995.

Puar, Jasbir. *The Right to Maim: Debility, Capacity, Disability.* Duke UP, 2017.

Reber, Dierdra. *Coming to Our Senses: Affect and an Order of Things for Global Culture.* Columbia UP, 2016.

Reeder, Jessie. *The Forms of Informal Empire: Britain, Latin America, and Nineteenth-Century Literature.* Johns Hopkins UP, 2020.

Rey, Roselyne. *The History of Pain.* Translated by Louise Elliott Wallace, J. A. Cadden, and S. W. Cadden, Harvard UP, 1995.

Ricardo, David. *The Works and Correspondence of David Ricardo, Volume 1.* Edited by Piero Sraffa and Maurice H. Dobb, Cambridge UP, 1973.

Richardson, Ruth. *Death, Dissection, and the Destitute.* 1987. 2nd ed., U of Chicago P, 2000.

Robbins, Bruce. *The Servant's Hand: English Fiction from Below.* Columbia UP, 1986.

Robinson, Cedric. *Black Marxism: The Making of the Black Radical Tradition.* 1983. U of North Carolina P, 2005.

Rothschild, Emma. *Economic Sentiments: Adam Smith, Cordorcet, and the Enlightenment.* Harvard UP, 2001.

Samalin, Zachary. *The Masses Are Revolting: Victorian Culture and the Political Aesthetics of Disgust.* Cornell UP, 2021.

Sanders, Mike. "From 'Political' to 'Human' Economy: The Visions of Harriet Martineau and Frances Wright." *Women: A Cultural Review,* vol. 12, no. 2, 2001, pp. 192–203.

Sanders, Valerie. *Reason over Passion.* Harvester Press, 1986.

Santner, Eric. *The Royal Remains: The People's Two Bodies and the Endgames of Sovereignty.* U of Chicago P, 2011.

Scarry, Elaine. *The Body in Pain: The Making and Unmaking of the World.* Oxford UP, 1985.

Schaub, Melissa. "Sympathy and Discipline in *Mary Barton.*" *Victorian Newsletter,* vol. 106, 2004, pp. 15–20.

Schuller, Kyla. *The Biopolitics of Feeling: Race, Sex, and Science in the Nineteenth Century.* Duke UP, 2018.

Schwartz, Pedro. *The New Political Economy of J. S. Mill*. London School of Economics and Political Science, 1972.

Sedgwick, Eve. *Touching Feeling: Affect, Pedagogy, Performativity*. Duke UP, 2003.

Shelley, Percy. *A Philosophical View of Reform*. 1820. Oxford UP, 1920.

Sherwood, Marika. *After Abolition: Britain and the Slave Trade since 1807*. I. B. Tauris, 2007.

Shuttleworth, Sally. *George Eliot and Nineteenth-Century Science: The Make-Believe of a Beginning*. Cambridge UP, 1984.

Singleton, Jon. "The Dissonant Bible Quotation: Political and Narrative Dissension in Gaskell's *Mary Barton*." *English Literary History*, vol. 78, 2011, pp. 917–41.

Smith, Adam. *The Theory of Moral Sentiments*. Edited by D. D. Raphael and A. L. Macfie, Liberty Fund, 1984.

———. *The Wealth of Nations*. Edited by Edwin Cannan, 5th ed., Methuen and Company, 1904.

Soares, Rebecca. "The Spirit of Labor: Spiritualism and the Industrial Novels of Elizabeth Gaskell and Elizabeth Stuart Phelps." *Religion and the Arts*, vol. 26, 2022, pp. 112–35.

Spencer, Ashley. "A Young Adult Author's Tweet Went Viral—But Somehow, Dr. Fauci Got the Credit." *Oprah Daily*, 26 Aug. 2020, https://www.oprahdaily.com/life/a33547008/viral-dr-fauci-quote-caring-for-others.

Spengler, Joseph. "Adam Smith on Population." *Population Studies*, vol. 24, no. 3, 1970, pp. 377–88.

Spinoza, Benedict. *Ethics; On the Correction of Understanding*. Translated by Andrew Boyle, Everyman's Library, 1959.

Steinlight, Emily. *Populating the Novel: Literary Form and the Politics of Surplus Life*. Cornell UP, 2018.

Stewart, Kathleen. *Ordinary Affects*. Duke UP, 2007.

Stoler, Ann Laura. *Race and the Education of Desire: Foucault's History of Sexuality and the Colonial Order of Things*. Duke UP, 1995.

Stone, Harry. "Charles Dickens and Harriet Beecher Stowe." *Nineteenth-Century Fiction*, vol. 12, 1957, pp. 188–202.

Taylor, Christopher. *Empire of Neglect: The West Indies in the Wake of British Liberalism*. Duke UP, 2018.

Thompson, E. P. *William Morris: Romantic to Revolutionary*. PM Press, 2011.

Tribe, Keith. "'Das Adam Smith Problem' and Modern Smith Scholarship." *History of European Ideas*, vol. 34, no. 4, 2008, pp. 514–25.

Valencia, Sayak. *Gore Capitalism*. Translated by John Pluecker, Semiotext(e), 2018.

Vargo, Gregory. *An Underground History of Early Victorian Fiction: Chartism, Radical Print Culture, and the Social Problem Novel*. Cambridge UP, 2018.

Viner, Jacob. *The Long View and the Short: Studies in Economic Theory and Policy*. 1927. Free Press, 1958.

von Mises, Ludwig. *Human Action: A Treatise on Economics*. Liberty Fund, 1996.

Webb, R. K. *Harriet Martineau: A Radical Victorian*. Columbia UP, 1960.

Weheliye, Alexander. *Habeas Viscus: Racializing Assemblages, Biopolitics, and Black Feminist Theories of the Human*. Duke UP, 2014.

Williams, Raymond. *Culture and Society: 1780–1950*. Columbia UP, 1983.

Winch, Donald. *Malthus: A Very Short Introduction*. Oxford UP, 2013.

———. *Riches and Poverty: An Intellectual History of Political Economy in Britain, 1750–1834.* Cambridge UP, 1996.

Wood, Laura. "The Domestic Chaos of Mrs. Jellyby." Web blog post. *The Thinking Housewife,* 15 Nov. 2018, https://www.thinkinghousewife.com/2018/11/the-domestic-chaos-of-mrs-jellyby/.

Wood, Marcus. *Blind Memory: Visual Representations of Slavery in England and America, 1780–1865.* Routledge, 2000.

Woodmansee, Martha, and Mark Osteen, editors. *The New Economic Criticism: Studies at the Interface of Literature and Economics.* Routledge, 1999.

Yeazell, Ruth. "Why Political Novels Have Heroines: *Sybil, Mary Barton,* and *Felix Holt.*" *NOVEL: A Forum on Fiction,* vol. 18, 1985, pp. 126–44.

INDEX

—————

as problem, 7–9, 30–37; as violence, 44. *See also* infanticide; Malthus, Thomas; population

Ricardo, David, 4, 6–9, 16, 19, 27–28, 30, 107n9

riots, 46–47, 55–56, 79

Robinson, Cedric, 154

Rothschild, Emma, 5

sadism, 99–100, 104, 152–53

Samalin, Zachary, 129n4, 143n10

Schaub, Melissa, 53, 60–61

Schuller, Kyla, 81n15

Sedgwick, Eve, 161

Seigworth, Gregory, 18n31, 62–63

self-interest: abdication of, 23, 61, 132, 134–40, 156; individual, 5, 24, 64–66, 76, 133, 147–48, 153–54. *See also* desire; *homo economicus*; invisible hand; private property

Shelley, Percy, 8

Silas Marner (Eliot), 1

Singleton, Jon, 66

slavery, 3–4, 12–15; in Dickens, 95n3, 99n5, 106; in Morris, 142–43, 147. *See also* racism

Smith, Adam, 3n2, 4–9, 19, 30, 56n1, 86, 144; invisible hand, 16, 133; and sympathy, 17–18, 21, 53–54, 61, 64–67, 89, 119, 151

Soares, Rebecca, 66n6

social body, 20–22, 29–36, 49–50, 88, 93–94, 111–12, 120, 132–35. *See also* population

socialism, 4, 23, 59, 87–88, 122, 141–42, 144–47, 149–50, 152, 154–56

Spinoza, Benedict, 18n32, 21, 63–65

starvation, 9–10, 31–32, 55–60, 68, 70–72, 74, 81–83, 85–86, 124

Steinlight, Emily, 8, 11–12

Stephens, Reverend Joseph Rayner, 41–42, 44

Stewart, Kathleen, 15

Stoler, Ann Laura, 14, 93–94

strikes, 30, 40, 53–59, 67–68, 70n7, 72, 74–75, 155. See also *Manchester Strike, A*

surplus population, 11–12, 32n10, 39n13, 105–6. *See also* population

sympathy, 17–24, 76–89, 133, 139, 149–52, 158–60; barriers against, 67–75; cross-class, 53–54; as insufficient for social change, 60–61; as problem for capitalism, 26, 36–39, 60–67, 141; and slavery, 99n5; within working class, 38–39, 70–71, 81. *See also* feeling; Smith, Adam; Spinoza, Benedict

Taylor, Christopher, 14

Theory of Moral Sentiments, The (Smith), 5, 17–18, 64–65, 67, 119, 133

Thompson, E. P., 145

trauma, 118–19, 149

unions, 56, 72–75

utopia, 7, 23, 27, 89, 122, 132, 137, 146–57

Valencia, Sayak, 13

value: biopolitical, 11, 31–32, 86 (*see also* biopolitics); of human lives, 93–94, 120 (*see also* racism); of narrative, 16–17, 54, 161; surplus, 3, 24, 146–48; of women, 77 (*see also* gender). *See also* money

Vargo, Gregory, 20, 26n2, 29, 38, 41–42, 45

von Mises, Ludwig, 56n2

voting: as buyable, 126, 134, 136, 140; and politics, 135–37, 140n9; working-class, 139. *See also* reform

Weal and Woe in Garveloch (Martineau), 30–32, 39

Wealth of Nations, The (Smith), 4–6, 30n7, 56n1, 58n4, 133

Weheliye, Alexander, 94–95

Winch, Donald, 10

Woman in White, The (Collins), 2

Wood, Marcus, 99n5

workhouse. *See* poor relief

working-class organizing. *See* socialism; strikes; unions